NEGOTIATING COHESION, INEQUALITY AND CHANGE

Uncomfortable positions in local government

Hannah Jones

First published in Great Britain in 2015 by

Policy Press
University of Bristol
1-9 Old Park Hill
Bristol
BS2 8BB
UK
t: +44 (0)117 954 5940
pp-info@bristol.ac.uk
www.policypress.co.uk

North America office:
Policy Press
c/o The University of Chicago Press
1427 East 60th Street
Chicago, IL 60637, USA
t: +1 773 702 7700
f: +1 773 702 9756
sales@press.uchicago.edu
www.press.uchicago.edu

British Library Cataloguing in Publication Data
A catalogue record for this book is available from the British Library

Library of Congress Cataloging-in-Publication Data
A catalog record for this book has been requested

ISBN 978 1 44731 004 4 paperback

Cover design by Qube Design Associates, Bristol
Front cover: image kindly supplied by www.alamy.com
Printed and bound in Great Britain by CMP, Poole
The Policy Press uses environmentally responsible print partners

Contents

List of acronyms

BME	Black and minority ethnic
BNP	British National Party
CLG	Communities and Local Government Department (also known as DCLG)
COIC	Commission on Integration and Cohesion
DCLG	Department for Communities and Local Government (also known as CLG)
EHRC	Equalities and Human Rights Commission
ESRC	Economic and Social Research Council
EU	European Union
GOL	Government Office for London
LAA	Local Area Agreement
LBH	London Borough of Hackney, also known as Hackney Council
LGA	Local Government Association
LSP	Local Strategic Partnership
MPA	Metropolitan Police Authority
PVE	Preventing Violent Extremism (also known as 'Prevent')
RAT	Race Awareness Training

Notes on the author

Hannah Jones is an Assistant Professor in Sociology at the University of Warwick. She previously worked in local government in inner London, and has held positions as a Visiting Scholar at the Institute for Public Knowledge, New York University; Research Associate in the Faculty of Social Sciences at The Open University; Teaching Fellow in the Department of Sociology, Goldsmiths, University of London; and Research Associate at the Centre on Migration, Policy and Society, University of Oxford. Her research interests include identity and belonging, urban studies and regeneration, local government, migration policy and community development. She is co-editor of *Stories of cosmopolitan belonging: Emotion and location*.

Acknowledgements

It has taken a long time to get this book into this form, and many many people have helped me to get here, directly or indirectly. The importance of the warmth, support and generosity of the colleagues and friends I have gained through working on the research in this book can't be underestimated. I was fortunate enough to be working on this research in a collaborative, supportive and exciting cohort of postgraduate researchers in sociology at Goldsmiths, and in other research networks, particularly NYLON and the Race, Ethnicity and Post-colonial Studies Group, which together created a research culture and group of friends without whom the work on this book would have been a much harder, less enjoyable and less fulfilling experience. Too many people to mention, but I wouldn't have enjoyed, and may not have survived, the intellectual (and beer-soaked) ride quite so much without Vanessa Arena, Alex Rhys-Taylor, Christy Kulz, Naaz Rashid, Ben Gidley, Suzi Hall, Adam Kaasa, Malcolm James, Kim Keith, Joe Deville, Allan Day, Yael Gerson, Will Davies and Anamik Saha. I want to thank Emma Jackson in particular for being an excellent colleague, sounding board and support, especially in these treacherous post-PhD years, as well as a fabulous friend.

Other friends have also helped me to survive, listened to me whinge, made me relax, tried to guess the title of my PhD thesis through the medium of charades, held the kick pads week after week, and generally allowed me to be a human being – as well as occasionally being drafted in to remind me when my writing, talking or thinking turned impenetrably academic. Special thanks for their work at keeping me sane are due to Anne Malcolm, Anneliese Dodds, Jennifer Sheddan, Rachel Bate and Ambia Ali.

I really appreciate the support, encouragement and love of my family. I couldn't have done this without Judith Kahn's emotional support, inspiration, emergency financial aid, laughs, scrabble and hugs; without Carla and Gwen Jones' sisterly support, sisterly teasing, mind-reading, in-jokes and friendship; without Rick Jones' and Nicky Roy's support, interest and sustenance; or without Hrishikesh Jones taking me on his adventures, sharing his ideas and discoveries, and being the best brother ever.

The book, and I, owe a massive debt to both Michael Keith and Marjorie Mayo, who not only guided my research and intellectual process, but did so with generosity, care and responsibility that is a model for what academics, public intellectuals and good colleagues should be.

A big thank you to Joanna Sumner, who supported me to develop my research while I was working at the London Borough of Hackney, appreciated the value of critical research, and championed the project throughout my studentship. Thanks to the London Borough of Hackney for its institutional support for my collaborative studentship, and to the Economic and Social Research Council which supported the research through grant award number ES/F032692/1.

Finally, I must thank all of the people who agreed to be interviewed for the research. Some researchers get offended when people decline to take part in research. I am always amazed that anyone agrees to be so generous, with their time, insights and stories. Thanks to everyone whose words and experiences I use in the book, and also for the stories that got left out – it is all appreciated.

Introduction:
Getting uncomfortable

HANNAH: Do you think your background or identity affects how you think about cohesion?

RACHEL: God it must do. It must do! I suppose I think that it's not really about me, you know that it's something other ... we talk about communities ... I probably think about ethnic minority communities, and people who are poor.... And it's something other, to me ... something that I watch rather than partake. Although actually, that's just so not true, I mean for me personally.[1]

Working in policy and government can be uncomfortable. It can be uncomfortable to recognise inequalities of power and discrimination, to challenge these inequalities, and to find limitations on what can be changed. As someone working on policy, it can be uncomfortable to recognise that one is in a relatively privileged position compared to many of the people for whom one is working. As this excerpt from an interview with a local authority officer in London points out, people working in local government can think of their work to meet public needs as separate from their own personal lives. But, as this book will show, they are often constantly aware that their own lives outside of work are bound up in what they do, and vice versa.

In the interview with Rachel, I asked about her understanding of community cohesion policy. This is a set of ideas and interventions that became significant in England and Wales in 2001 in response to concerns about the fragmentation of society, particularly along ethnic lines. Its meaning is fluid and shifting, and context-specific, but it circulates with ideas about identity, belonging and local government in ways that are recognisable in policy discussions in other times and places.

Starting with the questions provoked by community cohesion policy is a way of getting at a number of different concerns – how identity and belonging are understood in (local) government; how individuals relate their own personal struggles to the broader institutions in which they are embedded; the importance of feeling and emotion in how policy operates; and how power and inequality interact with each of these concerns. Using community cohesion policy as a focus highlights the importance of shifting and unstable meanings in policy, and creates space to engage with larger themes including the nature of society, identity, inequality, migration and belonging.

Community cohesion became a common term in Britain after the summer of 2001, emerging as a government 'agenda' in reports, explanations and suggested responses that followed a series of violent disturbances in the north of England in May, June and July that year. News coverage and government and independent inquiries, both local and national, found that much of the violence had been between groups of white men and British Asian men. Although the detailed inquiries attributed these outbreaks to a range of complex factors, the catch-all term for the problems was a lack of 'community cohesion', with people living 'parallel lives'. That is, there was a fear that people were living close to one another in the same town, but never meeting or mixing with nearby residents seen as from a 'different community', usually defined along crude ethnic lines.

In Chapter Two, I go into much more detail about the way that 'community cohesion' emerged as a policy catchphrase, the different ways it has been defined and measured, and the ways its resonances have changed since 2001, to encapsulate different formations of 'community cohesion problems', from the minor electoral successes of extreme racist parties, to radically new patterns of migration into the UK and reactions to these changes. It is notable that in all of these formations, the phrase 'community cohesion' continues to be critiqued as vague, misleading and confused (Robinson, 2005; Alexander, 2007; Husband and Alam, 2011). Both in policy documents setting out community cohesion work and in the practice and talk of people working in local and central government, community cohesion is constantly being defined and contested, and from many different political standpoints, as I outline in Chapter Two and throughout the book. However, to give a flavour of the definitions of community cohesion policy, here is the first definition of the term published by the UK government:

> A cohesive community is one where:
> - there is a common vision and sense of belonging for all communities;
> - the diversity of people's different backgrounds and circumstances are appreciated and positively valued;
> - those from different backgrounds have similar life opportunities; and
> - strong and positive relationships are being developed between people from different backgrounds in the

workplace, in schools and within neighbourhoods. (LGA, 2002, p 6)

On the surface, this is a vision that should appeal to everyone. Who could disagree with the positive sentiments being expressed here, if we assume that there is a broad consensus that equality and diversity are good, and conflict and separation are bad?

With a more focused critical perspective, however, the problems with this vision as a workable policy become clear. The statement uses the central idea of 'community' (twice) without ever being clear what it means (people who live in the same area? people who share the same cultural heritage or religion? people who support the same football team?). It repeats the term 'different backgrounds' that makes the policy all-encompassing, but also makes it unspecific (is this a euphemism for ethnic background, since that is where the focus of 'parallel lives' originated? could economic or class position be considered a 'background' that should not affect one's life opportunities?).

There is also a lack of clarity about whether community cohesion is being seen as something that produces other desirable outcomes (with more community cohesion we would not have riots), something that is a result of those other desirable outcomes (if we don't have riots, we can develop better community cohesion), or something that is measured by the absence of other negative outcomes (we know we have more community cohesion because there are no riots). In practice, it seems to slip between each of these uses, sometimes being cause, sometimes goal, sometimes overarching measure, and sometimes all three.

A great deal of work has been done critiquing the vagueness of the term, and the presumed motives behind it (discussed in more detail in Chapters One and Two). The point here, however, is that 'community cohesion policy' became, from 2001 onwards, a way of talking about issues of community, identity, belonging, connection and conflict. Discussion of community cohesion came to mean discussion of race equality, economic inequality, differences in beliefs, discrimination, tolerance and what role public authorities ought to have in each of these realms.

Activities branded as 'community cohesion work' might include celebratory festivals or other public events bringing people together; training in cultural diversity for public service staff or others; direct work with residents, perhaps by youth workers or mediation services, to identify and reduce minor conflicts; discussion in town planning meetings about new housing or business developments and their effects on residents; or a range of other interventions. Community cohesion policy might be seen as focusing largely on ethnic divisions, or on other factors. From starting out as a term that was critiqued as assimilationist and aiming to undercut multiculturalism (Kundnani, 2002; Alexander, 2007), it has become, in 2013, a term that is no longer in the current government's lexicon, but which is now embedded in local policy vocabularies as a defence against policies and practices that are seen as divisive. Despite the constantly changing government landscape, community cohesion as a term has become at least momentarily institutionalised in England and Wales, through job titles, policies and plans, through a statutory duty on schools to promote community cohesion, and in the stated aims of local authorities and their partners.

The broad aims of community cohesion policy, then, are that people 'get along' with each other in a context of cultural, or other, differences. By definition, this makes 'getting along', people's feelings about one another and behaviours towards one another, a government concern. Community cohesion policy seeks to shape such feelings and behaviours. Because of this, it is useful to think of community cohesion policy using theories of governmentality. Michel Foucault described governmentality as concerned with 'the conduct of conduct' (Foucault, 1982, p 221) – that is, with the ways that people behave. He used the term 'governmentality' to describe a form of power in which authority is exercised by requiring individuals to see themselves as responsible for their own lives and circumstances. This is contrasted with sovereign power, where government or authority controls people's behaviour by punishing them if they do not behave correctly (Foucault, 1991 [1978], pp 100-1). Where the politics of governmentality is operating, individuals absorb values and 'right' behaviours, and then strive to conduct themselves in those acceptable ways (Rose, 1999b, p 188).

How does this translate to community cohesion policy? In the thinking behind it, everyone has a responsibility to get along with people from different backgrounds, but they also have the freedom to choose not to. Government and public agencies can do things to encourage respect and mingling – organising opportunities to meet, for example, or providing information to help different communities to get to know one another. If people, or 'communities', still choose not to value diversity in the ways expected of them, they will not be forced to do so. But they will be considered not to share the 'common values' of society, and so they become personally responsible for a lack of community cohesion. In the process, structural factors that might have led to a separation between distinct communities – such as legacies of discrimination and oppression institutionalised in housing, education or employment – are removed from the equation; a lack of community

–

cohesion is ultimately seen as a failure of individuals and communities, rather than society as a whole.

Governmentality enables us to think about government not just as a process of the state, but as something that is undertaken at the level of the individual self (Foucault, 1991 [1978], p 103). This is often viewed negatively, a technique used by those in power to shift perceptions of responsibility from societal structures to personal failings of individual citizens, as described. But the dynamic process of governmentality can also leave space for radicalism. The all-encompassing language of 'different backgrounds', 'community' and 'values' offers opportunities for reinterpretation. In this sense, it is not simply the documents and official definitions of community cohesion that are important in understanding how community cohesion policy works; it is also the ways these documents are understood, interpreted and reacted against. The documents themselves are produced by active and self-conscious agents who are aware of many of the contradictions of the documents they produce, and also of the multiple ways they are likely to be used. As I explain in Chapter One, this study goes beyond simply analysing documents, to consider the lived practices of people working within local and central government and related organisations. These are the people who are operating policies of 'governmentality', but they are also subject to governmentality themselves; they are reflexive and self-governing selves, finding ways to relate their own views and commitments within their policy roles. Throughout the book, I coin the term *policy practitioner* to describe this role.

'Policy practitioner' describes local government officers and politicians, civil servants, members of think tanks, employees of other public sector bodies and local community organisations. It is more accurate than the more common term 'policy maker', which assumes that policy is something that is made in one place, enshrined in a document and implemented elsewhere. It draws attention to the *doing* of policy and government, the reinterpretations and negotiations that are not always recorded or accounted for officially. It recognises that 'implementing policy' is not simply a matter of doing what is instructed, but is about translation between contexts, understanding and priorities.

Studying policy as a dynamic, ongoing practice gets closer to understanding government as shifting and interpretive rather than commanding. By studying the day-to-day encounters of policy practitioners, my research follows in the tradition of scholars such as Lipsky (1980), who studied the world of 'street-level bureaucrats', and more recent work by Hoggett et al (2006a, 2006b), Ahmed (2012) and Hunter (2013). This empirical approach tests existing theorisations of governmentality that rely on documentation, and applies the theory directly to the engagement of individual's self-making activities in governing and being governed.

By engaging with policy practitioners, I draw out the understandings and negotiations they undertake in making political and bureaucratic decisions, translating between national and local contexts, and managing existing relationships between and within agencies and with the public. It becomes clear that policy practitioners hold several frames of reference, commitments, objectives, hopes and limitations as they go about this work. An element of this, for many, is relating structural social issues to individual lives – both the lives of their constituents, and their own lives. In this sense, I argue, many of the people I encounter in this book are demonstrating a sociological imagination, as described by C. Wright Mills (1999 [1959]). This application of a sociological imagination in everyday life and encounters is, I believe, an important form of public sociology. The movement for public sociology more usually outlines a mission for academics to share and apply their knowledge and critique in the wider world (Burawoy, 2004; Calhoun, 2005). In Chapters Six and Seven particularly, I make the case that it is also important to recognise how sociological thinking is used beyond the academy, and to consider the uncomfortable positions that are produced when applying such understandings as a practitioner.

To understand this discomfort, it is important to have an understanding of the relationships between *emotion and power*. As outlined already, community cohesion policy clearly aims to intervene at the level of *feelings* among individuals and populations, encouraging belonging, tolerance and a sense of shared values. In practice, many interventions made under the banner of community cohesion policy have been at the level of discourse and work on emotions, such as festive celebrations and encouraging dialogue between groups seen as otherwise separate and disconnected from one another. However, there is a more central way in which the interconnectedness of emotions and power are important to negotiations thrown up by community cohesion policy.

Emotion and relationships are central because they are central to how organisations, and specifically governing organisations, work. Organisations depend on people persuading one another to follow particular courses of action, by drawing on resources that sometimes include coercive power, or self-regulation based on acceptance of differences in power and status, or using elements of desire as tools of persuasion. All of these resources operate at the level of *people* doing the persuading, choosing and self-regulation – within structural constraints. The workings of organisations are thus mediated through embodied relationships, and experienced in emotional terms. But recognising this does not mean that governing and organisations are being reduced to the irrational, inexplicable or ineffable. Emotions are powerful, and power operates through emotions.

The operation of this type of persuasive, emotive power often works through narrative, or the telling of convincing stories. To reach agreement or compromise, people construct narratives that demonstrate connections between different points of view or priorities, and mask or overcome continuing differences (Bonnett, 1993, p 79; Christie, 2006). The most obvious way in which narratives appear in policy practice is in policy documents which provide an account of an institutional standpoint, plan or set of options, with a starting point and a desired destination or 'ending'. In Chapter One, I suggest that policy practitioners also use narrative techniques to negotiate their work in other ways – for instance, to describe their work as a process that makes sense and has a logical progression, or to remember why certain decisions are made. If we think of strategies, plans and speeches as persuasive stories with a beginning (the problem), a journey (proposals to address the problem) and an ending (the expected outcome an intervention), then policy and government can be understood to be about creating and disseminating compelling narratives. The research follows multiple narratives of how community cohesion policy has developed, of the reputations of particular places, of how policy practitioners understand and explain their own encounters within government.

In the making and remaking of community cohesion policy, it has become a way of telling stories about places, as well as framing shifting sets of issues – from 'parallel lives', to shared values, to countering extremism, to dealing with the consequences of migration and population change; from pressure on services to a sense of shared belonging. Chapter Two traces four different inflections of community cohesion policy in the UK, each of which tends to be connected to a particular locality in England within policy discourses; firstly, the idea of parallel lives lived by separated ethnic groups; secondly, the development of concerns about a disgruntled 'white working class' separated from 'shared values' of tolerance; thirdly, the impacts of new migration patterns in areas imagined as unused to change or diversity; and finally, these difficult situations can be contrasted with an ideal of unproblematic community cohesion in super-diverse inner-city areas, rehabilitated from the image of fear and danger to one of desirable, successful multiculture and cosmopolitanism ready to be presented to as modern Britain's Olympic brand, and where community cohesion is, on the surface, unproblematic.

As Chapter Two demonstrates, in official government definitions, community cohesion policy has moved from being imagined as a part of race equality work (Cantle, 2001, p 21; Community Cohesion Review Panel, 2004, p 57, to being positioned as quite separate from and different to work on equalities or on race equality specifically (DCLG, 2008, p 11). National government has also argued that community cohesion work should be quite distinct from measures to counter extremism, particularly extremism in the name of Islam (DCLG, 2008, p 11). These continued statements of how community cohesion is distinct only highlight that there would otherwise be an expectation that equalities work, particularly race equality work, and work to counter extremism, are directly related to community cohesion where community cohesion is about finding ways for everyone 'from different backgrounds' to 'get along'. The origins of the policy – as a reaction to ethnically defined tensions – also suggest that such relationships between policies should be key.

Despite the repeated attempts at separating out these streams of work, throughout my research I found that policy practitioners, both local and national, whether working directly on 'community cohesion policy' or not, continued to associate the policy primarily with questions of racism and race equality, and as bound up with counter-terrorism measures. In Chapter Three I explore this by engaging with ethnographic data from my experiences of working within a local authority at the moment when national government mandated local authorities to take an active role in the Preventing Violent Extremism (PVE) programme. This programme was part of broader counter-terrorist policy, and explicitly aimed to 'win the hearts and minds' of 'Muslims in our communities' (CLG, 2007b, p 3). The reaction of many local authorities was to argue that such an approach could endanger good relations among residents, not least because of the specific focus on one (diverse) religious group, and that as a result, it countered the aims of existing community cohesion work. By unpicking local and national debates and experiences, I demonstrate how the negotiations around community cohesion policy can shed light on much broader questions about the operation of government and policy, and the relationships between levels and agencies of government.

Place is a less dramatic element of community cohesion policy than countering extremism, but it has nonetheless been a continuing emphasis, on finding shared belonging in local places, developing relationships with neighbours, trusting local institutions and developing connections through everyday shared spaces at a local level. Understanding 'the local' and local identity is not simple, however. In Chapter Four this is demonstrated through an in-depth engagement with the attachments to and experiences of a particular place – Hackney – where the majority of my research was focused. Thinking about how this place is understood in government and policy, and how community cohesion is thought through in relation to Hackney's 'super-diversity' (Vertovec, 2006) as well as its extremes of economic inequality (LBH, 2006a), its rapid change in population, fortunes and image, and the desire and fear it simultaneously evokes, draws out some alternative understandings of community cohesion, as potentially a way of highlighting structural inequality which creates conflict. In Chapter Five, the theme of place, reputation and 'brand' in local government is developed further by exploring three other places – Oldham, Barking and Dagenham and Peterborough – which are often used as markers of cohesion debates in the UK. As well as highlighting the relationships between stories told about places and the management of reputation in local government, the chapter shows how emotive stories about place become important in managing the external reputation of places in government circles. I suggest that this is partly because the limits on local government powers to effect structural change can lead policy practitioners to focus on developing positive local feelings, without being able to address underlying issues that can lead to negative feeling; and to use positive narratives (or narratives of struggling against the odds) to win national government support for investment in their local area.

Chapter Six brings us back to the 'governors' themselves. I consider how power inequalities and the recognition of the power of simplifying narratives make many policy practitioners uncomfortable, particularly when reflecting on these issues in the research interview. I argue that the recognition of systematic discrimination and disadvantage of particular gendered, classed or racialised groups has become embedded in policy worlds to the extent that practitioners often note potential discrimination almost as a reflex action. But the result is not always emancipating. Indeed some interviewees used this starting point to re-establish themselves as privileged (for example, as a middle-class heterosexual white man) and therefore 'neutral'. Others, however, reflected on the desirability but impossibility of neutrality and what this means for the role of the bureaucrat. Some found community cohesion policy, or associated subjects, difficult to talk about because of the risk of exposure of their own privileged position in society, and many sought to find a more comfortable speaking position by demonstrating how they, too, had somehow been marginalised and therefore could speak authentically about oppression. I close this chapter by suggesting that perhaps the most powerful techniques for considering the inequalities and consequent tensions which community cohesion policy (sometimes) tries to address came from those practitioners who recognised their own uncomfortable position but spoke in solidarity with (rather than on behalf of) groups they saw as oppressed.

The majority of the research for this book was carried out in a period of change, between 2005 and 2010, when community cohesion policy was a hot topic for local and central government in England and Wales. The policy landscape continues to move on, not least with the election of a new UK government in 2010 and the continuing repercussions of the global economic crisis. Nevertheless, the central findings of this research continue to be relevant to policy negotiations in this field. Chapter Seven sets this out in four ways. First, understandings of governmentality as *process*, examining the negotiations of policy in practice (the conduct of the conduct of conduct) and how governors themselves are also subject to processes of governmentality and self-regulation. Second, the construction of narratives, what they allow to be said and what is silenced, can have the effect of masking power relations. In the case of community cohesion policy, my research demonstrates that attempts to expose and address inequality can be reincorporated into narratives, silencing attempts at more progressive imaginings of society. Third, the role and functioning of local government is an often unspoken subject of struggle in the negotiations I have mapped, and this constant questioning of what local government should be, or is, able to do – a mixture of promise and frustration – creates uncomfortable positions for policy practitioners working within it. Finally, the linking of individual moments and relationships (often experienced through emotion) and societal power structures is not limited to the imaginations of professional sociologists or academics. I argue that many policy practitioners encountered in this research made such links, but that their role was not simply to develop such understandings, but to attempt to *use* them in the negotiation and exercise of power. As my research shows, doing so is not easy or comfortable. It is often navigated through the use of narratives that draw on unspoken resonances and emotional reactions. Developing, interpreting and using such narratives is a skill in itself. The importance of understanding the power of emotion in policy is not so much about emotion as an output of policy, or an abdication of attention to material relations. Rather, it is about understanding how material relations of power are mediated *through* personal relationships and emotional reactions, and that to influence power inequalities it is necessary to understand such emotional resonances, and the uncomfortable positions they engender.

ONE

Negotiating cohesion, inequality and change

Community and community cohesion

Community cohesion policy is a collection of ideas, practices and texts which touches on a whole host of other subjects – difference, inequality and discrimination along lines of class, race, gender, religion, age and geography, conflicting values, questions of nationhood, community, belonging, trust, power and governance. Negotiating the meanings and resonances of community cohesion policy provides many opportunities to take up or avoid uncomfortable positions. Meanwhile, its supporters' insistence that it should be considered in all areas of public services, and of life (COIC, 2007), allows us to consider how far it morphs and changes in different contexts.

Community cohesion policy emerged in 2001-02, at the height of the British New Labour government and the influence of 'Third Way' ideas in British politics. The Third Way met the failure of state socialism and the need to regulate capitalism with a compromise between socialism and liberalism (Giddens, 1998) that influenced the electoral successes of centrist social democratic governments in the UK, US and elsewhere. It emphasised pragmatism over ideology, and populism over redistribution (Temple, 2000; Lister, 2001). The defining element of this politics seemed to be ambivalence in policy and rhetoric; this ambivalence was key to its electoral success, but has also provoked criticism (Hall, 1998; Lister, 2001; Back et al, 2002).

A central lever in the Third Way of governing became 'community'. As Schofield put it, 'the very attractiveness of community to policymakers lies in its ambiguous potential' (2002, pp 679-80). In these policies, community is treated as a seemingly fundamental social and historical concept, which can be 'allowed too easily to become an explanation rather than something to be explained' (Alleyne, 2002, p 608). For example, 'community involvement' continues to be used as a condition of state support for poorer areas, so that the requirement to *create* 'community' becomes a form of government at a distance (Levitas, 2005, p 199). The increasing use of the concept of 'community' – as

11

both a rhetorical technique and a way of shaping processes of governing – has been a particular focus of sociological attention. As Ruth Levitas points out, the concept's popularity has increased in academia as well as in government, with a similar lack of conceptual clarity (2005, p 89).

The use and power of language in reimagining and reinforcing social categories in the 'New Labour project' in Britain, and Third Way approaches more generally, is pinpointed by Stuart Hall as part of 'its efforts to be all-inclusive. It has no enemies. Everyone can belong' (1998, p 10). Yet claiming 'everyone can belong' still depends on the existence of 'others' who refuse, or threaten, 'everyone's' common values.

Early critiques of community cohesion policy described and participated in the struggle over its meaning. They pointed out how power relations were neglected in the way that theories of community cohesion were being developed, and identified inconsistencies in the policy, its practice and its identified subject matter (Burnett, 2007; Wetherell et al, 2007). These critiques show that the ideal of 'shared values' with which it appears easy to agree can actually stand for a multitude of shifting meanings (Yuval-Davis et al, 2005; Fortier, 2010). They identified a mismatch between the description of inclusive cohesion alongside a repressive criminal justice response, particularly to young Muslim men (Bagguley and Hussain, 2003a; McGhee, 2005); the association of cohesion policy with migration, and latterly with terrorism (Cheong et al, 2007; Husband and Alam, 2011); inconsistent attention to the social and economic factors underpinning unrest (Kalra, 2002; McGhee, 2003); the de-racialising and re-racialising effects of 'community' discourse and the implications of cohesion discourse for the construction of gender and family (Worley, 2005); and the assumption that consensus will always be a positive goal, that communities or identities are static and bounded, and that any of these questions can be separated from struggles over power and disadvantage (Alexander, 2004; Cheong et al, 2007). But how does community cohesion policy actually do this?

In 2005, as chair of the Commission for Racial Equality, Trevor Phillips suggested that 'integration is a learned competence – like maths or driving a car.' If integration (closely associated with the language of cohesion; see COIC, 2007 and Spencer, 2011) is simply a skill or craft to be learned, then the task of government is to provide the means to learn; the responsibility of citizens is to learn and apply this skill. The following extract from a Home Office cohesion strategy exemplifies this approach:

> *his is not something that the Government can do alone*, but it is an issue on which we can give a lead: *helping people come together* from different backgrounds; *supporting people to contribute* to society; and taking a stand against racism and extremists who promote hatred. (Home Office, 2005b, p 5; emphasis added)

Here, the role of government is to 'help' and 'support' people to make the right choices and to behave in an appropriate way. People are expected to do this not (only) for their individual benefit, but for the good of society; their responsibility for doing so, however, is an individual responsibility. These desirable behaviours are specified by the state, but ensuring they are followed is an individual responsibility.

To understand this type of governing, we need to take a step away from much of the traditional study of government in political science, public administration and state theory. Political science traditions tend to focus on national rather than local scales (see, for example, Rhodes, 1988; Jessop, 2003, pp 108-9), and on institutions rather than people (see, for example, Wolman, 1995; Stoker, 2004). They tend to either describe or prescribe ideal types of institutional models (see, for example, Dunleavy, 1991, p 259; Hood, 1991, 1998; Stoker, 2004, p 168). Finally, they tend to remain silent about their research methods (see, for example, Stone, 1995; Stoker, 2004, p 78), reinforcing their understandings of government as institutional, abstract and perfectible. Local government studies can appear to operate without people or places – the stuff of social interaction. By contrast, but following others (Back, 2007b, pp 160-3; Burnett and Duncan, 2008; Keith, 2008b, Hunter, 2013), the research in this book begins from an understanding of government, governing and policy making as messy, unruly and contingent, involving *people* and happening in *places*.

Thinking about the practice of policy through the lens of governmentality allows us to rethink government beyond easily divisible and mechanical workings of discrete nation-states, to take account of new flows, challenges and undercurrents. In this less certain world, a

> ... new ethical politics ... refuses the idea that politics is a matter of state, parliament, election and party programme ... demanding that individuals, families, communities, employers take back to themselves the powers and responsibilities that ... have been acquired by states, politicians and legislators. (Rose, 1999b, pp 2-3)

Rose argues that this is the mode in which government operates – through shifts, interactions and reinterpretations between a range of different actors, rather than through clearly delineated mandates of institutions carried out more or less efficiently. This does not mean that each actor has equal ability to navigate the rules and limitations of society, or equal resources to do so; it simply means that an attention to the micro level of interactions is important *alongside* a consideration of how institutions operate at a macro level.

Most writing about governmentality focuses on ways that citizens are subject to state power, and how they conduct themselves in response to regimes of governmentality. There is less research into how individuals are implicated in *creating* regimes of governmentality to govern others. A radical reworking of the relationships of self-government could recognise and embrace the constant struggle and re-evaluation of norms and values. Nikolas Rose's term for this is an 'agonistic politics of ethics' (Rose, 1999b, p 194); it chimes with Chantal Mouffe's call for an 'ethics of the political' (2005, p 113). By this they call for a recognition of struggle (agonism), continual weighing up of choices and possibility (ethics) and attempts at intervention (politics).

So governmentality theory can be used as a way of understanding the functioning of government by looking at these individual and group shifts in meanings and practice, as well as at official policies, requirements and sanctions. Governmentality is also useful for understanding a particular genre of policies that make the focus on individual 'freedom' and 'responsibility' their starting point. This is a genre of which community cohesion policy, with its focus on values and feeling included, is a good example. Such policies depend on the autonomy of the individual, while reinforcing norms (the 'shared core' of values) that strongly encourage individuals to behave in a certain way, to produce beneficial outcomes. But the sharing of norms and responsibilities, couched in an appeal to a morality of 'community', does not eliminate the possibility for tension, or the need to negotiate the diversity and difference of individuals in a population (Rose, 1999b, p 170). Devising and practising interventions that draw on self-government involves some level of sociological imagination, some analytical consideration of the relations between individual and society.

Sociological imagination

Sociological imagination is a concept coined by C. Wright Mills. Believing that dialogue and questioning are central to sociology, he conceived of the sociological imagination as:

> ... a quality of mind that will help [people] to use
> information and to develop reason in order to achieve lucid
> summations of what is going on in the world and of what
> may be happening within themselves. (1999 [1959], p 5)

and

> ... the capacity to shift from one perspective to another ... to
> range from the most impersonal and remote transformation
> to the most intimate features of the human self – and to see
> the relations between the two. (1999 [1959], p 7)

That is, Mills saw sociology's key contribution to be the relation of individual lives to societal issues, and vice versa. Mills argued for an imaginative and engaged craft of sociology, as opposed to rival sociological traditions of 'methodological fetishism' and Grand Theory, and their stifling disciplinary fixity (Gane and Back, 2012). Previous work on community cohesion policy has identified how sociological categories are used in its construction, for example, how the ambiguity of language allows categories of race and gender division to shift in and out of focus (Worley, 2005), or how the idea of managing populations through individual feelings is an essentially sociological project (McGhee, 2003, p 376). However, I will show that it is not simply in the surface rhetoric or in the schemes, plans and projects of community cohesion policy that individual and structural factors are related. In a potentially much more radical way, individual policy practitioners reflect on the structural power relations within which they function, and find ways, within this, to manage their commitments to principles, experiences in their own lives and relationships to other people within these structures, as they shape what effects community cohesion policy actually *has*.

In this, I argue, we can see a form of public sociology. This challenges the popular caricature of faceless bureaucrats acting out the will of a monolithic state. But it also challenges what often seems to be an implicit assumption of sociological studies of policy (see, for example, Strathern, 2000) – that academic thinkers have unique access to tools of social analysis, and that the ultimate use of such analysis is critique. For many policy practitioners, such analysis can also be used to make sense of their work within and outside government, and to influence that work.

It is important to recognise not only that non-sociologists sometimes think in similar ways to sociologists, but also that in some cases it is not so easy to draw a distinction between who is 'a sociologist' and who is not (Farrar, 2008). Sociological theories and ideas can be translated and reinflected outside universities with or without the academy's 'consent'. Non-professional sociologists have their own insights and expertise – for example, about how other, perhaps more radical, forms of social science could be transformed into practical tools for use within governing and policy, or challenging government and policy.

Calls for 'public sociology' gained momentum in 2004, when the American Sociological Association's then president, Michael Burawoy, made an impassioned call for the greater availability of sociological insights to the wider public (Burawoy, 2004). Burawoy's idea of public sociology meant sociological thinking made available outside of universities. He distinguished this from the kind of sociology commissioned by governments or other bodies, which he termed 'policy sociology'. For Burawoy, sociology used in policy is instrumental, focused on particular goals, but limited because it is entwined in the agendas of large organisations, whereas 'public sociology' must be critical, and critical thinking cannot be tied up in policy goals. He made a similar distinction within the university, between professional sociology (academic practices which focus on solving specific problems) and critical sociology (challenging and rethinking the foundations of the discipline).

I take issue with Burawoy's central assumption that the use of sociological thinking by the state or other public bodies must necessarily be unreflexive, or even malign. In my view, following C. Wright Mills, an important goal of public sociology should be to create the possibility of discussions that question power relations and their workings, in all realms of society (see also Back, 2007b, p 114). In the process of my research, the understandings of social problems that participants expressed were rarely described with explicit reference to social theorists or theories (although sometimes they were). But they were very often inflected by them, either by 'folk sociologies' (Sayer, 2005, p 20) or by half-remembered insights from books, radio, television or newspapers – or policy documents and conferences. Occasionally, participants would express frustration at the limits of the models at their disposal for understanding the complex social problems we were discussing. They would often describe the workings of government in pragmatic, ethnographic terms that emphasised the everyday and contingent, alongside their presentation of the formal model of how governing is supposed to work. They would provide their own theorisations about these forms of cognitive dissonance.

The focus of this book is on *how* policy practitioners create, maintain, obstruct, manipulate or change policies and institutions – including, often, by doing work on themselves. Simply identifying the contradictions and ambiguities of language in policy limits the possibilities for sociological imagination to have influence in the public sphere. The existing literature on community cohesion policy that provides this kind of analysis does not tell us very much about how alternative worlds might be imagined (or brought into being). In response to this tendency, Newman and Clarke (2009, pp 185-6) call for the re-articulation of concepts such as 'public', 'equality', 'bureaucracy' and 'welfare', to nourish counter-discourses towards an egalitarian form of publicness. They argue that such counter-discourses challenge the undertones and genealogies that undercut many of these terms, in a more effective way than simply rejecting a term such as 'diversity' because it has become discredited by some politically problematic usage. Throughout this book, I explore the extent to which such counter-discourses co-exist, refract and reinterpret existing meanings and echoes, in the everyday negotiations of policy practitioners.

Emotional work

As described earlier, feelings and their management are an explicit focus of community cohesion policy. In policy documents and most scholarly analysis of community cohesion policy to date (see, for example, McGhee, 2003, 2005; Wetherell et al, 2007; Flint and Robinson, 2008; Ratcliffe and Newman, 2011), it is the feelings and experiences of 'the public' that are in question. Similarly, much work on emotion in government has concentrated on the management of the feelings of the general public or of the welfare recipient (Barnes, 2008). I want to make the case for examining the emotional work that takes place at the level of the policy professional when negotiating cohesion, inequality and change.

Policy practitioners at once govern and are governed; they are subject to the policies they develop as well as explicitly active in the development of policies as tools of government (Hunter, 2003). Their awareness of this double positioning, as well as their sometime awareness of the ambiguities of processes, practices and policies of governmentality, their negotiation of their professional roles in research encounters with me, were to a great extent also concerned with their negotiation of their own sense of self. Analysts of government and politics tend to understand the individuals who work within and make up such institutions only in their professional roles, and their motivations are thus reduced to their professional commitments (McKee, 2009, pp 478–9). My study takes this further by engaging with these practices as both participant and observer.

I draw on the developing field of psycho-social welfare studies, which attempts to introduce feminist perspectives on the importance of affect and attachment to questions of power and knowledge (Barnes, 2008; Scanlon and Adlam, 2008; Stenner et al, 2008). This is not the approach to understanding emotion and well-being in policy making which has recently gained a spike in publicity in Britain and internationally (see, for example, Theodoropolou and Zuleeg, 2009; Wilkinson and Pickett, 2009), which is characterised (sometimes unfairly) as 'measuring happiness'. Within that movement there are differences, not least between those interested in a more developed sense of how to understand 'well-being' beyond economic aggregates (Stiglitz et al, 2009), and those more interested in quantifying 'happiness' while ignoring power relations (Layard, 2005; Mulgan and Davies, 2011). Nor is it a direct critique of these approaches, although work such as Ahmed's (2010) unpicking of how obligations to pursue 'happiness' can be detrimental to social justice is valuable here.

An attention to emotional decision making does not mean that decisions are made without reason; it means abandoning the fantasy or ideal type of rational choice theories to recognise that human beings make decisions in specific contexts and within relationships of power and connection. Hoggett (2001) challenges Giddens' celebration of the possibilities of rational choice by highlighting how choices can be made in 'urgent and contingent encounters' (p 40), in which 'our capacity to be a reflexive agent is often constrained by the difficulties we have in facing our own fears and anxieties' (p 42). By considering the importance of emotion in decision making, we may therefore be better able to consider the ethical dimension of relations to others that more scientistic accounts seem to remove.

The body of work on emotion in the workplace (see, for example, Hochschild, 1983; Fineman, 2000; Greco and Stenner, 2008) and within governing institutions in particular (see, for example, Cooper, 1995; Rose, 1999b; Hoggett, 2000; Lewis, 2000; Ahmed, 2007b) looks at the relationship between individual and organisation but less at how senior individuals in organisations relate emotionally to their powers to change that organisation or its effects (Barnes, 2008, p 477; although see Lewis, 2000; Hunter, 2003; Mayo et al, 2007). The existing literature on the 'public sector ethos' (du Gay, 2000; Le Grand, 2003; Hoggett et al, 2006a, 2006b) considers one element of this, an element traditionally thought of as about impartiality of service delivery and equality of citizenship rights. There has been less research into how processes of identity and subjectivity are invoked by those acting within governing roles, as a technique which allows practitioners to undertake and make sense of their work, whether protecting or attempting to disrupt the prevailing power dynamic (although see, for example, Lewis, 2000; Puwar, 2001; Hunter, 2005; Cooper, 2006; Ahmed, 2012).

The idea of emotion as a motivating force is an anathema to some theorists of bureaucracy (in particular, du Gay, 2000, 2007). Du Gay argues that the personae of bureaucrat and individual should be kept separate. He suggests that attempts of New Public Management and psychological theories of management to integrate feeling into public services have undermined the commitment to impartiality that is a central tenet of the public service ethos. Du Gay has a fairly positive view of the ideal of an impartial bureaucrat, implementing rules without personal reflection. While he acknowledges the political aspects of bureaucratic work – the negotiation and interpretation that is necessary for, in his main case, the civil service to develop politicians' ideas into workable policies (du Gay, 2000, p 141) – du Gay argues that for these negotiations to be successful, bureaucrats must conform to an impartiality which allows them to work with governments of changing political persuasion. My argument is that this is an ideal type, or a useful fiction, rather than what actually happens, or can happen, in practice (Mayo et al, 2007).

Focusing on the difficulties experienced by relatively powerful people can all too easily be dismissed as self-justification and the re-enforcement of privilege without action towards greater social justice (Ahmed, 2004b, p 118; Berlant, 2004, p 11; Skeggs, 2004, p 131). But indulging the narration of privileged selves is not the point. Rather, the point is to seek out whether, and where, there are possibilities for such privileged selves to take a position that recognises their (our) privilege, and uses it to improve the equity of social relations, without simply reinforcing a colonising relationship. Whether such a position might be possible is as relevant to debates about the role of the sociologist and academic as to debates about that of the policy practitioner (Skeggs, 1997, p 15).

Telling stories, imagining places

Both policy practitioners and academic sociologists make sense of the world using the powerful persuasive tools of narrative. Narratives are accounts of a series of causally connected events, usually involving a main protagonist. There are continuing debates over whether a 'narrative' is different to a 'story' (Paley, 2009, pp 18-21), but those arguments don't really concern me here. What I want to emphasise is that narratives/stories are accounts which are constructed, and that telling them is intended to have, and has, effects on social relationships (Samuel and Thompson, 1990, p 8; Gunaratnam, 2009, p 55). Through narratives, people make sense of the world, make arguments about the world, and remake the world (Trouillot, 1995, p 23). To reach agreement or compromise, people construct narratives that demonstrate connections between different points of view or priorities, and mask or overcome continuing differences (Bonnett, 1993, p 79; Christie, 2006). To find a way through difficult terrain, people try to imagine how the path they are constructing will lead to their eventual goal.

Narrative is important in policy practice in at least four connected ways. First, there is the narrative that appears in textual documents, providing a coherent and fully formed presentation of institutional or political standpoints, plans or options, with a starting point and destination or desired 'ending'. These narratives can be studied and their internal contradictions, assumptions and exclusions demonstrated. Their production and publication is used to structure histories of what happened, when, and why. The narratives *in* the document are important in that they are the product of negotiations, as well as being texts on which further negotiations work. But this does not in itself address the work involved in constructing and using these documents, or how that work entails negotiations with a range of 'stakeholders'; with existing policies, discourses and institutions; and with resonances of language and form that determine what is possible.

Second, the process of negotiating policy can be thought of as a narrative. It involves writing, reading and translating; talking, remembering and revising; meeting, not meeting and excluding. It is conducted by policy practitioners embedded in organisations and institutional practices. There are narratives of how it is *supposed* to work (toolkits, guidance and performance plans), and occasional analyses of why it does not work, but the fragmentary, variable and intangible is difficult to capture. This is not unique to policy processes, and is true of many aspects of life (Law, 2003). For the purposes of understanding these negotiations, this book draws on my own experiences as a policy practitioner in local government, as well as the first-hand accounts given by others in interviews. My research translates these negotiations into narrative – reframing memories which are themselves assembled through technologies of notes, documents and artefacts (Rose, 1998; Coffey, 1999). My reconstruction of these encounters into narrative is inevitably partial, embodied and embedded. My account is itself a technology (Paley, 2009) for understanding the processes of policy practice and governing in the context of the research account (Gunaratnam, 2009).

Third, I found that a central tool policy practitioners used for talking about the difficult subjects connected with community cohesion policy was to anchor discussion in an understanding of the self. Interviewees used biographical narratives, or elements of them, to claim a space from which to speak about issues where questions of power and situated knowledge were near the surface. This is *not* intended to suggest that this direct attention to identity reveals some more complete or authentic truth about the processes and negotiations of policy, or practitioners' understandings of them, than would be found through other means of observation or research (Atkinson and Silverman, 1997). Rather, the interviews present one form of data on the *ways* that policy practitioners negotiate these difficult subjects. This data is *itself* a negotiation, and it is a dataset that is produced by, and dependent on, the interview methodology that I used (Skeggs, 2002). More detail of the methodology and methods of data collection for the study can be found in the Appendix at the end of this book.

The fourth type of narrative is spatial, a shared 'folk knowledge' that explains the concept of community cohesion evolving over time and space. Policy practitioners often explained community cohesion with reference to places whose reputations stood in for a specific set of meanings and histories (see also Keith and Pile, 1993, p 37). As this spatial narrative was so strong, I adapted my research strategy to follow the threads of narrative to places that appeared as symbols. The intention was not to prove or disprove the 'truth' about local experiences of community cohesion represented in this narrative. Rather, by focusing on negotiation between competing claims to tell the stories of particular places, I examine how policy practitioners who are constructed *within* the narrative, negotiate their way *through* these narratives, and narrate their own place in relation to cohesion.

At a general level, narratives are built around (and create) reputations of places, and these reputations become metaphors for more general policy design, markers of what problems exist and how they might be solved. Policy practitioners can at once recognise and use such metaphors, and dispute their accuracy when talking about their own local area, claiming more detailed knowledge of neighbourhoods and towns than 'outsiders' might have. Thus, in policy practice as elsewhere, multiple understandings of a place (for example, as a metaphor for racialised segregation and as a place of everyday lived multiculturalism) can be invoked, without necessarily begging the question of which is more 'real' (Edelman, 1977, p 15).

Sociological and geographical critiques have considered place shaping in light of neoliberal frameworks that emphasise self-reliance and the requirement of places to compete for *private* investment (see, for example, Urry, 1995; Ward, 1998; Shaw et al, 2004; Evans, 2006). However, locals' attachment to place became a measurement of the success of UK local government work in the early 21st century,[1] as part of an increase in promoting well-being and affective goods as a government role, within a framework of targets and quantification. Much local place marketing by local authorities still marries the imperative of attracting private investment with an imperative of appealing to *local* residents. This is typical of the ways social democratic governments working in neoliberal frameworks have built social well-being concerns into adaptations of market and entrepreneurial principles for (local) government.

In the late 1980s, David Harvey (1989) examined (with cautious approval) how some Labour local authorities in Britain were seeking ways to work a prioritisation of equalities and elements of socialist principles into the dominant entrepreneurial logics of local government at that time. This required competition between municipalities for investment, residents and central government support (an early Third Way logic). By the end of the 20th century, this proto-Third Way had become the framework that local practitioners *must* negotiate. Alongside the traditionally business-minded imperatives of efficiency and productivity, New Labour's league tables and development of performance measures (already established under the previous Conservative administrations) were designed to make various measurements of well-being and public good the 'outcomes' which organisations would compete to deliver.[2]

This is not just about claims to 'be the best'. In the UK and the European Union (EU), Third Way quasi-marketisation of governance with government programmes in the 2000s measured poverty and deprivation and targeted national resources to areas most in need. Local authorities attracting private capital were still favoured by central government, but demonstrating need became an important tool in attracting financial and other support, thus the measurement of poverty reduction was a question to be negotiated carefully. If a borough attracted a growing wealthy population, the resulting increase in overall or average wealth in the borough might mean that central government support would be reduced – although the lot of the poorest residents may not have changed at all. Thus describing the status of a place as one of the poorest areas in the country became a matter not simply of highlighting an area of challenge, but also of staking a claim to a share of national resources.

An important measure of 'success' at a national level includes 'customer satisfaction' measures of approval of the council, and, during the period in which my research took place, more general questions such as the community cohesion indicator measured in national surveys ('Do you agree that people from different backgrounds get along well together in this area?'; CLG, 2007c, p 5), which translate affective judgements into quantitative measures. Local authorities were judged not just on the prosperity of their area, but also on the satisfaction of residents both with where they live and with the local authority as arbiter of this. This would, of course, have always been the case at some level, elected members being accountable for resident satisfaction at local elections, and officers' careers benefiting or suffering from association with a council seen as successful or otherwise. Such pressures grew exponentially with inspections and publicly available league tables on local authority performance, and reputational devices such as 'beacon status' and being regarded as a site of good practice. Since 2010, although the Coalition government removed many of the systematic auditing measures of local government, it has continued to value 'local opinion' of public services and their management, through more voluntarist means such as petitions and bids to take control of local facilities (Clarke and Cochrane, 2013).

In this context, belonging also became something to be quantified and audited. The attention to shared belonging which community cohesion policy prioritises is thus tied up directly with attempts to develop a shared, geographically based sense of 'belonging' at a neighbourhood level, which relates, of course, to somehow presenting a sense of place that appeals to, and rings true for, the variety of existing residents. The emphasis on shared sense of place is also related to political concerns that global flows of people and capital have removed some of the certainties of life, thereby risking fractures between different sections of society (whether along lines of class, race, ethnicity, religion or some other factor).

This returns us to the importance of narrative, explicitly recognised in the local–central government relationship, albeit in a peculiarly measurement-oriented sense. The Local Area Agreement (LAA) process in operation at the time of this research required all local authorities to provide an 'evidence-based story of place' which 'should present how groups of outcomes and performance indicators connect with each other ... so that in telling the story of place GOs [Government

Offices] and central government can understand the relationship (cause/ effect) between indicators and targets' (CLG, 2007a, p 17). The brand of place is thus seen within these frameworks of governance as at least as important as (and tied up intimately with) how place is experienced through material factors such as health, housing, education, and so on. An attachment to, and positive impression of, a place may rely in part on these material services and amenities – but those services and amenities could also be thought of as entirely separate to the feeling of the locality, or the emotional attachment to the place (and, in theory, the local authority). A guide to branding for local authorities, produced by the Improvement and Development Agency (IDeA), states:

> The LGA's [Local Government Association] analysis in 2007 of best value performance indicators (BVPI) data found that *resident satisfaction with council services had no impact on public perceptions of the council* improving lives and local areas. It also found that residents who feel informed by their council are far more likely to feel their council is making their local area a better place to live. (IDeA, 2009; emphasis added)

Here, the advice to local authorities is that beyond simply improving the lives of their residents or the services they provide, they must *publicise* this success – must tell a persuasive story – to ensure that residents associate positive changes with interventions by the local authority. If this association is not made, satisfaction with the local authority (as measured by surveys) will be low, and this will count against the organisation in national league tables of the 'best performing' authorities. It is also likely to adversely affect the prospects of the council's leadership in terms of career advancement or voting patterns.

Negotiating the research

I came to the academic research in this book from working as a policy manager in a local authority (the London Borough of Hackney). This experience meant I already had a 'feel for the game' (Bourdieu, 1990 [1980], p 103) of policy practice and institutional life within the organisations of local government and their interactions with other organisational forms. By taking a step outside of this common-sense framework to study these processes with an element of ethnographic distance I changed my role and involvement. But I also recognised that research participants – those people I am 'studying' – are able and liable to think analytically about their everyday practices, in a similar way that I understood myself to be doing. And perhaps this ability to step outside and reflect on one's choices is also part of the 'game' of policy practice. The space between what organisations do, what they say they do and how they appear is not simply something for critical social research to expose. It is something that practitioners also recognise and work with (Ahmed, 2007a).

Doing the research has formed part of the negotiation of difficult subjects. In Chapter Three I analyse some of my experiences as a policy practitioner, working on the Preventing Violent Extremism (PVE) programme. Moving to the role of researcher gave me the privilege, time and space to consider those experiences more analytically.

The majority of the research for the book draws on interviews where other policy practitioners were invited to reflect on their work with me. Uncomfortable positions emerge when reflexive subjects are faced by contradictions between their taken-for-granted understandings of the world and their empirical experiences. The interview encounters I engineered often enabled policy practitioners to occupy such uncomfortable positions, whereas in day-to-day life, they might have less time to dwell on these positions, because of the demands of fulfilling professional duties. This is not to say that such discomforts were not present in daily interactions, just that a space to examine and elaborate on them was created in the interview encounter.

The interviews gave participants an opportunity to reflect on, as well as to engage in, these negotiations. In my analysis, I treat the interview encounters as constructed space in which I take seriously what the interviewees say. I do not dismiss their arguments as simple self-justifications ('they would say that, wouldn't they'). But nor do I take the interview transcript as a straightforward explanation of 'how it really is'. Rather, taking seriously the interview encounter means understanding it as a negotiation, in which both interviewer and interviewee reflect on *and reproduce* elements of the policy- and self-making process. Interviews thus provide concentrated access to such negotiations in process, rather than an unquestioned explanation of the situation 'from the horse's mouth'.

Having worked as a policy practitioner in Hackney, I had existing relationships with many research participants, and perceptions about how policy negotiations work. This experience informed and enriched my data, and provided credentials that helped me to achieve access to interviewees, both within and outside Hackney. But there is a risk that these connections could lead to over-familiarity or lack of questioning of norms and practices. Relationships with participants, research sites and research projects shift, and involve emotional investment as well as time and professional energies (Coffey, 1999, p 46). For me, these shifts involved negotiating a position that created, at times, perceptions that I might be moving between roles of friend, colleague, adviser, 'spy', auditor or competitor. In the role of researcher, I could (be seen to) occupy all of these roles, and yet none of them.

This type of work does not easily fit into the methodological discussions either of researching 'up' or 'down'. The research participants *are* powerful, and could be considered 'elite' in that they are opinion formers and being researched precisely because they are powerful. However, their powerful or elite status is in many cases directly comparable to that of the academic. Indeed, in many cases they may have been colleagues; or the same person may cross 'between worlds' at different points. Although many of the interviewees with whom I spoke had been senior to me, they were also colleagues I had worked with and advised directly. Thus the usual methodological concerns about accessing and being manipulated by elite research subjects, while relevant, do not fit neatly here. Feminist methodological concerns with listening and engaging with research participants, with not exploiting one's power as researcher, similarly do not quite fit. It is about finding a space between the assumption that power needs to be shared with the research participants, and that the researcher is manipulated by the participants. This is another precarious position, one that I attempted to negotiate as a researcher by paying close attention to participants' accounts, being clear about the contexts of these accounts and explaining the grounds for my analysis and findings, so that they can remain open to challenge from the reader.

My proximity to many of the research participants, not just in terms of shared professional and personal biographies but also in terms of social positioning and political or analytical outlook and skills, emerged most strikingly in interviews when the analysis an interviewee put forward was almost exactly my own. This is a different experience from an interviewee saying something which one knows will illustrate perfectly, when quoted, a point that is becoming clear from the research. Rather, she produced statements that I would have been happy to include in my own authored analysis. If I had been using interviews as sources of information about 'what really happened', I might have been encouraged by this, seeing it as definite confirmation that my analysis was correct, because participants agreed with it. But my approach to the interview and other data was to treat them as performances and tools intended to produce particular effects in particular circumstances. As such, maybe the convergence of our analysis was a warning that I was too close to the material and the participants?

On reflection, I took it to be evidence that researchers are *not that special*. I do not mean to undermine myself too much at this point. My research for this project had a much broader reach than a single interviewee's experience, and my analysis draws on more (and different) theoretical frameworks. I have spent more time and given attention to different things than my interviewees might, or than I would have in other circumstances (that is, outside of my researcher role). So I believe I can claim additional value for this study and its conclusions beyond simply reflecting and repeating the layperson's views, but I want to emphasise that this privileged position comes from the particular purpose and context of conducting the research. It also comes from a particular intellectual training, which in large part is shared with many of the participants in my research. In this sense I am in the uncomfortable position of an 'expert', whose expertise remains open to challenge from others who have different, but perhaps equally valid, grounds for expertise.

As noted, it is not my intention to privilege an 'authentic self' or to use the interview method as a confessional tool through which this self is revealed. Rather, it is the biographical work in my interviews in which I am most interested (Atkinson and Silverman, 1997, p 322). The negotiations that policy practitioners make to comprehend and to re-present difficult subjects in terms they find manageable and acceptable very often involve work on their own biography and its re-presentation as narrative, connected to and orienting narratives of policy. This is a 'focus not on what language *means* but on what it *does*' (Rose, 1998, p 178).

Debates about discomfort and impartiality are as relevant to my research process as much as they are part of what my research participants are doing. Both bureaucrats and academic researchers can risk using reflexivity as a way of trying to absolve themselves from mistakes (Strathern, 2006, p 200). But by being clear about what research was done and how it was analysed, I hope to leave this work open to challenge from others (and for more detail on what methods were used, see the Appendix at the end of this book).

More than this, it is hoped that with this transparency about how the knowledge was produced, it is possible to develop analytical insights about the relationship between the production of academic and policy knowledge. Both academic researchers and policy practitioners are in the business of producing knowledge and analysis. Often, policy practitioners use research produced by social scientists in their work. This cross-over can be difficult to negotiate for researchers concerned about maintaining critical distance from their subject matter. For example, in Marilyn Strathern's (2000) discussion of the relationship between higher education and government policy, she seems adamant that critical research on the one hand, and audit and management on the other, should be maintained as two separate roles. Even when positions of both critical researcher and auditor are occupied by the same person, Strathern argues, it is 'absurd' to consider these selves as able to interact and reflect 'face-to-face' on the same knowledge (2006, p 193). She suggests that policy documents are a form of shield used in negotiation between institutions and government. She does not acknowledge that what is important might not be the contents of a document, so much as how it is used (Rose, 1999b, p 29).

By contrast, Riles' (2006) analysis of being an anthropologist at a United Nations (UN) meeting on gender provides a more engaged understanding of the connections and difficulties between policy and research. She found that although bureaucratic and political discussions used the same terms as academic debates (gender, discrimination), these terms were being used to denote different things – or more importantly, to achieve different goals. As a result, the anthropologists in this case found that their expertise was silenced as they were left without their own language. Riles argues that these silences should be paid greater attention, rather than trying to avoid the problem by separating academia from policy. There can be, then, a useful knowledge created by crossing these boundaries. As Bonnett puts it: 'contradiction needs to be understood at the level of lived experience' (1993, p 177).

Ahmed (2012), Puwar (2004) and others discuss the problems of being required to 'speak for' under-represented groups within governing institutions. In parallel, struggles to find ways to critique social inequalities while also being embedded in these inequalities (indeed, in some ways able to critique inequalities because of the privilege those inequalities provide) have concerned researchers in traditions of feminism, anti-racism and post-colonialism (Spivak, 1988; Ahmed, 2000; Skeggs, 2002, p 362). bell hooks invites the privileged subject – in stronger words, 'the oppressor' (hooks, 1990, p 146) – to 'choose the margin', as a 'site of radical possibility' (p 149); to 'enter that space' (p 152) of constant change, struggle and resistance. She suggests that people who have been marginalised – because of their gendered or racialised identities, for example – can make a virtue of their ability to see the world from an outsider's perspective, able to disrupt dominant categorisations. This echoes du Bois' conception of the 'double consciousness' of those whom racism has subjected to a 'sense of always looking at one's self through the eyes of others' (du Bois, 1994 [1903], p 2). Du Bois sees this as a resource, a source of knowledge of ambiguity and power struggles. hooks wrestles with the necessities of using language which 'carries the scent of oppression' (hooks, 1990, p 146) to reveal and resist that oppression. Her essay is hopeful that by *choosing* – rather than being relegated to – a marginal position outside of the dominating centre, one might be able to reinvent that language and, through this, alter the relations of domination. One might find in the shared margin a 'radical creative space that affirms and sustains our subjectivity, which gives us a new location from which to articulate our sense of the world' (p 153). Her call to the reader – both 'oppressed and oppressor' – suggests that this marginal space could be an opportunity to reimagine and reinvent unequal power relations by constantly unsettling and transforming perspectives on non-marginal space.

The ambiguity of occupying a marginal and contradictory position is difficult, perhaps sometimes impossible – it can provide a productive tension. The production of *public sociology*, as I envisaged it earlier, means entering these precarious positions and opening oneself up to possibilities (which might include the possibility of being wrong) (Back, 2002). As Gunaratnam puts it:

> The fundamental problematic of interpretation … is that it is always a risky, emotion-laden and ethical business … [to] practise our … crafts in ways that aspire to the honing of technique and skill and that give recognition to our being touched … while all the time remaining faithful and vulnerable to the unknown. (Gunaratnam, 2009, p 59)

This point about the role of emotion in uncomfortable positions is important. As Gunaratnam suggests, one can be at once skilled and technical, and aware and responsive to emotion and vulnerability. Emotions are embodied responses to situations (Sayer, 2005, p 37), attached to commitments which *mean* something to the individual, and which are part of the self – not just a preference. As such, they should be taken seriously. If commitments come into conflict (for instance, professional and political commitments) then we might expect this to produce an emotional response as much as a rational or articulated one. Hence we should not be surprised if difficult subjects create situations in which individuals *feel* uncomfortable; and we should not necessarily dismiss this discomfort as self-indulgent or self-protecting. We should take into account what provokes such emotional reactions, and how these reactions can motivate action, including within the policy process.

My research strategy takes the study of policy off the page, and into the practices, negotiations and *uses* of policy documents and their ambiguities by using participant observation and semi-structured interviews with policy practitioners where they are given the space to reflect on their policy practice by stepping slightly outside of their everyday negotiations.

To a great extent, the conduct of the research had many parallels with the subject of analysis. That is, the very action of developing this research project draws into question the roles and identities of both researcher and participant. This parallels one of the main threads of the research, about what it means *to govern*, and how this is best understood by attention to the actions and experiences of those engaged in governing. As I discuss at greater length in the following chapters, building relationships of trust (in order to influence action) appears to be at the heart of governing, and doing so requires both technical and emotional skill. Very similar processes are at work in building research relationships.

These relationships between individuals are of course always experienced within structures of differential power. As I have emphasised, the attention my research strategy gives to emotions as part of the process of governing is not intended to obscure or mask power relations. Rather, it is a recognition that *power relations and structures are lived through emotional reactions*. Emotional labour is used in the processes of governing, and expected in the responses of those being governed.

Nor are emotions, commitments, morals or ethics necessarily conservative. They can be, but they can also provoke resistance to dominant norms (Sayer, 2005, p 100). As Berlant, writing about compassion, notes, emotional complexes have 'powerfully material and personal consequences' (2004, p 11), whether these are progressive or conservative. Emotions, and the emotionally uncomfortable positions of policy practitioners, are worthy of study not simply as experiences within the self, but for their impact on social relations (Skeggs, 2002, p 350).

TWO

Contradictory narratives of cohesion

Introduction

This chapter narrates the landscape of cohesion through four narratives with geographically anchored reference points. This is a figurative landscape; it is imagined from material geographies, but only partly related to lived experience (Keith and Pile, 1993, p 6). Each of the four overlapping policy narratives demonstrates a relationship between community cohesion (the problem, description, cause or prescription) imagined through place ('they' experience community cohesion problems 'over there', but 'we' do not have problems 'here') and imagined through time (problems of the past which have now been solved, or problems of the present which never used to exist). Barnor Hesse has written about how imagining such problems as 'elsewhere' and of a different (past) era is typical of a colonising, Eurocentric approach which imagines the position of the speaker/viewer/analyst/ governor to be superior, modern and central (and those they speak about or view to be inferior, primitive and marginal) (Hesse, 1993, p 175). The narratives I discuss here are partial. I am not claiming to tell the whole story, but to provide some context for how community cohesion policy is thought about and performed in national and local policy practice.

John Solomos has shown how policies 'construct definitions of the problems to be tackled which exclude certain issues from serious consideration' (1988, p 142), where 'coded terms' such as 'urban problems' and 'pressure on services' are used to talk about violence and disorder, and about race (p 105; see also Hall et al, 1978). But it is also important to note how these coded terms shift over time and context (Solomos and Back, 1995, p xi). For instance, Bagguley and Hussain (2003b, p 3) read official reports on community cohesion as 'an "index" of changing racialised discourses' that reflect shifting government attitudes to community. And my research is most of all concerned with how *awareness* of these codings is practised. Once we recognise that policy practitioners, journalists and citizens may be aware, to various extents, of the coding or silencing they are doing or receiving, matters take on another order of complexity. Community cohesion policy is a particularly good example of this because (at least in some of its formulations) the difficulties of communication about 'sensitive issues' are at its heart (Cantle, 2001, p 18; Lewis, 2005, p 555).

Throughout, I refer to 'community cohesion *policy*' rather than 'community cohesion' because this emphasises the whole set of ideas which are collected together and given the label 'community cohesion' in order to construct a legible policy narrative (or multiple narratives). Part of the power (and the difficulty) of this sort of concept is that it so easily slips between meanings. Sometimes 'community cohesion' is used to describe an existing condition, or a condition that is being aspired to. At other times 'community cohesion' (or its lack) is treated as a cause of other conditions (such as educational achievement or poverty). Building on both or either of these meanings, commentators can prescribe a set of actions to engender community cohesion as required in a particular situation. Finally, 'community cohesion' can be treated as a political construct, and it is largely in that sense that I use the term.

Prescriptive, technocratic policy documents treat community cohesion as an object or condition which can be measured, as in the first two senses outlined here (see, for example, DCLG, 2007b). Attempts to map community cohesion policy as a policy prescription (the third sense outlined above) sometimes present a chronology of important moments and documents in its development, which illustrate that approaches have changed over time (see, for example, Cantle, 2005). There is a developing literature critiquing such unproblematised chronologies, and policy definitions of community cohesion that begins to consider community cohesion policy as a political construct (see, for example, Kalra, 2002; Burnett, 2004, 2007; McGhee, 2003, 2005; Robinson, 2005, 2008; Khan, 2007). However, in the main this has depended on archival discourse analysis of policy documents, which stops short of attention to my particular interest in the resonances and contradictions of how policy is understood, practised and lived (see also Bonnett, 1993, p 180; Solomos and Back, 1995, p xi; Husband and Alam, 2011, p 13).

In brief, the four narratives explored in this chapter are: first, the (familiar) idea of the unfamiliar Other, and how community cohesion policy has become closely associated with ideas of 'parallel lives', much discussed following the reports of inquiries into violent disturbances in northern English towns and cities in the summer of 2001. In more recent developments, associations of the 'alien other' have shifted to focus on a newer 'folk devil': the young Muslim (Asian) man (Alexander,

2000, 2004). Religious labelling of the outsider was less central to the initial stages of community cohesion policy, but following attacks on New York and Washington later in 2001, and the ensuing 'War on Terror', Islam has become increasingly problematised in community cohesion policy and its associated programmes (Husband and Alam, 2011, p 2).

The second set of coordinates locates a different folk devil – the 'white working class'. This term has become associated with nationalistic racism and particularly with the electoral successes of the British National Party (BNP) in the 2000s. This framing of debate allows racism to be situated with the white working class, outside or on the outskirts of London, and not in the capital city's middle-class, multicultural, metropolitan centre (Skeggs, 2005a, p 972). It also demonises and homogenises a section of society as backward and violently racist outsiders from the body politic and the national 'shared value' of 'tolerance' (Haylett, 2001, p 357; Hewitt, 2005, p 53).

Third, nostalgic ideals of national identity in Britain and specifically in England have long been associated with ideas of the countryside and rural landscapes and their links to idealised 'whiteness' (Williams, 1973, p 7; Neal, 2002, p 443; Garland and Chakraborti, 2006). Consequently, 'problems' for community cohesion were framed around how existing resident populations would 'cope' with increases in migration following the accession of new countries to the EU in 2004, particularly in areas previously unused to migrant or minority ethnic presence. Such areas become the focus for narratives of both a nostalgically imagined 'authentic' English identity, and debates about what multiculture could and should mean, particularly in changing contexts of power and difference.

Finally, I turn to a narrative of celebratory urban multiculture. The previous three narratives created racialised others, and situated the discrimination to which they were subjected within particular bodies and places (non-cosmopolitan, rural or provincial white working class – or self-segregating minority ethnic groups). They imagined places and populations lacking in community cohesion (in different ways). The final set of coordinates imagines a Britain that is cosmopolitan and multicultural, an image that does not overtake but sits alongside the other shifting referents of Britishness/Englishness. In this context, the inner city, previously imagined as a place of danger associated with poverty, crime, deviance and migration, becomes celebrated for its association with difference and change (Keith, 2005, p 121; Bonnett, 2010, p 129). The narrative of long-standing histories of welcoming newcomers becomes celebrated as part of the national story, representing 'British values of tolerance'.

These four narratives do not tell a straightforward story of community cohesion policy and its development. They converge, diverge, contradict and intertwine at various points. In the remainder of this chapter, I elaborate on each – beginning with their historical resonances, the more contemporary moments that connect these narratives to community cohesion, the policy developments that intersect with each, and the explanation for their associations with an imagined geographic location.

Parallel lives and 'the other'

History

A significant turning point in the UK both for government policy on race equality and academic engagement with racism and segregation was the 'moment' of urban riots in the 1980s (Keith, 1993; Solomos, 2003, p 36). That this 'moment' relates to events over several years is an illustration of how the complex yet mundane realities that led to those uprisings, the events themselves, and their aftermath can become distilled through narrative into 'the 1980s riots'. This phrase then draws in all the resonances and implications of black urban poor, state and casual racism, explosive reactions and government responses – while ignoring the questions of precisely who, how, why and what took place (nor is there room to discuss 'what happened' here; for detailed discussions, see Kettle and Hodges, 1982; Solomos, 1986; Benyon and Solomos, 1987; Keith, 1993).

Community cohesion policy was also a response to ethnically/racially marked 'riots', echoing the urban programmes of the 1980s, and their focus on ethnic residential segregation. But a new inflection of these debates in Britain in the 2000s was that the previous characterisation of 'good' and 'bad' migrant populations was reversed. Instead of African heritage groups being seen as the perpetrators of violence ('having problems') while South Asian groups were caricatured as responsible, quiet and dedicated to business and family ('having culture') (Hall et al, 1978; Solomos, 1988; Bagguley and Hussain, 2003a; Lewis, 2005), the 'problem' group or folk devil of the 2000s is the South Asian heritage Muslim, perhaps second or third generation migrant (Alexander, 2000, p xiii; MPA, 2007, p 51), although the 'problems with' Black Britons have by no means disappeared from policy discourse (see, for example, Blair, 2007).

Civil disturbances in the 1980s were initially led by the central government department responsible for local government[1] before this leading role shifted by 1985 to the Home Office, with its responsibility for law and order (Solomos, 2003, p 247). By contrast, the early responses to the 2001 disturbances were produced from the Home Office before moving back alongside community and local government matters.[2] Whereas law and order concerns apparently became more dominant in the 1980s policy responses, in the 2000s the change in departmental responsibility suggests an increasing emphasis on regimes of governmentality and behaviour-shaping activities rather than imposition of control. Increasingly, counter-terrorism measures were also split between these two departments, with Communities and Local Government (CLG) responsible for 'winning hearts and minds' of British Muslims (DCLG, 2007a), while information gathering and intervention remained with the security services (HM Government, 2006, 2009a; see also Chapter Three, this volume).

From the mid-20th century, rhetoric linking public disorder to failed immigration and integration policies contributed to immigration Acts limiting the rights of people from former British colonies to enter Britain, alongside Race Relations and Race Equalities Acts intended to improve the treatment of those already resident in Britain (Solomos, 2003, p 80). But racialisation is not only a project applied to those with darker skins (Miles, 1993; Bonnett, 1998), and folk devils are not always imagined through this lens. Although less centrally located in the race relations literature (Mac an Ghaill, 2001), an alternative 'folk devil' of late 20th-century Britain was the 'Irish terrorist', a trope that resonates with early 21st-century narratives of the 'Muslim suicide bomber' (Nickels et al, 2009). This was a community identified as outsiders by their religion and migrant heritage, and then associated as a whole with the dangers of the Provisional IRA's attacks on mainland Britain and separatist ideology. Longer histories of international domination led to systematic demonisation of the Irish in Britain as a specific danger to 'the nation' throughout the late 20th century through counter-terrorist legislation, police harassment and popular racisms (Hickman, 1998; Fekete, 2001).

The emergence of Muslim populations as alternative folk devils had its own 'moments' or turning points. These images had already become established before the appearance of community cohesion policy as a UK government agenda. One of these turning points was the reaction to the publication of Salman Rushdie's novel *The satanic verses*, which was seen as offensive by some Muslim leaders, with copies burnt in protests in Bradford and elsewhere, and a death sentence *fatwa* declared on Rushdie by Ayatollah Khomeini in February 1989 (Solomos, 2003, pp 212-13). These events re-energised political debate about multiculturalism, with a greater focus on ethnoreligious difference, integration and gender, problematising (South Asian) Muslims in particular, and prompting political mobilisations within Muslim communities as a specific political force (Solomos and Back, 1995, p 150; Solomos, 2003, pp 213-15). These were not new issues in British political debate. For example, controversy spilled over in the mid-1980s in reaction to Bradford headteacher Ray Honeyford's outspoken views against anti-racist education relating to the South Asian heritage children attending his school (Ball and Solomos, 1990, p 13). The first Gulf War, in 1990-91, also helped to congeal 'the idea that there was some kind of unitary Muslim community in Britain that could pose a threat to national identity' (Solomos, 2003, p 215). Thus the 'quiet and dutiful migrant' caricature attributed to South Asians in Britain had already begun to fade when community cohesion policy emerged (Fortier, 2007, p 109; MPA, 2007, p 51).

Contemporary moments

In 2001, violence broke out on the streets of northern English towns, most notoriously in Oldham (in May), Burnley (in June) and Bradford (in July). The news coverage produced strikingly similar images of burning cars and riot police that instantly drew parallels with the 1980s disturbances. Links between the two periods were drawn by policy practitioners (see, for example, Cantle, 2005, p 8), journalists (BBC News, 2001; Darbyshire, 2001) and academics (Kalra, 2002; Bagguley and Hussain, 2003a). The parallels were not just in the widespread and riotous nature of the disorders but in the involvement of racialised urban populations – this time Asian rather than black – although both sets of disturbances involved white participants too, and in more complex relationships than a simple 'white-against-black' scenario (Keith, 1993; Bagguley and Hussain, 2003a).

The government reports that emerged following the 2001 disorders identified a number of contributory factors for the violence, including economic deprivation, provocation from far right groups, crime and political disenfranchisement (Denham, 2001, p 8). But their greatest emphasis was on a diagnosis of 'parallel lives', that is, that 'Asian' and 'white' communities were living separate existences and rarely meeting (Cantle, 2001, p 9; Denham, 2001, p 13). This again was assigned a number of causes, including systematic discrimination in both public and private housing, and 'white flight' from schools and neighbourhoods, and to the choice of Asian people to live together for safety from discrimination and access to cultural resources (Cantle, 2001, p 28). The prescription was that 'parallel lives' needed to be addressed by developing greater 'community cohesion'. As the definition of community cohesion and how to achieve it has continued to be debated, there remains a reverberation around this central idea that established migrant heritage communities have remained separated from longer-standing (white) communities in many towns, and that intervention is required to bring these two groups together.

There were four key reports into the 2001 disturbances (Cantle, 2001; Clarke, 2001; Denham, 2001; Ritchie, 2001), and an additional report in Bradford that had been commissioned prior to the events there in July (Ouseley, 2001). The document that has dominated narratives of community cohesion is that produced by the Independent Review Team chaired by Ted Cantle (Cantle, 2001). This report refers to 'Asians' and 'the Asian community' (alongside 'the white community'), but places less emphasis on the designation 'Muslim' and only refers to 'the Muslim community' within the biographies of some of the review team members. The disturbances occurred weeks before the attacks on the World Trade Center in New York and the Pentagon in Washington on 11 September 2001, and the subsequent declaration of an international 'War on Terror'. The riot reports were being written at that time and published soon after, but it seems that the idea of Muslims as a focus of folk devilry, fear or discrimination was not yet fully crystallised as a concern in policy discourse in the way it became over the following years, with Britain's engagement in wars in Afghanistan and Iraq, and in the aftermath of bombings on the London transport system in July 2005 (although see Ritchie, 2001, p 10). Despite official insistence that the Preventing Violent Extremism (PVE) programme (also known as 'Prevent') which emerged following July 2005 was separate to community cohesion initiatives, in practice the two were inextricably linked (see Chapter Three). These public and policy developments occurred alongside widespread expressions of concern about 'parallel lives' of 'Asians' (now – problematically – equated with 'Muslims') as too different and separate to cohere with 'the wider population'.

As community cohesion policy was shaped by events and policy reactions, the messages about how precisely its relationship to race, racism and ethnicity should be understood also shifted. Despite being discussed as if its main focus was on segregation and separation, the Cantle report initially positioned community cohesion policy as specifically addressing racialised inequality. It aligned community cohesion work with race equality work, suggesting that local authority community cohesion strategies might be seen as part of meeting the duty to promote equality under the Race Relations (Amendment) Act 2000 (Cantle, 2001, p 21). The team made the first theme of their investigation 'the extent to which race issues are visibly and positively addressed by political/civic/community leadership and diversity is valued' (Cantle, 2001, p 56). Further, the later Community Cohesion Review Panel which was appointed by the Home Office to provide guidance on the development of community cohesion policy and strategies[3] stated in its final report the 'hope that the statutory duty to "promote good race relations" ... will be effectively discharged through the community cohesion agenda and will be regarded ... as *synonymous*' (Community Cohesion Review Panel, 2004, p 57; emphasis added). While these recognitions of the links between community cohesion work and race equality reflect the (implicit and explicit) understandings of many practitioners, most of the other documentation produced by national bodies attempts to separate the two or at least to remove the tensions of discussing race issues from community cohesion forums. An early example of this was in the first national guidance on community cohesion programmes: 'Community cohesion incorporates and goes beyond the concept of race equality and social cohesion' (LGA, 2002, p 6). Precisely *how* it might do so is not made clear.

Place

As described above, the rise of community cohesion policy as an agenda is connected to those places remembered as experiencing disorder in the summer of 2001. Disorder also occurred in other places around this time. Other localities with similar characteristics of population, geography and employment patterns escaped serious disturbances. But the three towns that experienced the most significant disorder were the ones that commissioned local investigations into their causes, and received the most national attention. This could be thought of as the process by which the moment of *fact creation* (the making of sources) gives way to the moment of *fact assembly* (the making of archives) (Trouillot, 1995, p 26; see also Wemyss, 2008). At each of these stages, some elements of history are remembered or privileged as facts, while others are silenced. Oldham, Burnley and Bradford in this process are recorded as places of parallel lives where attempts to find community cohesion are tested. They take an anchoring role from which the community cohesion policy narrative starts, as community cohesion is retold (the moment of *fact retrieval*). Silences and fact creation can manifest at any of these overlapping moments, or at a fourth, the moment of *retrospective significance*, the making of history 'in the final instance'.

Whether or not history is ever fixed 'in the final instance', the retrospective significance of community cohesion policy is not (yet). However, its association with this constellation of northern English towns remains, in their presentation at a national level through policy documents, conferences and media coverage (by both locals and outside commentators). Their names have, to different extents, become shorthand for ideas of segregated communities of South Asian Muslims and the 'white working class'. The transformation of cohesion agendas by connection with anti-terrorism reinflects these resonances, as do the broad West Yorkshire accents of the bombers of July 2005, who grew up as British Asian Muslims in nearby towns (Back, 2007a). The broader narrative this is used to construct is of northern England as a place where multiculturalism has failed – where migration of the mid-20th century stalled in its progress towards integration. This fits with the post-industrial landscape of popular films (for example, *This is England* [2006], *East is East* [1999] and *My Son the Fanatic* [1997]) which imagine a quasi-nostalgic, generalised provincial England stuck in the past of post-industrial hopelessness and depressed racism – in contrast to the super-diverse cosmopolitan harmony of *Cool Britannia* (read London) (Bonnett, 2010, p 130). Thus 'that' England of parallel lives is imagined as both spatially and temporally outside of the heart of government and power – and therefore simply unable to keep up, rather than left behind by others racing ahead. But this is not the only narrative which links places, events and times to a model of failed community cohesion.

The 'white working class': locating racism with the other Other

History

The second set of coordinates from which to trace narratives of community cohesion policy similarly locates problems outside, and in the past of, the centres from which such histories are told. The twist this time is that this is not a fear of an invading other, but of a relic of the past, the 'white working class' imagined as unable to adjust to a globalised world and therefore threatening national cohesion with a racist rejection of contemporary values.

The simple narrative is that Britain as a whole has become more at ease with itself as a post-imperial nation now able to celebrate its internal diversity. Racism and discrimination which were previously everyday have become unacceptable, indeed in many forms, illegal. The exception in this is the 'white working class', who are portrayed as either ignorantly racist or as articulating what others are too afraid to say: that 'multiculturalism has gone too far'. Either way, this figure enables a narrative in which racism has been eliminated from the nation but is still allowed to be spoken in response to concerns associated with this both marginalised and demonised figure.

Significant moments removing the acceptability of racist speech from British national discourse include the outrageous racism of Conservative slogans in the 1964 general election campaign in Smethwick[4] and Prime Minister Margaret Thatcher's 1978 comments about her fear of Britain becoming 'swamped by people with a different culture' (quoted in Solomos, 2003, p 177). These moments were significant not just in demonstrating xenophobia and racism at the heart of mainstream politics, but also in mobilising a critique of it (Solomos, 2003, p 69). Similarly, that extreme far right views were both present as a force in electoral politics, and a threat that could be defeated, was demonstrated by the election of the first BNP racist councillor in the UK in Tower Hamlets in 1993 and subsequent refusal of officers and elected members to cooperate with him, which with concerted efforts from local activists led to his removal (Wemyss, 2009, p 95).

Another significant element in this narrative is the idea of a 'backlash' from poor white communities already marginalised within capitalism and then threatened by labour competition from immigration; or, more recently, framed as neglected by the state in the privileging of minority ethnic groups through equalities policies and 'state multiculturalism'. This framing of concerns about immigration as spoken on behalf of the already economically excluded is most graphically remembered with reference to an infamous speech made by the Conservative politician Enoch Powell in 1968 (Solomos, 2003, p 61), but was also present in vociferous attacks on anti-racist education throughout the 1980s (see various essays in Ball and Solomos, 1990; Hewitt, 2005, p 119). These historic resonances are not necessarily place-based, except in that they call on images of both industrial and inner-city working populations struggling within competitive labour markets, and (less often) of agricultural or pastoral England/Britain.

Contemporary moments

If racism is now seen as unspeakable in public life, it is in large part due to outraged reactions – not just to the speech acts of politicians described above or institutional or banal racisms, but to specific incidents that have captured public and political imaginations. Perhaps the most significant of these events was the racist murder of a black teenager, Stephen Lawrence, in Eltham, South East London in 1993. The murder investigation was repeatedly compromised and, following an Independent Inquiry, this was found to be the result of institutional racism of the Metropolitan Police Authority (MPA) (Macpherson, 1999). A direct result of this was the Race Relations (Amendment) Act 2000, which created a positive duty for public bodies to promote race equality. The strongly worded outrage in the popular media at the racist nature of the murder and at the collapse of criminal trials[5] against the perpetrators was significant in demonstrating the unspeakability of racism (Hewitt, 2005, p 52).

Yet this condemnation was explicitly narrated through class. 'White working-class' housing estates become, in this narrative, the site of racist violence, condemnation of which enables the rest of society to claim its anti-racist credentials. As Roger Hewitt puts it, the 'message was that in looking for racism in the UK there was no need to look further' (2005, p 53). This enabled critics of the 2000 Act and its attempts to address institutional racism to claim a position of condemning racism – by locating it outside of institutions. Alongside this is a discourse that suggests (repeatedly) that concern about causing offence, or 'political correctness', is now the dominant mode of thought – an argument now made on the left of the political spectrum as well as the right (Ahmed, 2005). This counter-narrative echoes the attacks on multiculturalism and anti-racism through the 1980s (see later in this chapter), and is now apparently given a spur by the incorporation of greater race equality measures in law.

But political and media attention to the 'white working class' is not simply about characterising an incorrigibly and violently racist group. It is about designating them as a victimised and marginalised group whose racism is a reaction to their situation, about suggesting a resentment of attention they are said to feel is given to every disadvantaged group but them (Ware, 2008; Bottero, 2009, p 7). The category of 'white working class' is problematic particularly because the conjunction of race and class silences a proper analysis of inequality in either form. Indeed, the lack of clear specification of what actually constitutes being 'white working class' clouds the debate, particularly when statistics claiming to demonstrate disadvantage are invoked (Gillborn, 2009). The 'working class' label enables a claim to victimhood in economic terms, while the 'white' label enables the blame to be placed with government policies that are seen to champion only the ethnic 'other' (Hewitt,

2005, pp 126-7). Conversely, using the term 'white working class' to designate 'others' presumes a racialised and probably racist element to (white) working-class resentment, and hence to some extent discredits it. The 'working class' element serves to distance the (middle-class) commentator from such presumed racism and to reinforce their own (race and) class privilege (Haylett, 2001, p 365; Reay, 2008, p 1081; Garner, 2009, p 47). In terms of community cohesion discourse, having been coded as resentful, racist and backward-looking, the 'white working class' are constructed as outside the national community of shared norms and values.

In 2002, the fascist BNP won two council seats in Burnley, and over successive years increased the number of local council seats they held to a peak in 2008 of 37 across England and Wales (as well as gaining two seats in the European Parliament and one on the Greater London Authority in 2009). Although a very small number of the around 20,000 local council seats across England and Wales, the BNP's electoral success signalled that they had become sufficiently respectable to secure a viable voting base in some areas. The transformation was also visible in their increasing acceptance as a respectable political party by other major parties and the national media. Although still treated as more exceptional than fascist parties elsewhere in Europe, the appearance of the party's leader on BBC 1 Question Time alongside leading politicians from all main political parties,[6] and the cooperation of authorities to which they were elected, contrasts with the political mobilisation in response to the BNP's first election success, in Tower Hamlets in 1993.

Following this electoral resurgence of the party, the calls that 'multiculturalism', equalities work and community cohesion policy were 'playing into the hands of the BNP' became more vocal, reinforced by the BNP's own positioning of itself as standing up for a marginalised section of society (Back, 2002, p 36; Williams and Keith, 2006; Copsey, 2008; Keith, 2008a). Explicitly in reaction to this tendency, then Communities Secretary John Denham announced the Connecting Communities Fund at an event at the Institute for Community Cohesion in October 2009. Like the PVE Fund, the justifications and purpose given for this initiative appeared to contradict themselves, and to contradict broader government strategy on community cohesion. Like PVE, Connecting Communities was aimed at a specific group – in this case 'hard-working families' in 'predominantly white areas' who 'say "it's not my community any more". And feel helpless to do anything about it' (Denham, 2009) (rather than 'Muslims in our communities' who should 'identify themselves as a welcome part of a wider British society'; CLG, 2007b, p 3). Connecting Communities was aimed at 'addressing the legitimate fears and concerns which, neglected, can prove fertile territory for extremism' (Denham, 2009) (rather than 'isolat[ing] violent extremist activity'; CLG, 2007b, p 3). Both the Connecting Communities and PVE Funds aimed to encourage specified groups to feel more enfranchised by state investment, while in doing so attaching a stigma to them as a therefore problematic group (Kundnani, 2009; Turley, 2009). This also seemed at odds with the broader recommendations of the Commission on Cohesion and Integration (COIC) that '"Single Group Funding" should be the exception rather than the rule' (COIC, 2007, p 160, see also Chapter Three).

Proponents of the Connecting Communities Fund and other politicians and policy practitioners were trying to understand the existence of, and reasons for, discontent among particular sectors of the population, without appearing to pander to racism (or extremism). The problem is that many communities (identified as 'white working class' or otherwise) have found themselves without satisfactory employment, education, or (significantly) housing (Williams and Keith, 2006). That for many it has become easier to blame immigration and minority ethnic groups for one's own misfortune than to seek solidarity with others who are similarly disadvantaged makes this negotiation all the more difficult. Entering this difficult space means entering the 'grey zone' of attempting to understand discrimination without condoning it (Back, 2002).

Place

Although Burnley was the first place to elect BNP councillors in this wave of their electoral success, it is Barking and Dagenham that has become most associated with this narrative of disgruntled 'white working-class' communities turning to the far right. Barking and Dagenham had the largest BNP group on its council, with 12 councillors between 2006 and 2010.[7] Although it remained an overwhelmingly Labour council, the BNP was the most successful electoral opposition the local party had seen for some time. The borough came to symbolise, for both the national press and policy practitioners across the country, the problem of far right mobilisation among the 'white working class'.

As an outer London borough once reliant on social housing and dependent historically on manufacturing jobs (particularly at the Ford car plant) that have now severely declined, Barking and Dagenham has many similarities to northern towns that experienced disturbances in

2001. Within the borough, there is a noticeable difference between Barking, closer to inner London and capitalising on that proximity through developing retail, housing and transport links as part of the London Thames Gateway; and Dagenham, to the east and more firmly part of Essex, and suffering more markedly from a lack of alternative forms of employment. An important distinction between the post-industrial experience of Barking and Dagenham and that of ex-manufacturing towns in northern England is that Barking and Dagenham's population continues to grow. Much of the new population is made up of minority ethnic families moving outwards from inner London boroughs, particularly to family-sized former social housing (Williams and Keith, 2006, pp 3-4).

Proximity to the more established multiculturalism of inner London makes Barking and Dagenham a ready comparator to it, and a place against which national and local policy practitioners have tended to measure their relative success in managing ethnic diversity (see, for example, Muir, 2008). Employment and housing pressures are usually described within this narrative as at the root of racialised tensions in the borough. Yet this materialist framing has a nostalgic tendency which celebrates an imagined past of certainties of employment, housing and nuclear family values, a past of 'British culture' without immigration (see the debates between Dench et al, 2006 and Farrar, 2008; and Blond and Pabst, 2007 and Keith, 2007b). In this, it can mirror the nostalgic racist tendencies attributed to the 'white working class' (elided with BNP voters) who have become associated with Barking and Dagenham. The nostalgia of these narratives provides an easy-to-follow storyline that also silences alternative materialist framings. Shortage of housing supply is taken as a given, as is the consequent competition for resources, whereas alternative models of house building, distribution or ownership are not part of the debate – silencing any questioning of the models of power and resource distribution which *create* this competition.

Thus Barking and Dagenham can be made to represent the condition of post-colonial melancholia, in which Britain's white populations are stuck with an unrealised expectation of a promised white supremacy that has not materialised (Gilroy, 2004). Barking and Dagenham is thus the past that has only just met with the future, in the form of migration, and been found wanting. Such narratives can either mourn the past (as those populations are thought to), or construct the 'white working class' as necessarily backwards (and racist) because of their nostalgia (Bonnett, 2010, p 123). Either way, the narrative of 'white working-class' populations, subject to economic and social deprivation as a result of wider global forces, and as a result turning to far right racism, is represented through references to Barking and Dagenham, and this narrative situates its population as in the 'past' of a multicultural, convivial cosmopolitan future. Imagining the place (or any place) as somewhere populated by some violent racists but *simultaneously* by those deserving of sympathy does not provide so easy a narrative; it necessitates uncomfortable positions.

New arrivals: reimagining multiculture

History

A third narrative which intertwines with community cohesion debates is that of British identity, and its relationship to lived multiculture and prescribed multiculturalisms. The debate about national identity is of course ancient, but the narrative I concentrate on here is one that persistently imagines British identity as white and somehow unchanging, in defence against a reality of changing and emergent forms of 'Britishness'. Such a nationalist narrative is not, of course, unique to Britain. Nor, indeed, are the 'values' that are often claimed as particularly British. Part of the work of nation-building is defining an imagined community in opposition to outsiders (Anderson, 1991), and reimagining this shared community or solidarity is an ongoing process (Calhoun, 2007, p 166). The pastoral and agricultural have long been associated with an idealised nostalgia of Britain and Britishness (and more specifically, England and Englishness) and mobilised to promote this nationalism (Williams, 1973; Neal, 2002). While notions of national culture (and public services) being 'swamped' by immigrants are often invoked in relation to Britain as a whole (Solomos, 2003, p 66), this becomes much more potent when used in relation to the countryside which remains imagined, and often lived, as an implicitly white place (Bonnett, 1993; Knowles, 2008; Chakraborti, 2010) – where 'white' is also imagined as Anglo-Saxon, Protestant and heterosexual (Smith and Holt, 2005).

Attempts to reimagine Britishness as diverse and changing have been hampered by the necessity of confronting histories of nation-building which rest on racialised inequality and discrimination. A significant attempt at such reimagining pre-dates the community cohesion narratives by just a year. A race equality think tank, the Runnymede Trust, established an independent Commission for the Future of Multi-ethnic Britain in 1998, a launch initially endorsed by the then Home Secretary Jack Straw. The Commission published its report in October 2000, recommending that a new form of inclusive British identity be developed, incorporating flux and heterogeneity. It suggested this would involve negotiating the 'systematic, largely unspoken racial connotations' of Britishness (Parekh, 2002, p 38). The ensuing media coverage took this as a slur on British identity, replacing 'racial' with 'racist', and using this to suggest that the multiculturalist approach advocated by the Commission was one that would 'rewrite Britain's history' (quoted in McLaughlin and Neal, 2004, p 160). The response of the press was a nationalist and conservative version of multiculturalism, one that proclaimed a pride in Britain (and its professed tolerance and inclusiveness) before all else (Fortier, 2005, p 564).

This furore illustrates the difficulty of addressing issues of 'unspoken racial connotations' – when these connotations are unspoken precisely *because* they threaten underlying narratives of identity and location. The risk of examining these connotations is two-sided: both of being seen as straightforwardly reifying racial difference, and of being accused of reifying racism by pointing out its existence or potential. The apparent silencing of race while still talking about it in coded terms was notable throughout previous attempts to engage with discrimination and with new forms of common identity, particularly through education (Gilroy, 1990; Gordon, 1990). The narrative of a countryside invaded by immigrants invokes unspoken connotations of both race and nation, and creates risks for those who would attempt to negotiate these silences openly. Likewise, 'the rural' has classed connotations. Picturesque rurality might include 'salt of the earth' farmers alongside landed gentry and city dwellers fleeing urban bustle, but rarely do these images reflect a consideration of rural poverty, homelessness or exclusion (or the effects that rural isolation might have on making such struggles less visible).

Contemporary moments

There were several significant moments in the narrative of Britishness, Englishness and multiculturalism during the 2000s. These include the arguments of 'progressive patriots' such as musician Billy Bragg that the St George's flag and English identity should be reclaimed by anti-racists; suggestions by Gordon Brown when in government that a new bank holiday be created as a celebration of British identity; and the establishment under the Labour government of citizenship tests and citizenship ceremonies for new Britons. Under the Coalition government, since 2010, there has been a renewed focus on older models of nationhood drawing heavily on celebration of the royal family, with all the obvious connotations of class and race that that entails. Even as – or perhaps because – the borders of national identity and freedom of movement shifted, the debate about what it means to be British (or English) intensified.

That these debates are entangled in confusion about what 'multiculturalism' means only intensifies these silences – and the discomforts that emerge when they are made to speak. Multiculturalism has been a popular target within community cohesion debates, blamed for encouraging separation (Cantle, 2005, pp 10-11; Cameron, 2010), although some formations of multiculturalism share the emphasis on the need for a 'common core' of values that is at the centre of government-endorsed community cohesion definitions (Hickman, 2007; Modood, 2007). Unhelpfully, arguments centred on different philosophical models for understanding or living with difference or diversity, and the extent to which this is a desirable goal, are often confused with (much less frequent) considerations of 'actually existing multiculturalism' (Grillo, 2007, p 993). Stuart Hall points out these tangles of the debate, and suggests that a useful starting point is to distinguish between 'multicultural' as a description of societies where different cultural communities live together, and 'multiculturalism' as a type of strategy adopted to manage such societies (Hall, 2000, p 209).

Definitions of multiculturalism (as a philosophy, rather than as a lived reality) range from equal access to rights and services based on assimilation with majority customs, through cultural particularism in private coupled with universal public citizenship, to the allocation of group rights to different segments of society living alongside one another. Each of these rest on different beliefs about the relationships between solidarity and difference (Keith, 2005, pp 53-4); they differently balance the risk of either neglecting the particularities of individuals and groups by requiring too much similarity, or of emphasising difference to the extent that members of a society no longer see themselves as part of a shared whole. These arguments are not necessarily restricted to questions of migration, ethnicity, race or culture but can expand to other forms of difference such as gender, sexuality or disability and identity politics (Fraser, 2000; Cantle, 2005, p 159; Abraham, 2010, p 978).

Suggestions that multiculturalism has (or should have) ended (Kundnani, 2002; Goodhart, 2004; Phillips, 2005) are also entangled in the confusion about these differing meanings, and perhaps each attacks a different target. Journalist David Goodhart's intervention in the national press was identified as a landmark controversy[8] (Khan, 2007:49; Alexander, 2007:116), asserting a need to turn back from recognition of difference to a more assimilationist stance, describing a British identity as an ethno-historical one, to be learned, earned or born into, something pre-existing rather than alive and constantly remade (Goodhart, 2004, para 13). Here, multiculturalism is attacked as a position 'which rejects a common culture', and thereby puts at risk the social solidarity required to maintain a welfare state, and basic social cohesion. This suggests that in Goodhart's view, ethnicity remains central to an idea of Britishness, that ethnicity is fixed, that too much change to Britishness risks its disintegration and therefore that those who do not fit the current state of Britishness (whatever that might be) should adapt to it, rather than vice versa, and that the numbers of 'different' people entering the country should be limited.

Trevor Phillips (as newly appointed chair of the Commission for Racial Equality) denounced Goodhart's views as 'genteel xenophobia', which implied that 'some liberals have given up on the idea of a multi-ethnic Britain' (Phillips, 2004, para 1). A year later, however, he was launching his own high-profile attack on multiculturalism (Phillips, 2005). This speech *did* seem to recognise multiple versions of the concept:

> ... there has to be a balance struck between an "anything goes" multiculturalism on the one hand, which leads to deeper division and inequality; and on the other, an intolerant, repressive uniformity. (Phillips, 2005, para 38)

However, the message most widely taken from this speech was a warning that Britain was 'sleepwalking to segregation' (see, for example, Wetherell et al, 2007, p 47), and that a model of multiculturalism that emphasised group difference was a cause of this. The prescription was instead to pursue the goal of integration, based on equality, participation and interaction. Conversely, Kundnani (2002) opposes multiculturalism as masking underlying power relations and discrimination – he welcomes its 'death' as providing an opportunity for a renewed left-wing critique.

The ambiguities of both cohesion and multiculturalism debates make it possible for community cohesion to be seen as both a 'retreat to multiculturalism' (Brighton, 2007, p 3) and an indictment of it (Alexander, 2007, p 116). The argument about where and how boundaries of community should be drawn shifts between the local, national and global, while questions of whether boundaries should be drawn at all is seldom broached (although see Calhoun, 2002).

Debates about the meaning of nationhood have been tied to discourses about immigration throughout history, but narratives of migration to Britain which had for the second half of the 20th century been linked to former colonies (Gilroy, 1987; Mercer, 1994, p 7) were challenged in the early 21st century by different patterns of movement (Vertovec, 2007, p 1025). Aside from the expansion of freedom of movement within the growing EU, the inequities of global labour flows on which society depends were brought into focus through national attention at moments such as the deaths of 21 Chinese migrant workers employed to collect cockles in Morecambe Bay in 2004 (Back, 2007b, p 32). This is notwithstanding the daily tragedies of those fleeing persecution or risking life and family to come to Britain, within or outside the official migration channels (see Back, 2007b, pp 40-1). Migration is most often made visible through its demonisation, for example, by association with 'foreign prisoners' who 'escape deportation after release' (*The Independent*, 2006). Changes to policy on those seeking political asylum in the UK meant that, from 2000, applicants were dispersed to locations across the country to reduce concentration in areas of typical settlement, in turn creating new diversity in other areas (Home Office, 2005c, p 22). The biggest impact in terms of numbers of immigrants, however, was the expansion of the EU to include 10 new member states in 2004, with freedom to move and work throughout the EU. These developments plotted quite different patterns of migration from those used to understand migration through British colonial histories (Bagguley and Hussain, 2003a; Vertovec, 2007), and brought migration to areas of Britain previously unused to the settlement of 'new arrivals' (COIC, 2007, pp 31-3; Robinson and Reeve, 2007, pp 19-20).

The timing of the Communities Secretary's establishment of COIC appeared to coincide with increased concern about community cohesion linked to terrorist attacks on London in July 2005. However, when the report of the Commission was released in 2007 it focused much less on those attacks than on the challenges and opportunities of new migration (COIC, 2007). Providing a typology of five 'groups' with which local authority areas were encouraged to identify in order to consider their likely local cohesion challenges (pp 149-54), the report identified both changing and stable areas that are less affluent as being most likely to face cohesion challenges. The thrust of the whole report was reflected in its title, *Our shared future*, which emphasised that both new migrants and existing communities had responsibility for mutual respect and civility, as well as being entitled to a sense of trust in public institutions that demonstrate visible social justice. The name of the Commission – using 'Integration' as well as 'Cohesion' – seemed to be an attempt to draw attention to the specific measures that might be needed to enable new migrants to *integrate* into Britain (requiring government efforts, not simply efforts of migrants themselves) alongside *cohesion* as a more long-term process involving all residents or citizens.

Perhaps because of the connotations of the term 'integration', which suggest homogenising assimilation to some people, this term has not often been used in policy debates (Spencer, 2011).

Like the Commission for the Future of Multi-ethnic Britain before it, what the report became best known for was not what its authors necessarily intended as a central message (Keith, 2007a). The most headline-grabbing element of COIC's report was the proposal to move away from funding third sector groups and services which operated purely on the basis of group identity (COIC, 2007, p 160). This recommendation reflected older concerns that competitive structures for bidding for community grants could not only create bounded identity communities in order to present funding applications, but also that the ensuing competition between ethnic groups could further reinforce divisiveness (Ouseley, 1990, p 141). But the report became swept up within an 'end of multiculturalism' debate, and interpreted as insistence on an assimilatory approach towards nationhood.

Place

As I have argued, one narrative of nationhood in Britain relies on the countryside as an implicitly white symbol of history and identity. The image of this countryside being 'swamped' by immigrants is thus potent. Narratives of invasion were mobilised in response to the increasing presence of asylum seekers and refugees outside the main metropolitan conurbations (as a result of government dispersal policies) from 2000. The population of new asylum seekers was, however, tiny in comparison with the arrival of migrants from new EU member states between 2004 and 2006. While at its peak the asylum dispersal scheme had spread 54,000 migrants from London and South East England to other areas of Britain (Vertovec, 2007, p 1042), 427,000 migrants from the new EU states registered under the UK Worker Registration Scheme by 2006 (Vertovec, 2007, p 1036). Together, these new patterns of migration were a significant disruption to the narrative of an ever-stable rurality, as many migrants took up low-paid agricultural work in rural areas (Robinson and Reeve, 2006, p 6).

The narratives of areas previously untouched by migration, now struggling with sudden diversity and increases in population size, are less directly tied to a specific place than the narratives associated with Oldham and with Barking and Dagenham described earlier. However, Peterborough, in the East of England, *is* used repeatedly as an example of this narrative. Although a city, Peterborough sits at the centre of a subregion of market towns, and the local authority covers rural as well as urban areas. Aiming to compete as a growing city with expansion of higher education and environmental enterprises, the city is attempting to project its image as a growing regional centre. The city itself has for decades had established minority ethnic communities, was a national reception centre for asylum seekers and attracted new EU migrants to work in agricultural and food-processing industries. The pace of inward migration from international as well as national sources increased greatly in the years preceding this research, with an expectation that there will be a 21 per cent increase in the population aged 0–14 between 2008 and 2021, and a 57 per cent increase in those aged over 65 (Greater Peterborough Partnership, 2008, pp 7-8). The local authority was thus not only seeking to improve the quality of life of existing residents, but to understand the changing needs of a population that is growing rapidly in size as well as diversity, and in rural as well as urban areas.

Peterborough was a Community Cohesion Pathfinder Authority, a programme intended to develop early lessons from community cohesion initiatives. Subsequently, the city's experience has been used as an example of 'good practice' from which other localities can learn (see, for example, COIC, 2007, pp 96, 166; Home Office, 2005a, 2005c, p 50). Positioned as a place that has overcome difficulties, Peterborough represents the narrative of new forms of migration reaching parts of the UK previously equated with tranquil whiteness. Having experienced early difficulties associated with the arrival of asylum seekers, the town can now present itself as having learned how to overcome these challenges and establish new models of integration and multiculturalism, entering the present/future of mobile multiculturalism in a way to which others should aspire.

Super-diversity: where old problems become new solutions?

History

Throughout the previous narratives I have suggested that places with 'community cohesion problems' have been imagined as outside an idealised multicultural nation, and that these narratives allow those who use them to indulge in continued scaremongering about threats to national identity which are positioned at a safe distance. It may seem counter-intuitive to imagine the ideal of community cohesion within the inner city, given the histories of demonising this as a place of crime, violence and deviance. The change from seeing the inner city as a place of poverty, to a potential engine of growth, is relatively recent

(Keith and Rogers, 1991, pp 7-11). The flows of global capital which also require global labour flows have, of course, always passed through cities, but now the presence of populations with recent origins across the world provide cultural capital to be consumed, as well as being as a source of labour (Jacobs, 1996, pp 99-100).

The move from demonisation to celebration was not without struggle. In the 1980s, for example, political mobilisations by minority ethnic communities subject to harassment, discrimination and violence coincided with a movement of left-wing radicals in the inner cities, largely in response to the punitive policies of the Thatcher governments (Lansley et al, 1989). Among the most potent struggles of this time was the attempt by many local authorities in inner London (as well as urban areas outside of London, significantly Manchester) to develop anti-racist and multicultural policies. This gave way to the narrative of 'loony left' councils and many, largely spurious, tales of the excesses of 'politically correct' policies, such as attempts to ban the singing of *Baa Baa Black Sheep* in schools (Gordon, 1990, pp 179-80) because it was allegedly seen as 'racist'.

Early local policies designed to address racism within institutions received criticism not only from those opposed to their aims, but also from anti-racists and progressives who saw many of them as being counter-productive in practice. Race Awareness Training (RAT) became the epitome of this problem. Local authority officers who were regarded as racist would be sent on training at which they were encouraged to recognise their attitudes and overcome them. In practice, this was a punishment for those considered racist. But it also enabled them to become 'even more sophisticated at projecting themselves and covering up deficiencies and prejudices' (Ouseley, 1990, p 147). Meanwhile, RAT's focus on individual attitudes 'left the institution with all its power structures relatively untouched' (Ouseley, 1990, p 146). The reliance on 'guilt complexes' to regulate behaviour and 'the determinism of seeing all white people as inherently racist' provoked criticism of RAT from anti-racists as well as from the political right wing (Solomos and Ball, 1990, p 218).

The 'loony left' characterisation belies the fact that many inner-city local authorities had systematically discriminatory policies at this time. Housing in particular was a service in which severe discrimination on race grounds was found to exist in a number of inner-city authorities (Ben-Tovim et al, 1986; Jeffers and Hoggett, 1995; Lansley et al, 1989; Solomos and Singh, 1990). Hackney was one authority that became infamous, after action by the Commission for Racial Equality and pressure from local black communities engendered a review of housing allocations and management practices (CRE, 1984; Solomos and Singh, 1990, p 98). Indeed this, like many other policy narratives I have highlighted, was reincorporated by the local authority as an attempt to demonstrate good practice in *overcoming* institutional racism (Solomos and Singh, 1990, p 103). To some extent, the authority's eventual successes in improving practices and outcomes were recognised as such by others (Ouseley, 1990, p 151).

In the aftermath of these bruising struggles, there has been progress in addressing some of the more discriminatory policies and practices of local authorities and other agencies. Overt racism is no longer acceptable in most aspects of public life, but there remains a legacy of awkwardness about *how* to talk about discrimination and difference, and *what* precisely might be considered offensive or unjust. This leads to silences about these subjects and their histories, which can make negotiating this terrain both difficult and discomfiting.

The power of these associations and the way they were promoted in the national media are such that many councils, including Hackney, have found it hard to shake off an image of radicalism, incompetence and corruption in the ensuing years (Ball et al, 1990, p 86; Solomos, 1986, p 29). It has encouraged councillors to adopt policies intended to distance themselves from 'loony left' labels, particularly by emphasising diversity and inclusion rather than the more overtly oppositional anti-racism (Ball et al, 1990, p 90; Gordon, 1990, p 176; for more on the shift from 'anti-racism' to 'diversity', see Ahmed, 2007b; Faist, 2009).

Contemporary moments

The reinvention of the British Labour Party as New Labour was partly about distancing itself from the 'Old Left' label, from the idea that the party could not be trusted with the national economy, and from concerns such as racism and policing, which were 'seen as vote losers distracting public attention from Labour's "traditional" political heartland' (Keith and Murji, 1990, p 130). The shift towards neoliberalism, communitarianism and pragmatism all contributed to a massive increase in the culture-based regeneration of inner cities. Reconceptualising diversity as a virtue has been part of reimagining it as a capitalist asset, and as a governed and managed activity (Jacobs, 1996, p 87). In this process, the 'success story' is both 'neoliberal and multicultural', firmly in the present (if not the future), and 'aggressively forward-looking'. The 'brash multiculture of consumption' in Britain has a London focus, particularly in relation to its draw on competitive, young, highly skilled migrants, but this sheen is also to some extent lent to the rest of the UK (Bonnett, 2010, p 130), and with inner London treated as a model or laboratory for the future of multiculturalism (as in Butler and Hamnett, 2011, p 20). This narrative of forward-looking dynamic diversity centred on London (but enveloping the rest of the country) was central to London's successful bid for the 2012 Olympics (Vertovec, 2007, p 1025; Wetherell, 2008, pp 306-7).

One narrative of community cohesion, then, is that it is an attempt to roll out a post-racial settlement from London to the rest of the UK. The proclamation that chicken tikka masala was now 'Britain's national dish' by then Foreign Secretary Robin Cook (Cook, 2001) was based on an understanding that cultural mixing had become banal and ordinary, but it was also about promoting an image of Britain as slightly exoticised and no longer stodgily reliant on 'meat and two veg'. In 2006, David Miliband (as Cabinet Minister for CLG) gave a speech to the Scarman Trust in which he stated that 'diversity is a fact across all societies. All countries are multicultural and there is no going back' (Miliband, 2006). In the context of an argument to 'meet the challenges of a multi-ethnic society' by 'strengthening community', this was a moderate progressive speech, and more strongly empirical than Cook's. These comments are particularly interesting, however, for their resonance with the often-quoted (but difficult to source)[9] mantra of New Labour that 'we're all middle class now'. The assumption is that if 'we' are all middle class and multicultural, struggles with poverty and racism are over. Persisting power inequalities are silenced, as are struggles over ideology in a post-political age (Mouffe, 2005, p 35; Swyngedouw, 2010, p 214).

This leads to a technocratic approach to multiculture and diversity demonstrated in the implementation of community cohesion policy within government. In 2007, new national indicators were introduced that local authorities across England and Wales could choose to incorporate in their LAA with national government, as a way of measuring their impact on the local area. The set of indicators included three separate measures to monitor community cohesion. These were:

> NI 1: Percentage of people who believe people from different backgrounds get on well together in their local area
>
> NI 2: Percentage of people who feel that they belong to their neighbourhood
>
> NI 4: Percentage of people who feel they can influence decisions in their locality (CLG, 2007c, p 5).

These measures are given similar status and expectations for improvement to (for example) measures of the efficiency of refuse collections or the quality of public play areas. Yet they continue to rely on the collection of large-scale survey data about subjective measures, whose causes are much harder to isolate or manage. They are a 'technology of community', a device to make community or the experience of community real, and thereby something on which it is possible to operate (Rose, 1999b). The indicators were widely taken up by local authorities across the country, suggesting either that they were widely accepted as measuring local priorities or (more cynically) as easy-to-meet targets.

These relatively anodyne measurements of what it means to live well and safely within diverse communities emerged at the same time as the complexity of diversity itself was increasing exponentially (Keith, 2005, pp 177-8). 'Super-diversity' has been coined as a term to not only recognise the increasing number of locations across the globe from which migrants are now arriving in significant numbers in the UK, but also to emphasise that the word 'migrant' gives very little sense of the diversity of their experiences as it varies across different social positionings of class, gender, length of settlement, legal status, sexuality, family connections and so on (Vertovec, 2007). Developments in extending non-discrimination law to a growing number of 'protected groups' through the Equality Act 2010 and the merging of existing equalities bodies into a single organisation is one of the few ways in which policy or legal instruments explicitly attempted to address cross-cutting elements of diversity and their relationship to power. Legal protection from discrimination, and recognition that discrimination, disadvantage and inequalities of power can come in many forms and operate with different dynamics, have not been translated further into a discourse about commonalities of oppression, however (Gavrielides, 2011). The Act's duty for public bodies to promote 'good relations', building on the terminology of previous Race Relations Acts and Local Government Acts, produced little connection between equalities and good relations duties on the one hand, and community cohesion policy on the other, in either policy debates or academic literature. Since its election, the Coalition government has announced that it will scale back and delay many provisions of the Equality Act 2010, and reduce the budget and powers of the statutory, independent Equalities and Human Rights Commission that were provided for by the Equality Act 2006 (May, 2012).

Place

Hackney is associated with the narratives of the inner city not just because of its histories of migration and poverty (see, for example, Harrison, 1983), but also in relation to its histories of governance and engagement with racism and anti-racism. It is one of the local authorities whose names still act metonymically for the idea of the 'loony left'. It is also a place whose associations are strongly tied to the dangers of the inner city (see, for example, Bonnett, 1993, p 171; Oakeshott, 2008; Sinclair, 2009, p 9). Yet these connotations are also, in part, what has attracted growing creative industries and artists to the area, which have in turn contributed to its wider desirability. The marketing of London as an Olympic city on the basis of its multicultural associations is matched by the remarketing of its resonances of urban edginess, for instance, in the pirating of Hackney Council's municipal logo by Nike, to sell sports clothing worldwide (LBH, 2006c; Tran, 2006; and see also Chapter Four, this volume).

In the era of community cohesion policy, Hackney did not seem to fit any of the narratives of 'community cohesion problems' previously outlined. In part, this was because each of them has focused on challenges posed by new immigration (and reactions to it), or on the nature of 'parallel lives' defined by two separated communities. In this light, Hackney can be imagined as happily cohesive – in that the super-diversity of its residents might avoid large factional identity groups that could congeal into the rivalries of competitive identity politics. Ideas of multiculturalism could also, in some inflections, be broadened beyond migration and race to embrace other forms of diversity and discrimination. In this formation, the 'folk devil' is less the migrant (or sexual minority); instead it is the racist (or homophobe) who becomes the constitutive outside of the imagined national community. The past of far right activism in inner London, political infighting and struggles against institutional discrimination are forgotten, or at least less visible (Watson and Wells, 2005; Wemyss, 2009, p 94). And multiculture is frozen as an achieved goal, a cohesive community, rather than an ongoing, lived process. The inner city, and in particular inner London (with its proximity to national politicians and press) becomes a repository of hope rather than despair, for instance, as a symbolic figurehead for attempts to tackle some of Britain's 'most deprived and crime-ridden estates' when Prime Minister Tony Blair launched his programme of inner-city investment, the New Deal for Communities, on the Holly Street estate in 1998 (BBC News, 1998).

But this narrative of happily 'rubbing along' does not necessarily take account of power inequalities. Hackney, or the inner city, could come to symbolise the inequities of neoliberal forms of multiculturalism which allow 'difference' to be cultural capital for some, but to remain the source of exclusion for others (Ahmed, 2000, p 125; Bell and Binnie, 2000, p 86). In celebrating local diversity, it can become too easy to forget not only local histories of violent racism (Keith, 1993) but also the internal tensions, dynamics and injuries that a happy multicultural sheen might hide.

Conclusions

As I have shown, understanding community cohesion policy as bound to particular events, times and places conjures a set of easily digestible stories which can be readily referred to in conversation and negotiations (the riots in Oldham in 2001; the election of the BNP in Barking and Dagenham in 2006; new migration into Peterborough throughout the 2000s; long-standing diversity in Hackney). As I provide further evidence of how policy practitioners imagine and use such narratives in their negotiations, I suggest that in doing so they employ a form of sociological imagination that makes links between local, personal experiences and societal structures of power distribution. Within these narratives there is much to be learned from observing what is silenced, as well as what is spoken. In the rest of the book, I engage directly with the narratives of policy negotiation provided by practitioners in the course of my research. This chapter should provide both a factual background to the events and interventions to which they allude, and a guide to some of the ways these moments have been and can be fitted together to make sense of policy worlds.

THREE

"Is there anything the council did that distracted you from extremism?"

Introduction

The establishment of the Preventing Violent Extremism (PVE) programme in 2007 shows how far community cohesion policy, in one articulation, has been tied to the targeting of Muslims as a 'problem group', and refracted through the lens of religious and ethnic representation, privilege and stigma. As discussed in Chapter Two, some constructions of community cohesion position it as separate from PVE. This separation does not necessarily translate into the common-sense understandings of practitioners. In my experiences and interviews with local and national policy practitioners they suggest, based on the timing, presentation, implementation and funding of projects and their own professional and personal experience, that there are more complicated agendas at play than those laid out in official documentation. This chimes with much sociological comment on the subject (see, for example, McGhee, 2008; Husband and Alam, 2011). Yet the articulation of what community cohesion policy or PVE policy is 'really about' varies with circumstance as well as time and place – in negotiations between local and central government, power relations determine what can be said, and how. Through this chapter, it becomes clear that different levels of reality, information and argument become important at different levels and in different parts of governing organisations. These shifting terms of debate determine the most effective (or possible) forms for local policy practitioners to negotiate cohesion, inequality and change.

Preventing Violent Extremism lands on my desk

In early February 2007, the chief executive of the London Borough of Hackney received a request to attend a meeting of London local authority chief executives, called by the Government Office for London (GOL), to discuss the PVE Pathfinder Fund. At that time, I was working as a policy adviser in Hackney, responsible for maintaining awareness of policy, political and community developments, forming strategic alliances within and outside the local authority, advocating policy responses and ensuring the implementation of strategy agreed by the political and managerial leadership. Because I had a broad remit for 'inclusion' issues, I was asked to prepare a one-page briefing on the background to the PVE Fund, its significance for Hackney and a recommended response. The Fund was new, and the guidance note stated that Government Offices had been working with local authorities since the previous October to develop programmes. Having checked with colleagues in the community safety team that we had not been involved in those discussions, I suggested in the briefing that it seemed "unlikely they expect us to take part."

Nevertheless, I advised on the headlines of the funding programme: it was intended to 'encourage local approaches to preventing violent extremism'; 'this is to be separate from community cohesion activity'; and £2 million of the £5 million one-year fund would be 'available for bids from London boroughs with more than 5% Muslim population – this includes Hackney'. I also pointed out in the briefing that Hackney's 'large Muslim population (14% – compared to 8% in London)' was 'ethnically diverse, including Turkish and Somali communities' while 'only 1% of Hackney's population is Pakistani (2% in London), 3% Bangladeshi (2% in London) – the ethnic groups of Muslims the government appears to be most concerned about'; and stated that 'we have not noted any problems related to Islamic extremism in the borough' despite proximity to Finsbury Park Mosque (in Haringey) which had been associated with extremists. Finally, I suggested that:

> It seems unlikely that we would be involved at this stage as we do not have a history of problems with extremism and we would not want to highlight a particular community or group of communities as 'a problem'.[1]

I advised that we should attend the meeting to stay updated and see whether funds could be incorporated into existing community engagement programmes. I suggested we use the opportunity to highlight diversity within Muslim communities and to ask about the relevance of the Fund to extremism, beyond that claiming connections to Islam.

The chief executive sent an assistant director to the meeting as her representative, as did many of her peers.[2] After the meeting, I was briefed that it had been an uncomfortable affair. Representatives of the Department for Communities and Local Government (DCLG) and GOL were not pleased with the level of seniority of attendance from local authorities, and local authority representatives expressed a number of concerns about the scheme (see also Kelcher, 2007, and House of Commons Communities and Local Government Committee, 2010, p 226).

Local authorities expressed one very practical concern: the extremely short amount of time allowed to produce bids that fitted the PVE priorities. Guidance for the Fund was published on 7 February, the meeting with GOL was on 13 February and expressions of interest were due by noon on 2 March. Although local government bureaucracy is often criticised for the time it takes to reach agreement and to take action, the typical bureaucratic requirements for due process and consideration of financial, legal, political and managerial implications exist to ensure fairness and to avoid corruption or mistakes. The importance given to these checks and balances limits flexibility, but may be particularly pronounced in those authorities that still suffer from a reputation of incompetence or corruption from past decades (see also Chapter Two, this volume).

Nor can these practical considerations be separated entirely from the more politically sensitive issues that concerned local authorities (including Hackney) about the way PVE had been constructed. The framing of the Fund as exclusively targeted at extremism in the name of Islam without reference to other forms of violent extremism, the focus on Muslim populations only and the lack of any apparent basis for selecting eligible authorities aside from the proportion of their population that was Muslim, were raised not just in my briefing, but also by colleagues from other authorities. These were presented as not just problematic bases for the policy in themselves, but also likely to be counter-productive in that they might undermine relationships with local community groups, both Muslim and non-Muslim. These were not just questions of language but of implementation and process, which local authority officers suggested would be difficult to address, especially in the short time available.

However, it was made clear by civil servants from GOL and CLG at the February meeting and in subsequent correspondence that all 'eligible' authorities were expected to submit proposals to the Fund, and that non-participation would be seen as a sign of not taking seriously the threat of future terrorist action (see also McLean, 2008). It was hard for any local authority to refuse additional investment in services. In Hackney, being one of Britain's poorest areas made such a bold and apparently uncooperative move even harder, as did its still haunting history of municipal failures (see Chapters Four and Five).

Although their concerns about the Fund had not been addressed, the senior management and politicians in Hackney decided to submit an 'expression of interest' without necessarily committing to the programme. After all, this was still being described by CLG and GOL as a bidding process in which we may or may not be 'successful'. This decision was made after contact with peers in other local authorities, and indeed most authorities did present initial expressions of interest.

In Hackney, a potential project was developed with a local organisation, to 'undertake research with Muslim communities to identify experience and perceptions of Islamophobia' with subsequent work 'exploring the reasons for conflict and alternatives to conflict.'[3] Two weeks after this was submitted, the local authority chief executive received a letter from GOL saying that the borough would be 'offered' £90,000 to support that project. Despite the initial reticence of London boroughs reported in February, the letter stated that there had been high demand for funds; the £90,000 allocated to Hackney was thus 'not subject to further negotiation.' The first payment, the letter said, was to be made through the LAA[4] grant in April 2007 (two weeks from the date of the letter), and the programme was to be formally launched by the Secretary of State following an event at the end of March.[5]

The local political leadership repeatedly stated that they did not want to take the money if it would oblige them to run a programme ostensibly targeting Muslims – all local Muslims, Muslims in particular, and Muslims only – as potential terrorists. Yet there was clear pressure from CLG to show that the local authority was 'taking seriously' the potential threat of extremism. This was coupled with local pressure from Muslim organisations that saw PVE as a potential funding stream to develop their work. The senior management team and the council's cabinet (political leaders) developed an alternative local solution to this impasse. It was the end of the financial year and an under-spend had been identified within the voluntary sector grants budget. The cabinet agreed that this would be used to develop an alternative fund to the PVE programme in Hackney. They asked me to write a scoping document setting out its terms.

The proposed fund was 'to support vcs [voluntary and community sector] projects aimed at improving community cohesion ... in a Hackney-focused way, sensitive to our local population'. It was intended to prepare the borough to bid for future funding 'from other sources, including the Preventing Violent Extremism fund where appropriate' by developing 'a strong base of projects demonstrating success', to support projects addressing known areas of tensions between groups (socioeconomic divisions and regeneration; intergenerational issues; high levels of mobility and hidden communities; gang violence and area-based rivalries; and links between 'single community' infrastructures' and 'identifying new or unacknowledged sources of conflict'.[6] The underlying issue was that the local authority had no evidence of emerging extremism in the borough, but officers and politicians *were* concerned about sources of tension or potential tension. The administrators of the LSP (the local board of political, public and community leaders) advised their central government contacts of this, and that the local authority had therefore chosen not to accept the offer of PVE funding for 2007/08.

While it felt exceptional to refuse a funding stream from central government, I also felt, as an officer, quite proud of the compromise we had developed. Local politicians had taken a decision which they believed reflected the needs and wishes of local residents, and as officers we had found a way to deliver that. Between us we had done this in a way that did not reject outright the national policy, but questioned some of its premises and suggested constructive ways in which a local approach might differ. In theory, this also fitted with national agendas on localism, where authorities use their local knowledge to develop site-appropriate services. This didn't address, of course, what expectations might have been raised with organisations involved in the expression of interest for the PVE Fund, but there remained the opportunity for them to be part of the alternative Community Cohesion Fund.

However, this compromise did not satisfy those managing the PVE Fund nationally and regionally. In fact it did not appear to register with them at all. This became clear when the local authority received an email informing us of new indicators that would be included in the LAA to measure the delivery of PVE. The initial proposal for these indicators read directly off the aims of the scheme that were given in national guidance, and suggested that local authorities measure the impact of their activities by reporting publicly on the number of Muslims who had been diverted from extremist beliefs, among other things.[7] There were three immediate problems: we had not agreed to participate in PVE, yet were still being included in its measurement; the indicators were being inserted into the LAA without discussion; and the indicators themselves appeared impractical and offensive. As Emma, a senior officer in Hackney who I interviewed later, put it:

> EMMA: I don't know if they ever came up with a ...
> definition for that indicator about cohesion, and I

> think when it first came out I was thinking, well, what
> are you gonna do, you just going to go out and knock
> on … people's door and go, ooh are you a Muslim, is
> there anything the council did that distracted you from
> extremism?

Although Emma does not distinguish between cohesion and extremism, which have different indicators on which local government performance is measured, her point is a general one. Although Emma's comment is humorous, her suggestion does seem like a logical way to find out whether a project has helped "Muslims in our communities" to "reject violent extremist ideology and actively condemn violent extremism." But it is also absurd in that the question, much like the original design of the PVE programme, makes an implicit assumption that Muslims need to be dissuaded from extremism, and the question does not seem like one that a person who either remained an extremist, or had never been an extremist, would be likely to answer happily. The language and assumptions of the PVE programme expose fundamental differences in conceptualisation of communities, measurement, information and the role of government within and between policy practitioners, local and national.

It was quite clear to me that the council's political leadership would have a problem with including these proposed measurements in local plans for the borough, and this turned out to be the case. This made little difference, however. GOL asked local performance managers for Hackney's figures on performance against NI 35 (the PVE performance indicator). When they explained that Hackney had chosen not to participate in the scheme, officials at GOL replied that the money had been passed on to the borough as part of the LAA block grant, which it had, despite the local authority's protestations. The introduction of LAAs as a contract between local authorities and central government had been promoted as a way of devolving power to local areas, reducing the number of targets and separate funding streams for which they are accountable to central government, with one contact point through the regional government office (CLG, 2007a). Yet NI 35 was inserted into the 198 measures on which all LAAs across the country must report, after local negotiations for that year were completed. The only remaining element of choice for local authorities as to how to report was whether to make NI 35 one of the 35 headline indicators, for which improved outcomes in their local area would result in additional 'reward' funding from central government.

This precise question – whether to include PVE as one of the most important measures of success in Hackney – arose a year later when renewing the LAA. At this point, the borough commander of police presented a briefing for Hackney's LSP steering group, arguing that NI 35 should be included in local reward indicators because Hackney was a high risk area for violent extremist activity.[8] The police briefing posed the question, 'Why does Hackney need to build resilience to violent extremism?' and in response, quoted 2001 Census data on the size of the black and minority ethnic (BME) population in general. Although the report went on to observe that 'Muslims are not a homogeneous group', it then stated that 'Many Muslims may categorise themselves as having an Asian ethnicity, but this is not the case for all Muslims. Even within the category of Asian, there are huge cultural differences between Muslims from Pakistan, Africa and the Far East' [sic].[9] This suggests a lack of 'intelligence' within the police service, not just about community relations and local threats, but also confusion about ethnic, 'racial', national and religious categories as well as basic questions of geography.

The police briefing follows the national line pushed by both CLG and Home Office guidance on PVE that refers to past crimes, the size of the resident Muslim population and nebulous 'intelligence' that cannot be revealed, as evidence of threats of future violence. It then suggests that this should be prevented by actions to be carried out by the local authority at the behest of the police, security services and central government. The overall argument of the report was that local intelligence pointed to a terrorist threat in Hackney which should be tackled through PVE schemes *led by the local authority*, thereby turning the 'softer' tools of persuasion and self-government directly into the service of agencies of disciplinary control.

'Intelligence'

> BRIAN: And the police, because of their pragmatic approach, get there faster than the local authority.... We're aware this needs to be done, it needs to be done, and therefore we will drive it through. Because it needs to be done. We know it's gonna come, and I think the council know it needs to be done. But where they'd like to have a few more meetings and discuss it a bit further and go – and convince [*pause*] you don't always get that time, so.

I had asked Brian, a senior local police officer involved in community cohesion work in Hackney, about the inclusion of the PVE indicator in the LAA, as I knew the police had pushed for this to be one of the 'reward indicators' for Hackney. Brian's first response was to tell me that Hackney "hits all the boxes that [this is] where is your next radicalised extremist [is] gonna come from" because it has "huge levels of deprivation", and when people who have been in prison for extremism-related offences are released, "they all seem to come to Hackney". He saw the reasoning as quite straightforward, "it needs to be done, and therefore we will drive it through". Brian's view was that the local authority simply dragged its feet, but would eventually cede to the inevitability of the police's more quickly adopted approach.

While Brian framed the police's speed of adopting the PVE scheme as 'pragmatic', many of the objections to the scheme that I heard from local authority officials (and which I put forward myself when working as one) could also be framed that way. These objections were that the scheme would simply not address the problem it set out to solve, that even if extremism in the name of Islam was seen as an imminent threat, the focus on Muslims in general did not follow. While the parameters of their pragmatism differed, both local authority and police practitioners talked in terms of effectiveness, and of techniques that they saw as the most efficient to achieve desired outcomes.

In Chapter One I described the importance of governmentality, the promotion of self-governing behaviours, to the development of community cohesion policy. A simplifying theoretical framework might suggest that local government has promoted self-government, while the police focus on disciplinary government. Until well into the 1980s, local government and the police in England operated as quite separate entities, particularly in London. While some local authorities had police committees, in London the Greater London Council established the first such relationship in the 1980s, where the police had previously reported only to the Home Secretary (Lansley et al, 1989, p 68). From that period, work between local authorities and the police developed, albeit often in a situation of mutual distrust or misunderstanding (Lansley et al, 1989, p 51). Pushes towards *partnership* across government agencies, especially in the 2000s, brought developments in working relationships which meant that local authority chief executives and their local police commanding officers sat together on LSPs, with the two agencies held jointly responsible by central government for community safety targets (although more recently, the abolition of the statutory basis for LSPs and the creation of directly elected police commissioners has altered this relationship again). Although there is consequent blurring at the edges with exchanges of responsibilities, staffing and resources, the police service and local authorities remain quite distinct institutions, with distinct purposes and cultures. These differences become clearer when a controversy or crisis, such as the instigation of PVE, occurs. The police and security services (and largely the national government policy guidelines) present their viewpoint as 'pragmatic' and 'no-nonsense' as it aims to root out terrorists without worrying about causing offence. Conversely, the local government perspectives I consider position themselves as pragmatic, in that to achieve their goals of building trust with local residents they cannot be seen to form part of the police and security services' intelligence apparatus.

An increasing focus on counter-terrorism work with Muslim communities followed bombings in London on 7 July 2005.[10] National government established a number of working groups involving individual Muslims invited as private citizens, intended to find 'concrete proposals about how Muslim communities and the Government can further work in partnership to prevent extremism, and to reduce disaffection and radicalisation within Muslim communities across Britain' (Preventing Extremism Together Working Groups, 2005, p 97). To some extent this community relations focus did influence the PVE guidelines. The Working Groups proposed actions for engaging with Muslim women and young people, and support for community development and leadership, which appear as PVE priorities. But the Working Groups' ambition to promote understanding and dialogue about Muslim lives and religion – not just between Muslims but across society – was not developed further within PVE guidance (Preventing Extremism Together Working Groups, 2005; CLG, 2007b). There are also elements of the PVE priorities that do not relate directly to any recommendations of the Working Groups, around resilience and early intervention with communities (see also Bright, 2006, p 12). This demonstrates a move from treatment of 'Muslim communities' as potentially vulnerable in the Working Groups, to a treatment of 'Muslims in our communities' primarily as a potential threat within PVE, that is, from a 'community relations' focus to a 'security' focus.

These aspects of the relationship between local government and the police mirror, to some extent, the relationship between CLG and the Home Office on the national level. Within national government, it appeared that the security services and Home Office had won any debate about the balance between promoting good community relations and gathering intelligence on criminal terror-related activity. Although PVE was administered by CLG through local government, it emerged from the national cross-government counter-terrorism strategy, known as CONTEST. This was published in 2006, and revised in 2009 (HM Government, 2009a). CONTEST consists of four strands – Prevent, Pursue, Protect and Prepare. At the time the PVE programme was launched, the stated aims of the Prevent strand were threefold: to tackle disadvantage, inequalities and discrimination that could 'contribute to radicalisation' (HM Government, 2006, p 1); to deter facilitation of terrorism by 'changing the environment in which the extremists and those radicalising others can operate' (p 12); and challenging ideologies which are used to justify violence 'primarily by helping Muslims who wish to dispute these ideas to do so' (p 2).

The PVE programme was the community-based part of the Prevent workstream, implemented through local government, alongside policing and counter-terrorism work led by the police (HM Government, 2009a, pp 14-15). Although the overall counter-terrorism strategy draws attention to 'structural problems ... that may contribute to radicalisation', there are no specific efforts to address inequality or discrimination in the UK as part of the Prevent strategy. The PVE guidance even states explicitly that tackling disadvantage is to be considered elsewhere, and that PVE work is not to be directed to this end (DCLG, 2008, p 11). The original PVE guidance stated its aims:

> to develop a community in which Muslims in our communities:
> - identify themselves as a welcome part of a wider British society and are accepted as such by the wider community;
> - reject violent extremist ideology and actively condemn violent extremism;
> - isolate violent extremist activity, and support and co-operate with the police and security services; and,
> - develop their own capacity to deal with problems where they arise and support diversionary activity for those at risk. (CLG, 2007b, p 3)

This guidance, published, promoted and managed by CLG, directly translates an 'intelligence', criminalising and securitising discourse into the official policy of local government.

Similar themes can also be seen between the briefing that I produced as a local government policy practitioner responding to the PVE programme for Hackney, and that produced by the local police a year later (described earlier in this chapter). The most pressing argument of the police briefing was the risk of terrorist activity occurring in the borough, illustrated with information on previous arrests. The briefing also provided population data as a way of illustrating potential for violent extremism. But the way the data was used on ethnic and religious identity in the borough betrayed a lack of understanding of the information quoted. They confused ethnic, religious, national and 'racial' categories. The briefing stated the size of local Muslim (and minority ethnic in general) populations, but the author did not apparently feel any need to provide further explanation of why this was considered a risk factor.

The simple assumption of the national PVE guidance also seemed to be that 'the main terrorist threat facing the UK currently comes from Islamist extremists' (CLG, 2007b); that 'Islamist extremists' formed a subset within the larger population group 'Muslim'; that therefore reaching more Muslims would result in reaching more extremists as a percentage of that group; and that the most efficient way to reach more Muslims would be to work in areas where the most Muslims lived. In short, the assumption seemed to be that Muslims were a single group, and a set percentage of Muslims could be expected to be extremists or terrorists, distributed evenly across the population. There was no consideration of whether, for example, extremism might thrive outside of the larger concentrations of Muslim populations, rather than simply where the biggest numbers lived (see Finney and Simpson, 2009, p 109). This amounts to a question of how measurement is conceptualised at different levels and in different branches of government.

Conversely, a neglect of understanding the security intelligence on actual criminal activity could be attributed to my briefing, where I dismissed the suggestion that there was evidence of terrorist activity in the borough. Indeed, the local authority did not have any information to suggest this, but there may have been information available. For instance, the police briefing provided information on three individuals who had been convicted of terrorist offences, with residences or family connections in Hackney. The contrast between these two briefings was not just in the arguments each made, but in the types of knowledge available and valued in the two cultures of the local authority and of the police, and what information each framed as essential (or unnecessary) to make sense of the situation.

When the two organisations worked together, they each asked the other to take seriously their own form of knowledge and understanding of priorities – yet each retained their own overriding concerns. To caricature this difference: police officers appeared to see as self-evident that the most important ambition was finding and arresting (potential) bombers. Conversely, for local government officers, persuasion, trust and relationship building seemed the self-evident priority. It is also worth noting that, to some extent, techniques of persuasion and relationship building were perhaps the only ones *available* to local government in this context; while the police's more coercive powers were also limited by what information they had.

The lack of clarity about what 'intelligence' was available was important in blurring the roles between local government and the police or security services. This nebulous concept has been used both as an existing resource to justify the form and development of PVE, and as an output of PVE. Local authorities and individual service providers were expected to develop knowledge of local communities not just in terms of needs, priorities or tensions, but as information on risks that could be passed on to the security services. It is understandable that information on significant criminal investigations may not be made widely available. However, there was a feeling among local government practitioners in Hackney that those with access to this information (largely, the police locally) were using this knowledge to exert pressure on those without access. These fears were not confined to Hackney; for example, the Leader of Bradford Council appeared on BBC Newsnight in September 2008, stating:

> What they said was, that if we were willing to go out and monitor the Muslim community and use the resources of the local council to do that, then they would release an amount of money to us. The local council should be there to promote education, caring for elderly people, making sure we live in a safe place, and not become a wing of the security services.... We've had an enormous amount of pressure.... I think they are also trying to suggest that we're soft on terrorism, which is completely wrong. (Newsnight, 2008)

It is also worth noting the assumptions made in these comments about the self-evidence of local government's role being to provide amenities for residents – and not to be part of the security services. Throughout the life of the PVE programme occasional media coverage suggested that it encouraged local authorities to 'spy' on residents (see, for example, Dodd, 2009a), and other research reports based on interviews with local government practitioners have found them to be uneasy about working on a programme so closely associated with intelligence gathering for the security services (Kundnani, 2009; Turley, 2009; Husband and Alam, 2011). One element of PVE was clearly an intention to use trusted networks developed by local authorities to inform security intelligence, as illustrated further below. Yet, conversely, the police and security services only appeared willing or able to share a very limited amount of their own knowledge.

An example of this is extracted from my interview with Craig, another police officer who had worked with community cohesion and PVE issues:

> CRAIG: We've seen that there is a counter terrorist [sic] threat, we know that because we've had attacks ... we know that on account of the intelligence that's come in, I appreciate fully that most people can't – and I use the word can't with consideration, can't understand the intelligence picture ... that's not because they're thick, it's because they can't be allowed access to it ... but I think it's right to say that there is a tangible threat, and I ... have not yet found anybody of any note or significance or who has the ability to have an impact, who would disagree with the fact that there is a counter terrorist [sic] threat.

Craig noted first the history of violent attacks, which was not in dispute. He continued by alluding to 'intelligence' that suggested that there was an ongoing threat, but "most people can't be allowed access to". He was aware that there was some feeling that this intelligence may not be substantial, and countered this by suggesting that anyone made privy to this information was convinced by it. Such secrecy made the intelligence difficult to work with, but the seriousness imputed to it made it hard to ignore.

Later in the interview, I asked Craig what his views were about the specific focus on extremism in the name of Islam, rather than (for example) violent extremism linked to far right organisations. His first response was that a far right terrorist attack was "not gonna happen" because "we've never seen that". When I reminded him of a recent conviction of a far right activist for bomb making (Dodd, 2009b), and the bombings in 1999 by David Copeland targeting minority ethnic and gay communities in London, and of police statements about a growing threat of far right violence (Dodd, 2009c), Craig agreed that such acts of violence "need to be dealt with", but still insisted they were not "the real threat". He suggested that addressing far right extremism might be helpful in developing acceptance of PVE by demonstrating it was not a programme of victimisation of "people that happen to be Muslim", because "when we talk about the far right we're not talking about white people". Yet he then went on to argue that, "it follows ... [that] the preventing violent extremism agenda focuses on Muslim communities ... [because] the greatest threat comes from Al-Qaeda". The contradiction in this argument – that all white people were clearly not white supremacists, but that all Muslims *might* be linked to Al-Qaeda – is a straightforward reflection of the way the PVE programme was presented in national policy guidance. More broadly, these comments make clear how far 'whiteness' was taken by Craig as an invisible and normative way of being (Frankenberg, 1993; Ware, 2002).

Craig also suggested that far right extremists were less of a threat, and harder to target, because they "are acting alone, it's really difficult to target their infrastructure." This implies that the infrastructure of extremists acting in the name of Islam is accessible, although the only way this is targeted through the PVE scheme is by the broad focus on all Muslim communities. This is not to suggest that the rest of the government's counter-terrorism strategy did not have a more developed idea of infrastructure. However, the suggestion that the local government, community-focused part of the strategy should target extremism in the name of Islam because it has a more developed infrastructure, while remaining at the level of a religious identity, seems incongruous.

Whatever 'intelligence' did exist, access to it was restricted, and local government practitioners were expected to take on trust that what they were told by the police and security services was substantiated. They were then asked to promote this view among local residents. In addition, local authorities were expected to pass information to the police to supplement intelligence gathering, with very little reassurance about the need for this, or how information might be being used. David was one of the most senior local government officers in Hackney (if anyone within the local authority were to be made aware of security issues, it would be him), and he expressed his frustration at the way that 'intelligence' was being used:

> DAVID: The police saying ... you're ranked 6th [in terms of threat of violent extremism] in the country, but, can't get any evidence to prove why we are.
> HANNAH: [*laughs*] They won't tell you why, or?
> DAVID: No, they won't share the intelligence.... It seems to be based on [*pause*] numbers of people and numbers of educational establishments in the – so there's a completely flawed model about why.

HANNAH: Yeah. It's because lots of Muslims live … in Hackney.

DAVID: Yeah. But then I get told by the police, oh there are real threats out there but they won't tell me what they are.

David described the impression he had been given that the police model of 'intelligence' about extremism was flawed. The only explicit detail that had been given, even to a senior officer who was being asked to cooperate with the scheme, was that the threat level was based on the size of the Muslim population and 'educational establishments' (it is unclear here if David was referring to mainstream establishments or specifically Muslim education). Still, the spectre of 'intelligence' remained powerful, and David did not want to neglect, or be seen to neglect, 'real threats' – although it was unclear how threats could be addressed when they "won't tell [him] what they are". Part of the power of this nebulous intelligence was that those who were privy to it were confident that anyone who knew about it would agree with them about the threat. Here, 'intelligence' was another of those terms that slipped between discussion as a cause of problems (because intelligence was lacking), a source of knowledge of problems (when there was intelligence about a threat), a problem in itself (when the quest for intelligence threatened relationships with communities) and a solution to problems (if we had more intelligence, we could prevent threats). But while local government practitioners expressed concern that the way 'intelligence' was being used could cast unfounded suspicions on Muslim communities at large (see also Kelcher, 2007; McLean, 2008; Reading Muslim PVE Crisis Group, 2008; Kundnani, 2009; Turley, 2009; House of Commons Communities and Local Government Committee, 2010, p 226; Husband and Alam, 2011), national debates critiqued these practices from a quite different perspective.

Some media coverage of PVE derided both national and local government participation in the scheme for either excessive paranoia, requiring refuse collectors to 'snoop in residents' rubbish bins' (McGee, 2008; see also Dodd, 2009a), or of wasting money on projects such as 'thousands on producing t-shirts proclaiming "I love Islam"' (Reid, 2008; see also Newsnight, 2008). These stories are reminiscent of the critique of 'political correctness gone mad' in the public sector that is familiar from attacks on local government in the 1980s (see Lansley et al, 1989; Gordon, 1990; Dunant, 1994). Like the mythologies that developed at that time, they are potent because they are grounded in some elements of fact, coupled with exaggeration and ridicule. Some of these criticisms of supposed local government incompetence even echoed the portrayals of the nationally mandated PVE scheme by local policy practitioners.

A criticism that I did not hear from local practitioners, however, was a more serious allegation that PVE funding itself was being directed at groups with their own links to extremism (see, for example, Bright, 2006). This question draws on issues that go way beyond local connections or funding measures and back to international politics and the role of national and foreign policy in creating the context in which extremism erupts (Brighton, 2007; Thomas, 2010), and the lack of a viable framework at any level for understanding new forms of networks of ideology and violence (Bhatt, 2007, 2010). The suggestion that funding meant to prevent violent extremism could actually be used to support it is ostensibly quite separate from the problems of alienating Muslim residents. The knee-jerk reaction is to assume advocates of these critiques hold respectively right- and left-wing political viewpoints. However, both of these potential problems could be assigned to a shared cause: a lack of detailed knowledge about the actual functioning of extremist movements, and a push to be seen to take firm action, resulting in hasty and perhaps counter-productive policy. This connects to questions about how the PVE Fund conceptualised violent extremism, and potential interventions. These questions are not just about what interventions might be most effective in combating violence, but also about what it is practically (and politically) possible within existing frameworks of government, and ethical and social norms.

Measurement

> EMMA: As officers in local government, you're often from a sort of left-wing liberal-type background ... and the idea of enforcing anything, it is tough ... so community cohesion has a bit of a rebranding almost to do, because of its negative connotations, because government pushes can seem like spying ... it also stinks of a sort of white British versus Muslim.... And it's to do with extremism ... rather than in its wider sense about how communities generally, into race issues, into age issues, all sorts of issues ... need to be under the umbrella of cohesion ... it seems to be used and interpreted as, we need to guard against Muslim extremism. And if we don't, if we don't

do community cohesion, [*clicks tongue*] my god, what
will happen?

This comment from Emma relates to her discussion of the performance
indicators for PVE quoted earlier, and again she emphasised the
perceived links between PVE and community cohesion policies in
practice. What is of particular interest here, however, is the opening
comment in this extract, where she attributed her uneasiness with the
scheme to a feeling that it "seems like spying", that local government
was unused to "enforcing" things in this way.

Emma here drew on personal political and ethical commitments,
which she believed to be common among local government
officers, and which she described as "a sort of left-wing liberal-type
background". This is not a party political alignment, but what might
be described elsewhere as a 'public service ethos' – a commitment to
public service, social justice or some other general formulation of the
importance of the public good, and perhaps to the championing of the
vulnerable or those in need of support. The way that PVE had been
presented to her, particularly in terms of its elements of information
gathering, had made Emma wary that these commitments might be
subverted by the scheme. As discussed earlier, these were suspicions
shared more widely among local authority officers about the extent to
which the PVE programme might lead to them becoming informants
for the security services, or perceived as such.

Yet both of Emma's comments illustrate the fleeting nature of
managerial engagement with these issues. Despite her apparently strong
feelings on the absurdity of the project, she didn't "know if they ever
came up with a definition for that indicatorBlack to front and black
again". The PVE programme did not form part of her day-to-day
work and so her outrage did not necessarily translate into a practical
intervention. Rather, she demonstrated a level of knowledge of the
issue and her political relationship to it (to me, in the interview) but in
doing so, also abdicated responsibility and distanced herself from those
elements of organisations she worked within that were implementing it.

Despite Emma's suggestion that she and her colleagues were
instinctively uncomfortable with what she construed as "spying",
the local state has a long-established role in collecting and modelling
population data as part of planning services and predicting behaviours
of, and risks to, the local population (Foucault, 1991 [1978]).
As Husband and Alam (2011) observe, many local government
practitioners are fluent at integrating such statistical data with local
experiential knowledge about what it might *mean*. These interpretive

techniques were not always shared by the police service, as indicated by the police briefing discussed above. Nor were nuances of local knowledge always compatible with data considered as national aggregates, as in the guidance on PVE being aimed at those areas with the largest Muslim populations. Perhaps partly for this reason, the blunt ways in which the PVE programme was presented created difficulties at the level of definition and measurement of impact, and in implementation. These challenges were expressed to government in various forms (see, for example, Kelcher, 2007; McLean, 2008; House of Commons Communities and Local Government Committee, 2010), and eventually the initially proposed indicators (which mirrored very closely Emma's facetious suggestion) were replaced by more process-focused formulations (Rimmer, 2008). By 2008 NI 35 success criteria for PVE had been developed into a framework that focused on the achievement of internal goals by the local authority (HM Government, 2009b), judging levels of:

- Understanding of, and engagement with, Muslim communities
- Knowledge and understanding of the drivers and causes of violent extremism and the Prevent objectives
- Development of a risk-based preventing violent extremism action plan, in support of the delivery of the Prevent objectives
- Effective oversight, delivery and evaluation of projects and action. (HM Government, 2008, pp 55-8)

Alison, who worked for an organisation representing local government interests to national government and vice versa, suggested that these changes to the scheme's measurement and presentation were the result of dialogue between parts of government. She saw the process of negotiating the compromise itself as productive:

> ALISON: The feedback from some local authorities have been, we really hated this at the outset, we really felt that this was gonna do all sorts of untold damage ... and almost in the process of making that point back to central government, they actually did what they needed to do.... Because they had ... to go out into their communities ... and have a proper dialogue with them about, this is actually an issue, do we have a role in doing anything about it? And it started to draw out some of the more

unpleasant and difficult debates and tensions that you would have at a local level....Whether that's what CLG intended ... not a robust, you've gotta go out and stop the terrorists, is debatable but doesn't really matter 'cos I think the position they've arrived at now ... has got them to quite a sensible place.

What Alison's discussion does not address is that the changes to the scheme have framed it in terms that make local authorities more comfortable, a familiar move of 'polish[ing] the rough edges that do not fit neatly either side of the controversy' so that '[e]veryone seems to gain' (Trouillot, 1995, p 115). Producing evidence of 'knowledge and understanding', an 'action plan', 'oversight' and 'evaluation' relies on internal processes, and not on trying to measure levels of extremism or how they might have changed. What was viewed as inflammatory language in the earlier presentation of the scheme had been removed or was easier to keep to internal documents, while the premise of the scheme remained unchanged – that there was an unspecified threat from extremism in the name of Islam that should be tackled by activities focused on Muslims in areas with large Muslim populations. The existence of a government fund directed exclusively at Muslims persisted, and it did not only have the potential to risk relationships with Muslim communities that may feel victimised (whether this potential was in the anticipation of local policy practitioners, or voiced by Muslim community groups; see, for example, Reading Muslim PVE Crisis Group, 2008). It also created potential problems for other groups who were *not* eligible for the Fund to feel that Muslim populations were being unfairly *privileged*.

Impacts on local relationships

MARIE: Obviously there was counter-terrorism activity but there was also concern about a backlash ... against Muslim communities, but also potentially a situation where people might feel that they'd have to keep their heads down because they were scared of coming anywhere near the police about issues because [*pause*] the hunt was on for the bombers. And so ... we as a borough wanted to reassure people, that you could still contact us, you could still feed in those issues of harassment or incidents....What we discovered was there had been an escalation [in harassment] ... and the cumulative effect of those low level incidents meant that some of the services and people were in genuine feelings of fear.... But some of the feedback we got from mothers was that their sons were saying look we can see what's happening in Abu Ghraib....[11]

HANNAH: ... yeah....

MARIE: ... and we can we can see that what's happening in terms of their perception of an attack on civil liberties, and being really really reluctant to talk about people that they were suspicious of, 'cos ... they didn't have sufficient faith in the establishment to deal with suspicion....

HANNAH: ... yeah....

MARIE: ... without, from their perception, fitting people up. And putting them in a prison with suspended *habeas corpus* under the Terrorism Act. And never knowing if that person would get out again.

HANNAH: [*overlapping*] ... yeah, yeah....

MARIE: [*overlapping*] And if they did, their life destroyed.

HANNAH: ... yeah....

MARIE: ... And then ... after the [*pause*] killing of Jean Charles de Menezes we were asked as a borough to use the networks that we'd developed through that for community reassurance, to pass out information from the Met Police, which reassured the community about – the killing of Jean Charles de Menezes.[12] And I as an officer got in touch with my Cabinet Member and said I'm recommending we don't do this, because to put it bluntly I felt that what we'd got from the police was a – pack of lies, [*both laugh*] and ... it was a very very blatant [*pause*] the police version of the story, which by that time was beginning to unravel. We had to take the conscious decision at that point ... to decide that our relationships ... with our BME communities in terms of the reassurance and trust could have been massively undermined if we'd forwarded the whole set of stories about – what had happened in Stockwell.

In this account, Marie described some of the tension that had emerged from the attempts at partnership working between the police and local authorities when roles became blurred, as they seemed to around the purpose and implementation of PVE and related counter-terrorism work. Marie worked in equality policy, and in this interview extract she described her experience of working in a previous job for a local authority outside of my case studies, during the summer of 2005.

Marie first described her concern that some local residents might feel "scared" as a result of counter-terrorism operations. While not dismissing the need for police action on countering violence, she pointed out that a violent backlash against Muslims (and those assumed to be Muslim) also required intervention. Marie suggested that the local authority's work should focus on supporting residents experiencing harassment, and preventing further conflict, rather than searching for criminals. The importance of local authority services being seen as separate from security and police services was emphasised in Marie's account – people were "harassed" and "in fear", and some of this stemmed from feeling that "the hunt was on", and that anyone could be a suspect. It seems apparent from this account that Marie was quite sympathetic with that feeling, and indeed at other points in the interview she described feeling parallels to the way that she had experienced victimisation under anti-terror laws related to Irish people in the 1980s and 1990s, when she was married to an Irish man who was unjustly arrested under the Prevention of Terrorism Act.

Where the first part of Marie's account referred to the feelings within the community and how she as an officer tried to find ways to understand them, the second part relates even more directly to the relationship between local government and the police. Marie described receiving a request from the local police to pass out information on their behalf about the fatal shooting of a man at a tube station by counter-terrorism police. Given the local authority's role in community reassurance and the networks they had built, the police service were presumably hoping to increase the spread of their information, and to use what trust people might have in the local authority. Yet Marie was immediately wary of being asked to work in this way, for exactly that reason – because unquestioningly disseminating the police briefings would ally the two organisations even more closely for local people, and any trust (or lack of it) would be shared between the two organisations. This was not simply a disinclination to be allied with the police service, but a suspicion Marie had that the initial police information was "a pack of lies". She was quite clear that if her suspicion should turn out to be justified (which it did; see Knight, 2005), the relationships of trust between the local authority and residents would be severely damaged.

It is worth highlighting two other elements of Marie's account in contrast to the national and police understandings of PVE and related work. First, towards the end of the interview extract here, Marie referred to "relationships with our BME communities". Earlier in the chapter, I criticised the police briefing for appearing to equate the BME population with the Muslim population, thereby ignoring diversity within the category of 'BME', and also that some Muslim residents may not be categorised as 'BME'. Marie also moved from talking about Muslim communities to BME communities. However, the context of Marie's comment is a long history of difficult, distrustful and sometimes violent relationships between the police force and racialised minorities. Her argument was that an incident such as the shooting of Menezes drew on these wider histories and was likely to increase mistrust and fear of the police among a broader population of minority communities, not just among Muslims. Menezes, after all, was not Muslim but was targeted because he was mistaken for a terrorist suspect. Second, Marie's account suggested that she herself also shared some suspicion of the police force and their workings, based in part on her own personal experiences. This construction of her argument actually mirrors the 'intelligence' discourse of the police and national government, in that both are based on empirical events in the past that are attributed predictive power about future behaviours.

The tensions that become visible are a result of the different perspectives of national and local government. Yet another perspective exists among many voluntary and community sector organisations (as well as individual residents) who might be potential recipients of the Fund, as Saida, who was directly engaged with implementing PVE in Hackney, described:

> SAIDA: It's actually singl[ing] out a community, and if you're looking at trying to build community cohesion … then the last thing you want is to say oh hang on, we need to do some work with this community around counter-terrorism stuff … when you've got things like funding that can be an issue as well 'cos other people from other communities may feel, non-Muslim communities … oh they're getting all this money and why is that, when we might need money for this and that, so – it's about striking the balance so, in the sense of Prevent strategy it was quite sort of controversial and quite sensitive for some Muslim communities.

Saida clearly had some commitment to PVE as she was working directly within its remit. However, her comments here express a degree of ambivalence, which she attributed to local residents (PVE "sometimes can be seen as quite sensitive"). Saida was one of the few

Muslim practitioners I interviewed, and this could also have played some part in her relationship to the programme. While many of the white, middle-class professionals I interviewed were, to some extent, asserting their 'left-wing liberal-type' credentials by expressing their solidarity with Muslims targeted by PVE, perhaps Saida was performing a similar move in a different direction, asserting her understanding of the views of "other communities, non-Muslim communities". The difference between the positions available to different practitioners may also relate to their levels of involvement in the scheme, and to a need to justify one's own alignment with a particular policy (see Chapter Six for a more detailed discussion of this point; and Husband and Alam, 2011, pp 168-73).

While I was working to establish an approach to PVE in Hackney, one organisation contacted me about concerns that the local authority might *reject* the scheme, and that this would constitute *neglect* of local Muslim communities' needs. This might be understood in the context of a super-diverse local area in which policy practitioners perceived there to be multiple ethnic, religious and other identity groups with specific needs and different forms of access to power. For example, it is well-established that the borough's Charedi Jewish population is both relatively large[13] and vocal, with well-developed lobbying techniques for presenting their social, cultural and economic needs to local statutory organisations.[14] There is a risk that aligning need with identity groups in this way within a competitive culture of bidding for public funds could create community cohesion problems in itself.

This was a question raised in relation to community cohesion by both Cantle's original report (2001, p 24), and later in a different form by COIC (2007, pp 160-4). Where Cantle argued that area-based allocation of funds had created inter-ethnic tensions because different identity groups saw each other as being favoured by the local state, COIC focused specifically on funds allocated on the basis of group identity, which they argued had a similar effect. Both suggested that resentment could be inspired by targeted funding perceived to be privileging one group over another. Yet there is rarely a shortage of organisations wishing to receive these funds, however potentially divisive. In the economy of the voluntary and community sector in Britain, which through the 2000s received an increasing amount of public funds for provision of services (Flood, 2010), the imperative to maintain income to deliver organisational goals in a context of scarce resources means that funding, from whatever source, is highly sought after.

In both the systems critiqued by Cantle and by COIC, the majority of such funds are allocated on the basis of economic or social need, where the data that identifies inequality suggests it is associated with disadvantage of a particular geographical neighbourhood or identity group. They are not usually allocated *simply* on the basis that an area or identity group, in itself, should receive more funds. Yet this appeared to be *exactly* what the PVE Fund proposed. The documents that set out the rationale for the funding to local government and communities provided no evidence, qualitative or quantitative, that where it was targeted would prevent violent extremism; it just had to be spent on Muslims. It was not just a basic political or practical opposition to this aspect of the project that troubled many policy practitioners. As described, there was potential to incorporate funding directed at Muslims with other streams of funding for the general population that could have potentially overcome some of these difficulties. It was central government insistence that agencies be *seen* to be doing PVE, and that it be promoted in these terms, that caused the most difficulty for policy practitioners attempting to negotiate local sensitivities.

Communication and presentation

> Sam: We had quite a big fight with DCLG about the Preventing Violent Extremism Fund ... just the name made a number of boroughs say that they didn't want the money if that's what it had to be called and I think we were the one, the last one that held out, and said, well okay we'll take it only if we don't have to flag up locally that that's what it's called and as long as we don't have a minister rocking up and saying, if there was a particularly successful project, oh this is great and it's all part – to do with this.

The interviews I conducted with policy practitioners took place about a year after the initial negotiations over the Pathfinder Fund, in which I had been directly involved. Those memories still rankled, as in this interview with Sam, a senior politician in Hackney. The importance Sam placed on the language and presentation of the scheme was clear. This could be easy to dismiss as a superficial question of public relations, but issues of communication were particularly important to how practitioners perceived their role. Relationships with real people in local communities were at stake for officers and politicians, and I and many of those I spoke with felt strongly that the name of this scheme and some of its central tenets would not only undermine the potential to prevent extremism, but could also threaten broader relationships of trust within communities and between local government and residents.

Sam's account constructs this negotiation as a tussle between the local authority and central government in which the local authority is portrayed as both heroic and victorious (accepting the Fund but only on certain conditions). This is the same chain of events that I described in my own account earlier in this chapter. Sam seemed to be demonstrating a similar pride to that I described personally, at having at least tried to resist the problematic aspects of this scheme. And he also positioned himself in a way that echoes my account, describing a distinction between local and national parts of government and demonstrating a personal distance from the PVE scheme.

Sam and I were positioned differently in relation to these negotiations: he as politically responsible to (and reliant on) a local electorate and his national political party; I as interpreting national policy and local needs and framing possible responses as a functionary of the bureaucratic structures of the local authority. But we were both well aware that local residents and national organisations would make little distinction either between the differences in (for example) our two positions, or more importantly, between us as individuals acting within local government, and the local authority as a whole. Hence my 'pride' in seeming to have found a compromise solution, and Sam's insistence that "we held out." These are negotiations in which we (as policy practitioners) have both an institutional and a personal stake. The importance of presenting this as a struggle between parts of government is partly about demonstrating that the institution of which we form a part is capable of taking an ethical stance similar to that we might wish to have taken as individuals (see Chapter Six). By 'ethical stance' I do not mean to imply taking a moral high ground; rather, I treat ethical practice as a weighing up of choices, reflecting on and making – perhaps impossible – decisions between finite goods (Mouffe, 2000; Sayer, 2005; Mayo et al, 2007).

While my assessment of Sam's narrative may have sounded somewhat cynical, in that the 'victory' over national policy in this case was rather limited, the negotiations over the importance of language, communication and conception of the PVE scheme did appear to have some effects. This was the result of concerns expressed by local authorities across the country, not just in Hackney (House of Commons Communities and Local Government Committee, 2010). Alison, from her position between national and local government, reflected on these negotiations:

> ALISON: Somebody in CLG did actually say to me at one point, well if we let them call it community cohesion they'll hide behind [it] and they won't do anything about preventing violent extremism and I just think that's bollocks, I don't think that's the case at all, I don't [think] the reason that authorities call it community cohesion locally is because they don't want to deal with PVE, I think it's because they're uncomfortable with the language, they know that it won't play well with local communities etc etc, so CLG have shifted and said you can call it what you like locally but you're still doing PVE.

Alison was of the opinion that PVE work did need to be tackled separately to community cohesion, to deal with specific issues around involvement in violent extremism. But here she expressed some sympathy for the way that some local authorities attempted to rebrand (or debrand) PVE, and tried to promote a more sophisticated view than the CLG official she quoted. Thus Alison presented herself as between the central and local government sides of the argument (as indeed was her role), and as even-handedly understanding their different perspectives. Yet she also emphasised the power of the centre: "you're still doing PVE."

There were some signs, towards the end of the period covered by this research, that the approach of national government to PVE shifted slightly. In a speech in October 2009, Parliamentary Under-Secretary of State Shahid Malik indicated that the government had listened to local community concerns about the language of the programme, and that they would now refer to the scheme as Prevent, 'removing the "violent extremism" label from funding' to help local communities contextualise the funding (Malik, 2009) (although what else were they 'preventing'?). Although Malik reiterated that the main focus of work should remain on 'the Al Qaeda-influenced threat', a space was opened in the debate to consider other forms of terrorism and violent extremism. This echoed John Denham, Secretary of State for Communities' speech, a week earlier, in which he indicated that right-wing racist extremism would also become a focus of specific action by the CLG (Denham, 2009). How far this shift in political rhetoric was influenced by the arguments of local policy practitioners, or by other political calculations, is unclear. With the subsequent election of a new government, a significant review of Prevent was undertaken (Travis, 2010) which removed this ambivalence by ending all community development aspects of the programme and simply reinforcing the focus on security (HM Government, 2011).

Conclusions

The central criticism of the national PVE programme and the way it was handled and promoted locally by the police was that it lacked sensitivity to local populations or understanding of how people and organisations react to, interpret and engage with policy interventions. To engage with these weaknesses would have required a great deal more time and detailed work, and this appeared to conflict with an urgency to be seen to be 'stopping the terrorists'. This weakness led to criticisms such as those I have engaged with at length here, about the impacts on people placed unfairly under suspicion. It also contributed to criticisms elsewhere that PVE and the wider counter-terrorist programme were counter-productive because they were wasting money on pointless exercises or supporting damaging organisations (see, for example, Bright, 2006). The broader criticism – that the PVE scheme imagined that the causes and solutions to the problem of terrorism could be found by interventions at the level of local extremists – was raised at various moments, but in the end was silenced by the search for more pragmatic ways to negotiate the question, using vaguer language, less clear about this bypassing of causes of terrorism or extremism that might be found in more global structures of power.

While I have criticised in particular the police and security services' conceptions of communities and the ways that populations should be managed and talked about, I do not want to suggest that the approach more common among local government practitioners (with which I have aligned myself) is unproblematic. What surprised practitioners about the PVE programme was not the aim to collect information on Muslims or the assumption that all Muslims were potential terrorists. Most of those I spoke with through the research had varying levels of awareness of institutional racism and its histories in both the police and local and national government policies. This has often involved actions that victimise, demonise or otherwise have an impact on some racialised groups more than others. What was 'new' in PVE was that all of the guidance and monitoring of the scheme was *explicitly* targeted at one religious group. There was no attempt to hide this focus.

The local authority approach of incremental negotiation to try to meet the different sensitivities of different constituencies might be accused of masking, rather than dealing with, institutional discrimination. However, direct challenge may not be the most effective means of change from within government, given that the attempt to challenge national policy directly by creating a different local approach was simply ignored. The tactics of negotiation, which allow for reinterpretation and flexibility of meaning, may be more effective means of subverting problematic policies. We have also seen, in this chapter, how the meaning and purpose of local government is both treated as self-evident, and questioned by its juxtaposition with demands that don't fit a 'self-evident' role. The emphasis that local government practitioners put on *relationships* and *negotiations* may have been related to idealism about their role, or equally about identifying what tools were available to them in governing. When usually silent power relations became articulated as baldly as they did by PVE policy's suspicion of an entire demographic group, discomfort among policy practitioners was palpable. In this case, this overt language and practice was quietly modified back to a more ambiguous framework relating to internal processes. *Muslim* extremists were still understood to be the primary focus of PVE, but more 'polite' ways were found to discuss this.

FOUR

'I Love Hackney'/'Keep It Crap'

Introduction

A sense of place and shared belonging have been incorporated into considerations of community cohesion policy partly as a way of trying to negotiate the more difficult subjects of difference and belonging by imagining a neutral, shared, neighbourhood space. But this chapter demonstrates a set of competing claims about the meaning of a place – and about authenticity, narrative, histories, futures, power, class and identity. These debates suggest that far from providing a neutral ground for a simple shared coherence, places exist as both shared and contested meanings, grounded in and experienced through competing narratives in emotional registers.

This chapter explores a set of overlapping narratives about the meaning of a place – Hackney – and who is included or gets to speak for its local 'community'. Each narrative appeals to emotive associations with symbols of authenticity including claims to be marginalised or to understand marginalisation through identification with Hackney. I consider how the resonances of the local authority's branding strategies for Hackney reappropriated meanings and associations, and how others reinterpreted and subverted that Hackney brand. As I am looking specifically at meanings within policy practice, the voices of 'people on the street' are largely silent in this discussion. Although community consultation is required by national regulations to form part of local authority narrative construction, this does not necessarily mean that such street-level voices are heard directly in policy making, or indeed that if they were heard they would be as progressive as the people I interviewed sometimes imagined (Keith, 2005, p 153). These 'real people' are, however, frequently spoken *for*. Policy practitioners often presented their narratives of Hackney as being those of authentic residents, and as counter-claims against the perceptions of outsiders, or against other vocal image makers. The power of 'celebrity' critics was a particular preoccupation of many of the policy practitioners with whom I spoke, and two names in particular kept coming up. Michael Rosen and Iain Sinclair are both local residents, writers and public figures, and have both been involved in public arguments with the local authority over regeneration and change in the borough. Because of the significance these two figures appeared to have gained in local policy negotiations and narratives of place, I chose to interview them both, and I discuss those interviews in this chapter. Although neither Sinclair nor Rosen are 'policy practitioners', their interventions have become part of the narrative of place used by policy practitioners, and I wanted to give them an opportunity to reflect on these entanglements in the same way as the others whose narratives I consider here.[1]

For many of my interviewees, Rosen and Sinclair had come to symbolise a particular form of middle-class gentrification. The relationship of middle-class gentrifiers to the places they inhabit in the inner city (and specifically in Hackney) has been discussed at length elsewhere (see, for example, May, 1996; Butler, 1997; Butler and Robson, 2003a, 2003b; Savage et al, 2005; Reay, 2008).[2] Very often, there is a conclusion that many middle-class inhabitants of poor and ethnically diverse areas enjoy living there because they can choose to opt in and out of the excitement of multicultural inner-city life. That is, they are able to claim an affinity with what they perceive as 'exotic' or 'different', and thereby increase their cultural capital (knowledge of others, superiority over suburban 'normality') while remaining able (by virtue of their economic capital) to retreat into more privileged and safer environments (Bourdieu, 1986; Skeggs, 2004). My discussion in this chapter does not necessarily undermine that assessment, but I add to it in two ways. First, the negotiations over the meaning of Hackney are not separate from sociological analysis; they are not carried out in a closed environment, to which social theory can be applied from the outside. They might be understood as 'public sociology' as outlined in Chapter One, where sociological imaginations are applied outside the academic arena, and research participants are able to draw on sociological resources to negotiate their own place within government. For example, criticisms of the council's policies and place marketing often draw on arguments about appeals to private capital and neglect of communities which can be found in gentrification literature, and policy practitioners in turn accuse their opponents of exoticising poor and ethnic 'others' for their own benefit.

Second, many interviewees refer to a group of gentrifiers who are against (a particular type of) gentrification, and who are trying to protect a nostalgic past which maintains some of the difficulties of living in Hackney which made their own journey so 'pioneering' – and also exclusive (and therefore provided profoundly greater cultural capital). What is interesting is that, like 'the community', for the most part such unreflexive gentrifiers are always absent; none of my interviewees identified themselves to me as uncritical 'gentrifiers against gentrification'. Although, of course, the purpose of my research design was not to seek them out, it is notable that such views are always *attributed*, but never *admitted*. Instead, all of those participants I encountered discussed how to some extent they were implicated in and personally benefited from gentrification in the borough, but also wanted to highlight their motivations and why their own nuanced position was different, and superior, to that they perceived others to hold. This self-positioning in relation to an (imagined) outside resonates with the tendency (to be explored in Chapter Five) of many research participants to define their own sense of place (or achievement of community cohesion) in relation to perceived failings elsewhere.

I begin the chapter by providing a flavour of the mythologies of Hackney that circulate in policy and public discussions, through a 'collage' of artefacts representing Hackney in different ways. I do not claim to provide a definitive description of the place, but to provide a guide to the narratives and issues that constitute Hackney, and their various connections to different forms of empirical fact and experience.

What is Hackney?

(1) Hackney is an inner London borough in the north east of the city, 18.98 square kilometres of land,[3] 3.3 square kilometres of green space,[4] 247,000 people (LBH, 2012b) in 101,690 households (LBH, 2012a). 36% of the population is White British and the 30% of households speak a main language other than English (LBH, 2012b). 42% of the population aged 16-74 have a degree or equivalent qualification, and 20% of the same group have no qualifications; both of these are higher proportions than the London average (LBH, 2012b). House prices rose 176.6% between 2000 and 2005 (LBH, 2006a), the average house price is £426,470 (20% higher than for London as a whole and more than two and a half times the average for England and Wales) (LBH, 2012b).

The average male life expectancy is more than a year shorter than the London average (LBH, 2012b). Hackney was the only inner London borough without a tube line until the London Overground opened in 2010, and was one of the five London boroughs to host the 2012 Olympics.

Hackney is consistently ranked among the top four most deprived areas in the country (Noble et al, 2009). In

2009 78% of residents agreed that people from different backgrounds get along well in the area. (Ipsos MORI, 2009, p 39)

****

(2) Hackney has enormous strength and great opportunities. We are in the centre of London, one of the world's most thriving cities. The people who live here have come from many different ethnic backgrounds and brought cultural diversity and vitality to the borough. The population is young, so has real prospects to improve its life chances. The borough itself is, in many respects a good place to live, with busy vibrant areas, strong communities and attractive open spaces.

But many of the benefits of growing prosperity in the capital have not extended to us. While other parts of London experience pockets of deprivation, every ward in Hackney is among the 10 percent most deprived wards nationally.

There are many problems facing us: poor skills and attainment levels, high mobility, a weak transport system, high levels of crime and poor environmental conditions.

Increasingly Hackney is also experiencing a polarisation of its community between richer and poorer groups while those with moderate incomes choose, or are forced, to live elsewhere. This polarisation can only harm the prospects for our borough. It makes it increasingly difficult for people to see pathways out of poverty – to become economically active, successful *and* stay in the borough. It makes it more difficult to recruit to the jobs which are needed to service our community. (LBH, 2006b, p 3)

****

(3) In the interview, Smith, the first woman home secretary, was asked whether she would feel safe walking on her own around Hackney at midnight. She replied: "Well, no, but I don't think I'd ever have done. You know, I would never have done that, at any point during my life." Asked why not, she answered: "Well, I just don't think that's a thing that people do, is it, really?" (Oakeshott, 2008)

****

(4) Hackney is well known for being one of the most diverse areas in the country. It is a place where you can walk past Turkish supermarkets, Jamaican takeaways, fish and chip shops or Nigerian restaurants on one road. It is an area where mosques, synagogues and churches lie within five minutes of each other. Living in Hackney means having diversity at your fingertips.... For me, Hackney is a microcosm of multicultural Britain and there are many lessons the rest of the country could learn from community relations here. (Abbott, 2008)

****

(5) 'Ms Mop heroine sees off raiders: Raiders come unstuck in jewellery heist.'

'11-year-old girl raped on her way to school: Police arrest 46-year-old man after attack on Well Street Common.'

'Hitman, 15, moaned about fee, jury told: Youth complained he only got £200 for killing woman, court hears.'

'Gangland arms cache hidden in graveyard: Knives and skewers found after routine police sweep.' (*Hackney Gazette* front page headlines, 3, 10, 24, 31 March 2011)

****

(6) Hackney east of Well Street Market is where you'll find genuine bona fide artists in genuine bona fide crumbling warehouses. See through the dour landscape of flyovers, lock-ups and lap-dancing clubs, and you'll discover a neighbourhood of Somalian cafes and tasty Turkish grills, vast, atmospheric green spaces such as Victoria Park and Hackney Marshes, and a fierce local community. And prospects: the Olympics site abuts. (Dyckhoff, 2008)

****

(7) "So if you've got the council, Hackney, worst performing – now not! But you know, when it was, Hackney probably needed to hear that at one time [*laughs*]." (Interview with Rob, senior local government officer in Hackney)

****

(8) "Many people say I love Hackney but ... you put an image in front of them and they wouldn't necessarily know [that it's in Hackney]." (Interview with Angela, senior local government officer in Hackney)

As this collage illustrates, there are many ways to describe Hackney. I have presented this selection of representations not to cancel one another out, but to demonstrate how these experiences exist alongside, and are intertwined with, one another – and how they are negotiated in policy practice. I am not trying to expose a difference between an objective reality and representations of Hackney, nor do I want to argue for an extreme relativism in which all images of a place are equally valid (Keith and Pile, 1993, p 6; Keith, 2005, p 72). I do, however, want to give a sense of the empirical place for the uninitiated. I also mean to highlight that the representations of place used in government are themselves multiple; that they claim authenticity through scientific measurement or local intimacy; and that they are used strategically both to negotiate policy at national and local levels and to make sense of the personal positions, commitments and roles of individual policy practitioners within the institutions of governance.

As such, the opening extract in this section (1) is a representation of Hackney in which I present, through words and numbers, administratively important data derived from numerous sources of empirical enquiry. Like all of the sources, it could be criticised for its limited ability to capture reality, either from the point of view of methodology, timeliness, missing of particular populations[5] or missing of the point. This type of description is related to and co-existent with materiality, as are the various more literary, emotional or experiential descriptions I include below it. Just as the material realities that these descriptions attempt to represent are important in how individuals and populations live and experience their lives, so are the narratives and emotions that attach to them. As artefacts of data they are important to how government prioritises local and national interventions, and to how populations make choices about where to live, how to behave and who to vote for. And, like all of the elements of this collage, this representation is a snapshot in time, and made from a particular vantage point, to meet a particular set of interests.

The extract that follows, (2), is the local authority's attempt to condense this data into a narrative of place that encompasses both the difficulties and the positive attributes of Hackney. When working as a policy practitioner within Hackney, I became accustomed to producing such narratives. They are crafted to negotiate a precarious position, presenting the borough to a variety of audiences. Such narratives must be acceptable and recognisable to residents (who are, of course, a diverse lot themselves), and they must present Hackney as a place that is both attractive for outsiders, and deserving of support. To be overwhelmingly positive would not only belie the realities of local struggles, but would potentially put at risk political capital for national government support in addressing issues of deprivation, exclusion or poverty. To be overwhelmingly negative would again belie realities, and would alienate those with a deep attachment to Hackney. It could also risk suggesting the local authority had not been doing its job, and could put local private sector investment in jeopardy.

The next artefact, (3), is an extract from a newspaper profile of the then Home Secretary, Jacqui Smith, in which she suggested that she would not feel safe alone at night in Hackney. It does not seem, from the context of the interview, that Hackney was under discussion in the rest of the interview. Rather, the journalist used it as shorthand for the unsafe inner city. When Smith suggests that it's not 'a thing that people do', 'people' can be assumed to be those of a similar class, gender, age and perhaps ethnic background to herself. The potential political consequences of such a straightforward yet casual equation of Hackney with danger (and 'others' who are more routinely exposed to such danger) is reinforced by a later episode in the same newspaper article:

> Later an aide calls me fretting about these comments. The home secretary might have given the wrong impression and meant no slight to Hackney. In fact the boss went and bought a kebab on the mean streets of Peckham, southeast London, after dark the other day. (Oakeshott, 2008)

Here, as well as highlighting the politician's wish to avoid affronting an otherwise politically friendly local authority, the exchange makes it clear that Hackney was simply a metonym – not a place itself, but a stand-in for all those places that are avoided after midnight by those able to do so. This is reinforced by the retreat – that instead the minister was recently out in Peckham, where Peckham is equivalent to Hackney in its potential for danger. In my interviews with policy practitioners in Hackney they were very aware of the negative discourses that they felt still dominated outsiders' views of Hackney as a place of crime, deprivation and squalor, the typical sense of the abject inner city. The feeling that this portrayal was something to fight against was strong in my research interviews, but finding explicit examples of such depictions is not a straightforward task. The place has absorbed the connotations of the abject inner city to such an extent that it is unnecessary to spell this out in national discourse – a reference to Hackney in an article on knife crime, teenage pregnancy or street gangs, it seems, is sufficient to set the scene of fear, neglect or immorality.

But this characterisation is followed, in my collage, by an extract from a column in the local commercial newspaper, the *Hackney Gazette*, written by the Member of Parliament (MP) for Hackney North and Stoke Newington (and Britain's first black woman MP), Diane Abbott, (4). Entitled 'Multicultural marvel', this account was a typical celebration of Hackney's welcoming, exciting (ethnic and religious) diversity – as typical as the more negative *Times* piece quoted above it. These narratives are produced in conversation with one another. In Abbott's account, Hackney is proposed as standing *not* for the dangerous inner city, but as "a microcosm of multicultural Britain" from which others should learn. This is Hackney as the safe and celebratory multicultural ideal that as I argued in Chapter Two is one way various actors have tried to reposition Hackney in the wider geographic and political imaginary.

This ideal is disrupted by the set of headlines (5) also taken from the front page of the *Hackney Gazette*, during one month in 2011. These four headlines are shocking reports of violent crime in the area; the missing week's headline was an attack on the local authority's (potential) profligacy at a time of public spending cuts. The consistency of this type of coverage in the *Gazette*, coverage that presents Hackney as violent, dangerous and corrupt, was the source of much concern and anger within the local authority when I worked there. These headlines were all unmissable on the front pages.[6] However, they were usually accompanied by a smaller – and much more uplifting – picture story: for example, on 10 March, the headline about the rape of a schoolchild was offset by 'Cabbie Ishmail helps deliver Chloe's baby in the back of his taxi'. The 'gangland arms cache' story on 31 March was published alongside a large picture of a young child wearing tiger facepaint, with the caption 'It's fun in the sunshine', reporting on a community event held by a housing association. The prioritisation of shocking news to sell papers was offset by the need for a good picture and the appeal of heart-warming stories, which can also evidently be found in Hackney.[7]

These reports of crime and danger are interrupted by an extract from a property column in *The Guardian*'s Weekend Magazine (6), in which Hackney Wick is considered as a home relocation destination and investment opportunity. Although somewhat tongue-in-cheek with its references to 'genuine bona fide artists in genuine bona fide crumbling warehouses', this is also a typical estate agent or property speculator's assessment of the area. The 'dour landscape' presents an opportunity for the discerning homebuyer/explorer to discover exotic foods and hidden parkland, and to make money from the 'prospects' of the Olympic site. Thus this column neatly encapsulates the potential for those with sufficient (and the right sort of) economic and cultural capital to profit from investing in a part of the inner city with just the right amount of danger and exoticism – and civilisation.

The histories of Hackney Council's reputation as an irresponsible, incompetent, corrupt or a 'loony left' institution in the 1980s and as poorly managed (financially, politically and in terms of local services) in the 1990s (see Chapter Two) lie behind Rob's comment, (7). He suggests that Hackney (in this case, the council as an institution, rather than the place itself) has had troubled histories, from which it has learned and moved on. Not only is this improvement celebrated, but the journey from 'worst' to 'well' performing[8] is also considered a heroic achievement in a way that it would not be in an organisation that had always been well run. Like the other elements of this collage, Rob's comments take on specific meanings when understood in relation to the other narratives.

Finally, Angela suggested, (8), that while it is easy to elicit claims to 'love' Hackney, what 'Hackney' actually means to people who love it can vary widely. Angela was a senior local authority officer with responsibility for community development. She discussed in our interview how she had grown up in Hackney, which was unusual among my interviewees although a large proportion of them now lived in the borough. Angela only brought this up, however, when the interview turned to a discussion of school experiences in Hackney – she did not draw more generally on her long attachment to the place as a marker of authenticity (see Chapter Six). Instead, she demonstrated an awareness of how, as a middle-class manager, her experience of Hackney was simply one among many others, situated within power relations, time and space:

> ANGELA: It's a very stable borough in many, you know, on the surface but actually, you just go and stand in the market! [*all laugh*]…. You know, as policy people we might not always stand in the market and if you're out at particular times of the evening you will pick up stuff that you don't pick up ordinarily. And it's those things are just below the surface, I think, that [we] need to look at how we manage.

Although Angela had seen real improvements in Hackney, she suggested that there were other places not normally seen by her where the picture may be different. She not only implied that multiple experiences of the place co-existed, and that her own experience may be incomplete; she also reinforced a sense of authenticity of her own account *despite* this multiplicity. By recognising experiences that differed from her own, her narrative is made to appear more balanced and grounded, and potential criticism that her view may be partial seems to be neutralised. She incorporated alternative experiences, in order to assert a stable vision of place. It is an uncomfortable negotiation, but perhaps a necessary one in the managing and governing of place.

Butler and Robson's (2003a) research with middle-class residents of Hackney found that many of their interviewees identified with a 'Hackney of the mind' (p 177), which they suggest is connected to ideas of authenticity embedded in oppositional working-class histories (see also Butler and Robson, 2003b, p 1802). My data suggests there are rather more versions of this 'Hackney of the mind' than given credit by Butler and Robson. As Angela said, meanings of Hackney were shifting, overlapping, sometimes contradictory. They existed in tension with and relied on one another. They had similar themes at their heart, but they approached these themes differently. There is also a wealth of more detailed writing on the borough, ranging between literary, journalistic and social scientific engagements, but here I am most interested in how the borough is understood and the idea of it is managed in policy worlds. While my discussion suggests that these various policy-oriented 'Hackneys of the mind' do interact with the other uses and imaginings of Hackney that circulate in popular culture and social science, it is not part of this project to catalogue such reinventions comprehensively here, or to judge them as more or less accurate accounts. Instead, I suggest that these debates are *not* really about establishing the truth of either a symbolic or empirical meaning. As Trouillot (1995) demonstrates, history is not only about process or events, but also about the ways those events are remembered through narrative. Similarly in Hackney, the *idea of the place* itself – its 'brand' – becomes an 'organising theme of contradictory rationalisations' of urban change (Keith, 2005, p 71). This was demonstrated clearly through explicit conflicts about the control of meaning and brand related to the 'I Love Hackney' publicity campaign.

'I Love Hackney'/'Keep it Crap'

> LAURA: What do the people that at the end of the day have phenomenal power in the policy-making field … really think of Hackney? Have they actually been here? … we won't crack all of that, but because Hackney has such a dramatic, burning past, particularly I'm talking about the council now. You know, that is just burnt so deeply…. I've never before seen a brand that'd burn flesh, and you can still see the steam rising … you do feel that there literally is something about the absolute origin of brand and the cattle stamp…. Hackney, oh yes, Hackney has a

brand. People know that, people have heard of Hackney. And that's fabulous, there is a gut reaction and an instinct, and all sorts of emotional stuff about Hackney. And my only quibble with it is, is it accurate? And is it about the future, or is it about the past? And I think it's much much much more about the future, now, actually. And I think the Olympics is a massive driver in that.

Laura was a senior officer whose work was partly related to a recent publicity campaign based around the slogan 'I Love Hackney'. This began with an exhibition at Hackney Museum drawing on locals' memories of the borough, drawing together multiple narratives of place. A striking aspect of the exhibition was the use of a logo based on the 'I Love NY' iconography,[9] replacing Hackney in the motif, and later available on badges, mugs, sweatshirts, bags and other items. The publicity campaign was turned into a larger drive for civic pride, and was relaunched in response to the naming of the borough as the UK's 'worst place to live' by a Channel 4 property programme in 2006 (another example of the creative tension between the promotion of positive and negative images of the borough). This campaign was very popular, inside and outside Hackney – although perhaps only with certain people. When wearing my 'I Love Hackney' badge, people asked me (elsewhere in London) if I'd ever been there. Other people have reported seeing them worn in Brighton and Oxford, by middle-class Hackney exiles. The logo was thus worn as a fashion item, while also used as a more traditional municipal message, on posters promoting falling crime rates and encouraging recycling, and as the theme for a local photography competition celebrating the borough and what people loved about it.[10]

In the interview extract above, Laura was grappling with the Hackney brand as it related to national policy makers, rather than residents. Her concern was largely with existing ideas about the place, and the council, its "dramatic, burning past". The power of the place's reputation was described vividly ("burning", "burn flesh", "steam rising", "the cattle stamp"). Laura explicitly tied this to an affective, embodied impact, "a gut reaction and an instinct, and all sorts of emotional stuff about Hackney". Initially concerned that national policy makers may have a negative, outdated or inaccurate view of the borough, Laura's speech quickly turned to excitement about the potential for developing the brand. When she questioned whether the emotion that was drawn on by the Hackney brand was 'accurate', and began to talk about turning to the future rather than the past, Laura was describing the move that she and others had made for the local authority with the rebranding of Hackney. By taking the gut reaction and emotional draw, connected with the fear and desire of the inner city, and harnessing it to 'the future' as symbolised by the 2012 Olympic Games, regeneration and the 'vibrancy' that is so often invoked in the positive profiles of the borough, the statement 'I Love Hackney' uses the edginess of Hackney's prior associations to evoke much stronger affective ties than might come from a simple narrative of improving public services. As Laura elaborated:

> LAURA: There's something about defiance.... I think the 'I Love Hackney' thing is about – 'I know that you think that this is a dreadful place but believe me it's not and I love it, so there'.

Laura's view was that by aligning themselves with Hackney, residents and others found common cause and a sense of community, in opposition to those who did not know or love the place in the same way. In the formulation she described, people expressed pride and defiance through their claims to love Hackney, which may or may not relate to a reformulation of what the place was like. That is to say, loving Hackney in defiance may be about accepting and defending the aspects of it that others saw as 'dreadful', or about suggesting that these 'dreadful' traits were not the true Hackney. Which of these it is that Laura thought was taking place is unclear, and indeed it was probably both. Either way, she saw this emotional power as an important device for the local authority.

While the local authority and other agencies of governance (London Development Agency, Olympic Delivery Authority, Visit London tourist authority) have packaged 'edginess' as an attraction for residents, business investment and tourists, there is a vocal group of residents (writers, poets, artists, political activists and others) making their own claims to speak for the authentic place and to champion this 'edge' in a different way. Part of the defensive struggle for the authentic claim to love Hackney has been a tendency among some elected politicians and local officers to label as the 'Keep Hackney Crap brigade' those who term the council's regeneration as gentrification (or, occasionally, 'gentricide' or 'regenocide'), as in this interview with Joe, a senior politician in the borough:

> JOE: There's a great mentality across all of Hackney by a load of our political opponents, of actually bizarrely now,

right and left, that you know, want to keep Hackney crap, I mean Iain Sinclair, absolutely preposterous, he actually lives in Albion Square, sitting in Albion Square, saying Hackney had been ruined, it wasn't the kind of edgy place he moved to 30 years ago, look at all these flats springing up, it's like, alright, so you get to live in Albion Square, and the rest of us, and everyone else in Hackney, we should just keep it as nasty as possible so you get to feel really cool about it and write some edgy articles for *The Guardian*? Absolute bollocks. And offensive as well.

This interview extract makes clear Joe's sense that he and his colleagues had been striving to improve life for people in Hackney, and that their intentions, efforts and achievements had not been recognised. His anger was perhaps born of frustration at the lack of recognition – that the narrative of Hackney as 'crap' persisted, and that the changes it was undergoing now might not be seen as positive. He also staked a claim to authenticity ("the rest of us, everyone else in Hackney") to counter the critics' attempts to speak for the spirit of the place.

In 2009, such sentiments were expressed more publicly, in comments by the elected Mayor of Hackney, Jules Pipe, published with his permission on *The Guardian* journalist Dave Hill's blog about the borough. Pipe's comments were in response to a newspaper article written by the local poet and political activist (and former children's laureate) Michael Rosen, who had criticised the nature of the regeneration of the Dalston area of the borough, and the local authority's role in it. Rosen's piece was subtitled 'Regeneration has become a byword for New Labour's disregard for democracy and slavish devotion to business' (Rosen, 2008a). Pipe countered that Rosen's 'ill-informed stance against the Dalston development is just the latest example of the "Keep Hackney Crap" mentality so beloved of the borough's far left contingent' (quoted in Hill, 2008). In this exchange, the argument was much more clearly about the question of political and economic choices as to 'how best to bring prosperity to inner-city neighbourhoods', as Hill pointed out (Hill, 2008). Yet the rhetorical power of affective language, and in particular the label 'Keep Hackney Crap', was unleashed as another way of confronting these debates through the lens of attachment and devotion, as well as through the oppositional framing of nostalgia and progress.

Not long after Pipe's intervention, the iconic 'I Love Hackney' badges became parodied by the independent production of badges bearing the slogan 'Keep Hackney Crap'. Tony Collins, a spokesman for *The Eel* artists' collective producing them, suggested that:

> *The Eel* likes to celebrate that which is forgotten and marginalised. The 'Keep Hackney Crap' campaign is about retaining the things which genuinely make an area unique and loved. (quoted in Davies, 2009)

In the same interview, Collins accused Pipe of believing that 'what is currently there is not worth keeping', and countered this with his own statement that 'one person's crap is another person's gold'. In one sense, then, this was an echo of the municipal defiance inherent in the 'I Love Hackney' campaign, or at least Laura's characterisation of it recounted earlier ("I know that you think that this is a dreadful place but believe me it's not and I love it, so there"). It is also a struggle over what it means to 'love' Hackney – keeping an affection for the 'crap', or wanting to improve and change the place in some way.

Although the Mayor suggested the prevalence of the 'far left' in this type of nostalgia, Joe suggested in the earlier interview excerpt that this type of nostalgia came from political opponents of the local Labour Party on the right as well as the left of the political spectrum. Indeed, *The Eel*'s badge campaign was promoted on Andrew Boff's website, then prospective Conservative Mayoral candidate for Hackney, who ended his piece noting the campaign with the rhetorical question, 'Isn't it time we had a Mayor who loved Hackney?'. Pipe's accusation that the 'Keep Hackney Crap brigade' did not love Hackney enough to improve it was turned on him, to suggest that his desire for change showed a lack of love for Hackney (notwithstanding that Boff's own website was called changehackney.com).

These public debates quickly became oppositional and simplifying. But in the interview situation, my research created a space in which policy practitioners were able to reflect in more nuanced ways on how to negotiate shared (or contested) narratives of Hackney. As these debates emerged, I expanded that space to include the two figures who had become emblematic of a particular aspect of these arguments, to explore whether there actually was any shared ground within these negotiations.

"Improving for whom?"

Two writers and Hackney residents, Michael Rosen and Iain Sinclair, were frequently identified by policy practitioners as totems of the campaign to 'Keep Hackney Crap', as we have already seen. Although often mentioned in the same breath by local policy practitioners, and both long-time residents of the borough and well-known figures, the two have rather different positions in the struggles over meaning in Hackney. Iain Sinclair's writing about Hackney is part of his broader body of literary psychogeographical work, much of which focuses on London. Although he often speaks at local cultural events that are sometimes critical of the council, the position he has carved out for himself is as a cultural observer, rather than as a political activist. Michael Rosen, on the other hand, has long been active within left-wing politics. The article that embroiled him in the argument with Mayor Pipe outlined above was published in *Socialist Worker*, and he has produced artistic as well as journalist work on political themes, in particular criticising regeneration projects such as the model seen in Dalston (see, for example, Rosen, 2008b).

Those working in senior roles in the local public sector were well aware of criticisms that their efforts to improve conditions in the local area were aimed at, or resulted in, a simple displacement of poorer residents by wealthier gentrifiers. The dilemmas of how to improve local quality of life without thereby becoming subject to market processes that produce this demographic change led to evident frustration for many. Local politician Sam argued that those against change were trying to preserve some form of genteel urban chaos for themselves:

> SAM: But there is this body of people in the borough who say 'Oh no no! You should leave it as it is', the whole sodding Iain Sinclair nonsense and to my mind it's ... deprivation fetishism....

Here Sam was referring to the elegiacal tone of Iain Sinclair's writing on Hackney and particularly around changes being made to the Olympic site (see, for example, Sinclair, 2008b, 2009). He might be thinking of statements such as the following:

> There is no sense of regeneration here. Thank god. Not yet. Business as usual. Cornershop steel-shuttered like Belfast and bristling with handwritten warnings to schoolkids. Hooded chemical brokers start young. And finish young too, many of them. (Sinclair, 2009, p 9)

The passion in the narratives of Sinclair and others who claim to be voices of otherwise unheard Hackneys can be taken as nostalgia for a place of dirt and poverty, expressed as an angry polemic against those who would regenerate and clear up the place. The sigh of relief at 'no sense of regeneration here' may refer to some kind of distaste for a cleaning-up seen as antiseptic and inauthentic, but coupling this with an apparent celebration of the 'bristling', 'steel-shuttered' scene of young drug dealers heading for an early grave undermines this romanticism (similarly the drawing on another mythology of place, a conflict-hardened and depressed image of Belfast). This is the reading of many council officers and councillors such as Joe and Sam, who feel that Sinclair and other critics are sitting pretty in the 'nicer' parts of Hackney, wanting to preserve the picturesque poverty elsewhere for their own inspiration, without caring about the people who live in the majority of the borough.

A particular row erupted when an invitation for Iain Sinclair to give a pre-publication reading of his 2009 book dedicated to Hackney, in a Hackney public library, was withdrawn. This resulted, of course, in an eye-catching hook for his book's publicity (see Sinclair, 2008a). The general tenor of the book (which the local authority had not seen when the invitation was withdrawn) is, like much of his other writing, a self-professed love for the borough in which he has lived for 40 years. But this is an affection tempered with nostalgia, and a distrust of the organisations that govern the borough and the changes in its life and infrastructure (particularly linked to the 2012 Olympic developments). When I interviewed Iain, I asked him for his perspective on the way that the 'banning' of his book launch had created publicity for the book itself:

> IAIN: From my point of view, all of that was absolutely wonderful … what was in a sense a very Old Hackney event … a very small, 20 people in the library kind of [thing] … that would have been invisible and under the radar is suddenly big and it helps to sell an enormous quantity of books, in a way I couldn't have invented if I'd tried to do something myself [*both laugh*]…. It was an act of branding to have actually got Hackney into the title of the book and a map on the cover, meant that it became a branded artefact of a particular kind of argument which it wasn't even necessarily making, because a lot of it was just to do with uncovering and celebrating and testing mythology of the past.

Iain Sinclair pointed out that the clash with the local authority was unplanned; he had expected an 'Old Hackney event', of interest only to local history enthusiasts, and yet the local authority's clumsy attempt to avoid being associated with negative publicity for the Olympics had resulted in a national news story. In our conversation, as in much of his writing on the subject, he placed his concern with 'mythology of the past' in opposition to the workings of government, and of the future as imagined through regeneration such as that linked to the 2012 Olympic Games. And here he drew on two types of mythology: that which he was most interested in 'uncovering and celebrating', a nostalgic psychogeography based around Hackney's histories (see also Bonnett, 2009); and that of branding, which made his book, through its associations with Hackney (and its controversies) alone, an "artefact of a particular kind of argument that I wasn't even necessarily making". This "particular kind of argument" is, presumably, the anti-regeneration and anti-gentrification position that many officers and members of the local authority attributed to him. Here, he was arguing that his position was simply that of a cultural commentator exploring mythologies and their articulations in the present.

In Sinclair's dreams of Hackney, the 'unnoticed and unrequired ruin[s]' should be cherished (Sinclair, 2008b). For him, their renovation was a tragedy, profit conquering aesthetics, with Olympic legacy building as a driving force. Although he might argue that he was defending creativity and urban energy, it is easy to respond that this was self-indulgent in comparison with meeting pressing needs for affordable housing and decent services. But while mourning the loss of 'every previously unnoticed and unrequired ruin', he also recognised that some of the work of turning them 'to profit' had been done by the 'impoverished artists and free-livers' themselves:

> We have waved this disaster through, we have colluded: dozens of artists roam the perimeter fence soliciting Arts Council funding to underwrite their protests. It's so awful, such a visible horror, we can't believe our luck. (Sinclair, 2008b)

While Sinclair is nostalgic for the waste and ruin of a haunted landscape, he also recognises that this nostalgia is his subject, and that as it becomes built on and over-written, the material for his own writing expands. Further, the artists 'protesting' this 'horror' seek and find support for their work on it from the public sector in the form of Arts Council funding. The faceless state at once destroys and preserves the landscape;

the protesting artists at once protest and profit from this change. Both are implicated in patterns of regeneration and the gains and losses it can bring, and capitalise in different ways on its ironies.

As an author, Iain Sinclair's main concern is much different from that of local authority officers, politicians or other policy practitioners. He made this clear in the interview, when I asked "How would you do it differently?" and he replied, "You see I wouldn't ... if I responded to that then I'm actually putting myself up to be on the council!" He added that the local Liberal Democrats had asked him to stand as their candidate at the 2008 Mayoral election in Hackney ("... they said ... would you stand, because we saw you got all this publicity with this book and it doesn't really matter what your political beliefs are"), but he had declined ("I do see this as a real job! It's not just something you do because you can generate some publicity"). This suggests that Sinclair's view of himself is definitively *not* as a policy practitioner, nor would he choose to be one. Nonetheless, he and his work have become embroiled in political negotiations, and one reason for this is that brand and narratives of place leach between municipal campaigns, political movements, cultural artefacts and commercial development, as, more deliberately, have Michael Rosen's interventions.

Some months after the 'I Love Hackney' campaign was established, the reopening of Gillett Square[11] in the Dalston area of Hackney as a renovated urban space was greeted by the elected Mayors of London and Hackney, 200 saxophonists and an audience for an afternoon of celebratory music and dance. It also attracted a group of protesters with signs declaiming the 'gentricide' or 'regenocide' they felt the new space represented, with its repaved square and ban on public drinking. Their view was that the square's renovation was a privatisation of public space and another stage in the transfer of wealth and power from poor to rich, and in this process a neutering of some form of authentic Hackney-ness (Ben, 2006).

One response to this view came from Sam, a senior elected politician in the borough, when I asked his views about the effect of rising property prices on Hackney's diversity:

> SAM: I don't think it's a gentrification that's pushing out the local working-class people ... but some of these things with Gillett Square or whatever ... push out the grottier element, you know. There was the street drinking that used to go on there, and ... people that are there now ... want that moved on, understandably.

Sam's response seems to confirm suspicions of anti-regeneration(/ gentrification) protesters that the intentions behind Gillett Square and other developments were to move on "the grottier element", here referring to street drinkers, from public spaces. But Sam distinguished this 'element' from 'local working-class people', who were seen as regaining access to the urban environment by removing a threatening presence. The protest at the opening of Gillett Square was recalled by several council officers and elected members as typical of privileged gentrifiers wanting to preserve a sense of urban grittiness at the expense of those without the cultural and economic capital to insulate them from its ill effects. More than one council officer described to me a group of teenagers telling the protesters that they (the teenagers) were glad that the place was now "safer, more well-lit".

Gillett Square is in Dalston, the area of Hackney where poet Michael Rosen lives, and one undergoing rapid change associated in particular with the arrival of a new link to the Tube system, the opening of new cultural and entertainment venues and large-scale housing developments. Michael Rosen has been outspoken about these changes, the subject of his public spat with Mayor Pipe outlined above, and with comments published in *Time Out*:

> A demographic dream grew in the heart of the large white building: they could change the way Hackney is ... families out, young professionals in. Migrants' shops out, chain stores in. Blink and you'll miss the rising of another block of loft-style apartments ... Manhattan ... studio ... modern living etc.... A train linking Hackney to Croydon is on its way, reminding us that the great white building will preside over the Croydonisation of Dalston and no one really knows what the Olympics will bring. (Rosen, 2007)

Here Rosen suggests a sinister Town Hall dream of the displacement of the authentically local by the blank face of economic capital. His reference to the 'large white building' carries echoes of Iain Sinclair's characterisation of Hackney Town Hall as a removed, colonial and quasi-fascist building (Sinclair, 2009, p 24). Rosen noted the opening of new London Overground stations in Hackney, fearful of the 'Croydonisation'[12] of what was once the Hackney spirit, ushered in by preparations for the 2012 Olympics, which stood here for an uncertain and threatening future. The overriding tone was mistrust of the local state and of a model of regeneration which relied on global, homogenising capital that would 'change the way Hackney is'.

In light of such writings, many councillors I interviewed treated Michael Rosen as a symbol of those holding a nostalgic, preservationist attitude, wanting to keep a picturesque idea of ramshackle Hackney for themselves. But when I interviewed him, he criticised such views in very similar terms to them:

> MICHAEL: I think people think that they discovered Hackney in 1975 or something and then are really quite cross that people who look like them and sound like them and the same educational background or whatever, have turned up. But no, I don't have that attitude. I don't think that's THE problem.

Here, Rosen alluded to the 'pioneer' gentrifiers who valued Hackney for what they felt to be its exotic edge, some of whom are now characterised as the most vocal opposition to later stages of urban renewal. As more people "who look like them and sound like them" gain access to Hackney's inner London exoticism, it undermines the rarity and value of the cultural capital they have amassed through an exclusive association with the place. Rosen acknowledged that these attitudes existed, but distanced himself from them (again, they were the absent others who defined the speaker's position as an authentic Hackney resident). For him, such people were something of a sideshow: "THE problem" is the way in which urban change is progressing within a neoliberal capitalist framework.

Although Rosen pushed for greater attention to the preservation of older urban environments in Dalston in particular, he argued that this was not an outright opposition to urban change, but that he favoured more community-led and less capital-intensive development. He contrasted this to the local authority model of reliance on the capital and leverage available within the parameters of local government power and the vagaries of the property market. Rosen went on to describe an altercation with a council official in which their contrasting visions of Hackney collided:

> MICHAEL: I said, all you've done is just facilitate very large private capital to bulldoze the centre of Dalston, and create something that nobody has asked for ... of course there was immediate resentment from the woman, she said no, no, no, we're improving, and I said improving for whom? ... And she said 'look at Kingsland Road ... it's a mess, isn't it?' ... And I said, it's just people ... that's

life, it's not a mess, it's just how we live, and I could see
that there was absolute incomprehension, that we were
talking two completely different languages.

Rosen's question – "improving for whom?" – is at the centre of these
narratives and counter-narratives. The local authority practitioners I
spoke with saw the renovation of Gillett Square as benefiting local young
people (those who were reported as being pleased about better lighting,
paving and security), albeit relying on elements of private investment
and public–private partnership to do so. Michael Rosen (and, we might
presume, the 'gentricide' protesters) emphasised the role of 'very large
private capital' profiting from something that 'nobody has asked for'.
What seemed to Sam to be 'deprivation fetishism', aiming to retain
poverty as an artistic backdrop, was for Rosen an attempt to protect
'people', 'how we live', from the homogenising and excluding forces of
capitalism. Rosen sensed that he and the local authority representative
he encountered "were talking two completely different languages". But
I would suggest that the mutual incomprehension was not so clear-
cut. While Rosen and others were not championing poverty, nor were
the policy practitioners I interviewed uncomplicatedly championing
gentrification or free market logics. And people in both 'camps' were
aware of, if not comfortable with, the ways that their own fortunes
were implicated in the positions they took in these debates.

However, my interest is not in arbitrating claims about whether the
development of Gillett Square, or any other regeneration initiative,
was for better or for worse. Rather, I focus on how (and why) debates
about the future of Hackney, and about processes of regeneration or
gentrification, are played out through emotive narratives that call on
ideas of authenticity of place and of voice. Such decisions centre on the
question of who benefits from either changing the place or conserving
it, and suggest that there are limits to local influence over market-driven
changes to the area. The way these debates are articulated suggest it
is more comfortable for all involved to talk about emotive senses of
belonging and authenticity than to confront these limits.

Brand and cultural capital

Throughout these empirical encounters I encountered the language
of branding as a way of thinking about how place and narrative
are mobilised by different groups. While many of the participants I
encountered might have used this language casually, theories of branding
are apt for understanding the dynamics of Hackney's meanings, and

particularly for understanding them as a source of cultural capital, and therefore as a site of power and struggle.

The marketing literature distinguishes *branding* as a distinct approach to selling a 'product' that is not about a fundamental change in the product or an association with a simple abstract emotion, but attachment to a narrative (Holt and Cameron, 2010). Lury suggests that not only have brands become used as a way of organising the role of emotion in brand relations (between consumer and product), but that the use of brands relies on a shift in which '[i]nstead of a desire to keep up with the Joneses, consumers are believed to be more concerned with finding meaning in their lives' (Lury, 2004, p 38). Authors vary in the extent to which they acknowledge that such narratives rely on the reincorporation of existing mythologies. Aronczyk, for example, suggests that rebranding nations (as business products for tourism and investment) relies on creative destruction, 'in which old myths and memories are swept away and new ones instituted in their place' (2007, p 118). However, evidence from more traditional corporate branding exercises, such as those of the Starbucks coffee store chain or Nike sportswear, suggest that myth and counter-myth depend on and play against one another for effective communication, notoriety and relevance (Lury, 2004; Thompson et al, 2006; Holt and Cameron, 2010).

The reappropriation of brand myths can be thought of as a form of trading in cultural capital (Bourdieu, 1986), where identities or meanings that are otherwise seen as abject become a source of cultural capital for those people who are able to adopt appealing aspects of the identity, while avoiding abject connotations (Skeggs, 2005b). Skeggs suggests that the logics and techniques of branding are used in popular culture to commodify the culture and experiences of working-class British people, making identification with these 'products' an asset for middle-class people, which they can trade on as cultural capital (see also Skeggs, 2004). In the case of Hackney (and other places like it), the power of 'edgy' branding allows a place that is seen as dangerous and uncomfortable to be appropriated by those whose existing economic, cultural and social capital enables them to escape any actual danger, while profiting from association with local myths.

Throughout this chapter, such reappropriation happens at various levels, in an iterative way. The presentation of Hackney as an exemplar of successful multiculture under the slogan 'I Love Hackney' was powerful because of Hackney's prior negative connotations (its "dramatic, burning past"), and the campaign was reinvigorated in response to being dubbed Britain's 'worst place to live' on national television. Here, the first-order claims to 'Love Hackney' were being made in defiance, claiming an authentic knowledge of Hackney as *not* as bad as had been perceived, and therefore claiming knowledge of the place that exceeded that of outsiders.

But some residents took exception to this as a potentially disingenuous 'sanitising' of local difference, packaged to appeal to 'the middle class'. Their response, in the form of various rebranded cultural artefacts, was to declare their allegiance to another imagined version of the borough under a defiant slogan 'Keep Hackney Crap'. This second type of claim to 'Love Hackney' (as 'Crap') could be a claim to authentic knowledge similar to that outlined above – it's not crap, or 'one person's crap is another's gold'. But another, more ironic version of this reappropriation of the Hackney brand is that by identifying with a place seen by others as dangerous, 'dour' or down-at-heel, people gain a sense of excitement and edginess without actually being exposed to any danger.[13] As Iain Sinclair suggested, simply having 'Hackney' in the title of a book and a map of Hackney on its cover was 'an act of branding' that appealed to a group (or groups) of people who were keen to buy into (one version or another of) Hackney mythology. So the nature of the brand is that it is not straightforwardly controlled. Its draw on associations and emotion make it inherently unstable; 'it retains the margins of indeterminacy, and the activities of consumers can extend these margins' (Lury, 2004, p 162). In branding Hackney, the 'consumers' are residents, activists and others with claims to the place. While other studies of place branding have demonstrated the risk of a homogenising effect of place branding in a global market where every place vies to be 'unique' and 'vibrant' (see Philo and Kearns, 1993, p 3; Evans, 2006, p 203; Aronczyk, 2007, p 119), the questions raised in my empirical material focus more on the competing claims to local authenticity made by a range of voices for a range of purposes.

Philo and Kearns pose a confrontation between accounts of place and history produced '*in the name of* an urban-based bourgeoisie', and those '*in the name of* those "other peoples" of the city' (Philo and Kearns, 1993, p 26; emphasis added). Their assumption is that each of these groups speak for themselves, and are in competition, so that the stories of 'other peoples' are always silenced by the bourgeoisie. But all of the accounts provided here are accounts made *in the name of* the disempowered and marginalised, *by* middle-class urbanites. Philo and Kearns' model can only really work when histories of the working class, women, ethnic others, sexual minorities, disabled people and other marginalised groups are seen as uninteresting, irrelevant or threatening by those with greater power to command narratives of place. In the time, place and context where my research was conducted, this is not the case. Such stories are in fact the *most* interesting, their appeal lying precisely in an association with authenticity and the concern of consumers to find meaning in their lives identified by Lury (2004, p 38) as at the heart of branding strategies. The people I have quoted speak *in the name of* marginalised others, but also in the name of *solidarity with* those marginalised others. For example, let's remind ourselves of two such claims, the first from local politician Joe; the second from Michael Rosen:

> JOE: ... you get to live in Albion Square, and the rest of us, and everyone else in Hackney, we should just keep it as nasty as possible so you get to feel really cool about it and write some edgy articles for *The Guardian?*...

> MICHAEL: ... all you've done, is just facilitate very large private capital to bulldoze the centre of Dalston, and create something that nobody has asked for....

Both of these interviewees made a claim to be part of Hackney's (authentic) community, and to be defending either this community's future (in the first quote) or its past (in the second). They both positioned themselves as mounting this defence against threats from more powerful others (in the first case, artists and writers; in the second, property developers) who they positioned in turn as trying to profit from the cultural capital of Hackney. The claims to authentic knowledge of and solidarity with 'Hackney' that both speakers made were based on their existing stocks of cultural capital rooted in their own local histories and associations.

As the 'Keep Hackney Crap' badges, the artists who 'can't believe their luck' at 'such visible horror' of urban development, and the people who 'think they discovered Hackney in 1975' show, one aspect of the attachment to Hackney is to seek to protect the cultural capital it accrues by keeping this capital scarce. That is, something is only 'edgy' as long as most people still despise it (and the edgy people remain ahead of the crowd). Such a logic has been identified in more straightforward analyses of trends and marketing (see, for example, Thompson et al, 2006), but differs from the more general findings of studies such as Butler (1997), Butler and Robson (2003), May (1996) and Reay (2008), which uncovered a more explicit desire to enjoy observing 'otherness' while maintaining a definite distance from it.[14]

The difficulty is that so many of these claims to Hackney and its myths are rooted in claims of certainty, certainty of being right and of others being wrong. Even complexity and flux become reified by appeals to 'diversity', or claims that Hackney has 'always been a place of change'. The success of London's bid to host the 2012 Olympics is widely attributed to its foregrounding of the internationalism and multiculturalism of East London (Vertovec, 2007, p 1025; Wetherell, 2008, pp 306-7). One of the central motivations for making the bid was to attract funding to this deprived area of the city (*Evening Standard*, 2008).

The local politicians and officers might benefit by 'improving' the place – in their careers and reputation as well as their community-minded goals. And the artists make (and recognise that they make) a good deal out of it too, as noted by Iain Sinclair above. Academics (including myself!) are, of course, no less exempt from this, with Hackney's potency as an area of diversity and change, inequality and political history (and often personal associations) drawing a variety of scholars to produce studies embedded in the area (see, for example, Young et al, 1980; May, 1996; Butler, 1997; Butler and Robson, 2003a, 2003b; Mumford and Power, 2003; Markova and Black, 2007; Andersson, 2009; Manzi and Jacobs, 2009; Pratt, 2009; Sinclair, 2009; Watson, 2009; Wright, 2009; Rhys-Taylor, 2010; Wessendorf, 2010; Aldred and Jungnickel, 2010/11; Harris, 2012; Koutrolikou, 2012). The logics of audit and associated cultural and eventually economic capital apply to academic outputs as much as to those of local authority employees (Back, 2008). There are no easy answers about which narrative is 'most progressive', and this is complicated further, as the narrators themselves recognise – to different extents – their own privileged positions in negotiating and using Hackney's brand.

FIVE

"We spent a lot of time trying to be known for other things"

Introduction

Local policy practitioners are concerned to present a positive image of the place they represent (politically or professionally) because they perceive that its material conditions, as well as perhaps their own careers, are mediated primarily through presentation and reputation. So this chapter is dedicated to understanding the metaphors that policy practitioners use to make sense of, and work within, reality. These metaphors are important not because they *capture* 'reality', and not because they *disguise* reality. They are important because they are 'a means through which reality is rendered comprehensible' (Keith, 2005, p 70).

To remind ourselves of how narratives of 'other places' were used to demonstrate a relative lack of urgency of community cohesion policy in Hackney, here is an extract from one of the first interviews I conducted, with Mark, an assistant director there:

> MARK: But it [community cohesion] doesn't ... seem to me to be a big issue. Now I've no doubt that in the Peterboroughs of this world ... they sit in the pubs and they worry about all these East Europeans flooding in, picking all our tomatoes or carrots or whatever, or in Dagenham, they think that this is the final straw, Ford closes down, or nearly closes down, and nobody cares about us, and now they're dumping all these foreigners on us, and so on and so forth ... but I think that that's an atypical perspective for London. Now I've no idea whether it's appropriate for Oldham, clearly where there's a very different geographical mix of the ethnic groups kind of thing. And, yeah, you go to Bradford, you think, oh gosh, that's – this is – you know, it's quite different really!
>
> HANNAH: Yeah. [*both laugh*]

> MARK: [*laughs*] I can see why the Asians don't wanna live
> on some of the estates there....

This striking extract sums up "the Peterboroughs of this world" as places scared by the newness of Eastern European migration and fearful for their agricultural jobs; (Barking and) Dagenham as a deindustrialised wasteland whose residents feel neglected by the state and society and resort to scapegoating "foreigners"; and Oldham and Bradford, whose "geographical mix of the ethnic groups" does not even need to be elaborated to provoke a sardonic laugh of recognition from me about the segregated nature of their 'parallel lives'. A similar strategy of understanding 'types' of community cohesion in relation to place was adopted by the national COIC, which produced a set of archetypal descriptions rather than referring directly to empirical places as representative of particular problems (COIC, 2007, p 58).

As will become clear throughout the chapter, the three places to which I followed these narratives do not map universally onto the imagined geographies of cohesion. That is to say, for example, that Bradford was used as a reference to parallel lives and riots at least as often as Oldham; indeed, sometimes places which had not had civil disturbances in 2001 but whose name sounded similar (for example, Blackburn) were referred to in this way by interviewees. And as noted in Chapter Two, the association of Peterborough with community cohesion narratives was not as strong as for Barking and Dagenham or Oldham. Yet, consistently, all of these places *were* used as reference points for demonstrating shared knowledge of failures of cohesion and integration. And as I show in this chapter, policy practitioners in each of these places recognised that such associations were operating at a national level, and thought it important to address the negative associations this entailed.

The chapter considers each of the three 'other places' in turn. In each, attempts to appropriate an existing negative meaning and to use it to promote a place has a similar logic to the rebranding of Hackney discussed in Chapter Four. In this chapter, however, policy practitioners were looking beyond local affect and belonging, and trying to establish a positive reputation for community cohesion policy among other policy practitioners.

"Oldham? Riot town!"

Approaching Oldham

> ERIN: [We said] we need some funding from government to deal with this before we have a Oldham and Bradford riot.
>
> ANDREW: We would have had another Bradford riot if we hadn't have done this community cohesion work.
>
> SIV: Like in Oldham ... you know, when they had the riots ... people didn't even go to school together, the kids in the different areas in Oldham didn't even know, that it was a no-go area and you start getting that apartheid.

These interview extracts are examples of how Erin (speaking from Peterborough), Andrew (from Barking and Dagenham) and Siv (from Hackney) used Oldham and associated places to stand for riots and parallel lives – and experiences far removed from their own. These examples arose within interviewees' narratives without prompting, clearly linking Oldham (and Bradford) to 'riots' or 'apartheid'. I explained the design of my research at the outset of each interview, and some of the resulting exchanges shed light on how implicit the meaning of Oldham had become:

> HANNAH: ... part of the story of what cohesion means to people, so they were Oldham, Peterborough and Barking and Dagenham.
> SALLY: [*overlapping*] Oh right I wonder why! [*laughs*]
> HANNAH: [*overlapping*] For different reasons. [*laughs*]
> HANNAH: When people talk about cohesion there's certain places that come up....
> MIKE: [*overlapping*] "Right."
> HANNAH: [*overlapping*] ... in the story and Oldham....
> MIKE: Oldham is obviously, yeah.

Sally, who works in the voluntary sector in Hackney, and Mike, an interfaith leader in Oldham, were both unsurprised that the fieldwork sites I had chosen were being treated as of particular significance to community cohesion policy. More strikingly, neither they nor I felt the need to establish what this significance might be; the meanings have simply become 'common sense'. As discussed in Chapter Two, these associations stem from the violent disturbances of 2001 in those towns, to which government reports prescribed 'community cohesion' as a cure. Oldham (with other 'northern towns') has taken on a resonance that fixes it in time as a place of riots and ethnic segregation. Interviewees spontaneously referred to the 'problems of Oldham' without feeling the need to elaborate on what they meant by this. Those working within Oldham recognised the image they had, were frustrated by it, and suggested alternative narratives for understanding the town and its history.

Jim was a councillor in Oldham, and described his experience:

> JIM: People that come from Oldham, after the riots, wouldn't say they come from Oldham, they'd shy away, you know … come from near Manchester and things like that … and people used to say … where do you come from, I said Oldham, Oldham? Riot town! Well yeah, but – there's been a riot in Birmingham after, why don't you ever remember that one? …
>
> HANNAH: And why do you think that one's not remembered as much?
>
> JIM: Well, it's the national news, Oldham was great, weren't it, 'cos Asians were setting fire to cars, it made good news, you know … but I think we've got away from that now, nobody ever says it to me now…. Now and again it creeps up….Where do you come from…. Oldham, and … half a dozen people said, oh, riot town!
>
> HANNAH: [*laughs*]
>
> JIM: You know, other councillors, I said, No! … Not the riot town! The best borough in the country for cohesion!

Jim was clear here that the reputation of Oldham as a 'riot town' had been pervasive, to the extent that he believed many Oldhamers had become unwilling to identify themselves as local because of the negative response they expected this to elicit from other people. Jim noted how "Asians setting fire to cars" made "good news", and such images were, of course, not only dramatic in themselves, but drew on resonances with the past, such as the urban riots in the 1980s and all of their political associations (see Chapter Two, this volume). Jim suggested that these images made Oldham's disturbances more resonant in imagined geographies than the "riot in Birmingham after". Jim was referring to disturbances that took place in Birmingham in 2005 that were characterised by the media as being clashes between Pakistani and African-Caribbean groups arising as a result of revenge attacks for a rumoured gang rape (Muir and Butt, 2005).[1] Although it can only be speculation on my part, the difficulty of fitting the Birmingham situation into the existing narratives of migration, integration and cohesion (or their lack) may have contributed to this story not developing as a policy parable in the way that those connected with Oldham have (Bourdieu, 1977 [1972], p 170; Trouillot, 1995, p 82).

Inside Oldham

> ANNE: And I got quite fired up and said do you not think that we know that we had disturbances in Oldham in 2001, and do you not think that we've been doing something about it since? ... Do you not know that we've had so many weekends since then ... where we haven't actually had disturbances in Oldham ... and Ted Cantle actually said then, Oldham was unlucky.... It was a series of events that happened on that afternoon ... fuelled by known BNP members, and it happened in Oldham, but he said it could have happened in any of the northern towns with similar ethnic compositions.

In this extract from my conversation with Anne (a former Oldham councillor), she described an encounter at a national conference where a colleague had "wanted it all to be about the riots in Oldham, and not progress that had happened since". In this case, she had had the opportunity to disagree with him, and had been supported by Ted Cantle (who since conducting the national report on community cohesion is often presented as a 'community cohesion guru'). Anne's argument here was not just that Oldham was unlucky, but also that people in Oldham had "been doing something about it since". Like Jim, she expressed frustration at the association of Oldham with riots, and linked it to media coverage:

> ANNE: I think there's a frustration with the national press in that every time Oldham's on the telly you've got the blazing police car. The blazing police van, it was just a prerequisite and it's just shorthand, isn't it, it's journalistic shorthand, and the number of times where whenever people mention Oldham they talk about those events,

> I think the other thing that I was constantly batting off
> was the question about the BNP.

Anne noted another way in which Oldham's reputation had spread. She was not only expected to talk about problems with community cohesion at conferences, but also to dispense advice on how to deal with similar problems. And the expertise that was sought was not necessarily in areas that Anne felt were particularly relevant to Oldham's circumstances. Although she suggested that the 2001 disturbances were "fuelled by known BNP members", Anne denied that the BNP had been a significant presence in Oldham; mainstream parties had confronted them and they had not been elected to the council. She seemed angry that, nevertheless, there was an "assumption that we must have had a handful of BNP councillors", leading representatives of Barking and Dagenham to ask Oldham for advice after electing 12 BNP councillors in 2006. Anne was adamant that Oldham's reputation for riots should not seep into an assumption that the borough had a racist voting record. Thus, even where Oldham's association with community cohesion was as a source of good practice, Anne had reservations. Claims to know how to deal with problems could result in a continued association between the area and those problems.

A number of policy practitioners in Oldham argued that while it was true that there had been disturbances in 2001, the national narratives that stemmed from these were distorted. They provided more nuanced narratives, based on claims to authentic local knowledge. For example, Rafiq, who now works for an interfaith organisation in Oldham, described his personal experiences on the night of the disorders:

> RAFIQ: Riots in Oldham and as serious as they were ... were
> very very localised.... I know that because I was driving
> my taxi that night ... and I was all around Oldham ...
> it was very very localised ... this is the physical act of
> rioting ... there were bad feelings among people but it
> was, I feel, localised and whenever a news story is put
> out by news organisations ... there's this sense of déjà
> vu, that, we all say, here we go again! [*both laugh*]

Here, Rafiq demonstrated his awareness of Oldham as an empirical place and as a metaphor. He acknowledged that the rioting was serious, but stated his own physical presence in the town (indeed, driving around different parts of the town) as evidence of his authority to speak on the subject. Despite this, Rafiq suggested that the *narratives* of the riots, as opposed to the physical acts that took place, were important to the area. They had become commonplace in news coverage of Oldham, "whenever a news story is put out ... here we go again!" This suggests that what *actually* took place on the nights of the riots was less important than the aftermath in terms of how Oldham was treated by both insiders and outsiders.

Jim's position, on the other hand, was to state very definitely that the disturbances were wholly the result of rivalries between drug dealers. This was an explanation I did not hear from anyone else, although there were fleeting references to drugs in all three of the Cantle (2001, p 40), Denham (2001, p 11) and Ritchie (2001, pp 12-13) reports into the disturbances. Jim went much further, suggesting that the drugs trade in itself was the root cause of the violence:

> JIM: Everybody says that Glodwick, the Pakistani area, is a no-go area and ... it's not particularly the Asians, or the BME that are making it a no-go area, it's the drug [*pause*] lords, if you like ... making it into a no-go area, 'cos they don't want the police down there! ... What they do want is white people going in that use drugs ... to buy 'em off 'em, and that's part of what all that rioting were about. You know, a lot of it started off with a drugs war. Really. And people don't agree with me on that, but ... I'm different as a cabinet member, I'm a blue-collar worker ... you start listening to people and that's what's going on, a lot of it's drug-related.

Although he continued to talk about "the Asians, or the BME" and "white people" as distinct groups throughout the interview, Jim insisted that problems were not linked to racialised inequalities or tensions. His alternative explanation was that many of Oldham's problems stemmed from the drugs trade: "nothing to do with race or anything else, it's just thuggery." Jim suggested that he had access to privileged knowledge as a working-class councillor whose day job brought him into contact with many locals across Oldham. His underlying argument seemed to be that those council officers, national commissions and others who had concluded that tensions in Oldham were inflected by race and racism and associated with structural issues of social and economic inequality had missed the 'common-sense' problem of local criminal rivalries.

Even more prevalent was an attempt to turn the focus away from those events altogether, and to create narratives about Oldham that presented it instead as a leader in the field of community cohesion, or attempted to step outside the cohesion framework and to suggest that the town had moved beyond its dominance.

Rebranding: "best borough in the country for cohesion!"

> GLEN: If we had a repeat of the disturbances it would be absolutely catastrophic for Oldham ... we know the damage it did to the reputation, our reputation in 2001 ... if you talk to the average person in Britain now, what do you know about Oldham, an awful lot of people say oh yeah, didn't they have riots in 2001 ... we're not famous for lots of other things, and so we need to rebrand ourselves ... we don't want to be remembered as the place that had riots.

Glen was a senior local authority officer in Oldham. His reference to 'rebranding' was not just casual; the local authority had, at the time of my visits, recently undertaken a full corporate branding exercise using high resolution images of different positive faces, buildings and landscapes of Oldham alongside a new logo and the slogan 'One Oldham'.[2] A screensaver on this theme played on Glen's computer behind him throughout our meeting. This branding played on local pride and residents' 'sense of place' that has become important in local government policy and closely connected to community cohesion. Yet most of the responses to my question about how national views of Oldham had affected the interviewees' work did not focus directly on the immediate impact or feelings of local residents for the place. Rather they were concerned with outsiders' images of the place.

The corporate policy of both the local authority and its partners attempted to provide alternative narratives of the 2001 disturbances and to refocus attention on other aspects of Oldham. This appears to have begun soon after the riots, when Oldham speakers spent a lot of time promoting their work nationally, as Steve rather cynically described it:

> STEVE: A lot of paper evidence was accumulated and sent down to London ... in order to show that Oldham was really doing things, and Oldham speakers were encouraged to go around the country ... [the local authority] chief exec ... was asked to speak because he came from Oldham.... He wasn't able to reel off a lot of initiatives that had happened in Oldham but he very

successfully gave the impression that Oldham was in the forefront of dealing with community cohesion.

Steve clearly felt that much of the work to change perceptions of Oldham was carried out in the world of image management. The strategy of sending speakers to national cohesion events continued at the time of the research; I had initially made contact with Oldham interviewees through meeting an assistant director of the local authority at a local government event in London, where he and another colleague I would eventually interview were presenting on good practice for working with faith groups. Jim's comment quoted earlier that Oldham was "not the riot town" but "the best borough in the country for cohesion!" also highlighted how Oldham had turned national interest in their cohesion problems into a marketing virtue: Oldham as a place with more experience of thinking about community cohesion than most, and hence as a place to seek good practice.

Yet several interviewees described a shift in this strategy (linked to a change in chief executive) towards promoting aspects of good practice besides work on community cohesion, because even talking about community cohesion continued to raise the spectre of the troubled past. For example:

> RON: What I don't think we should be is a one-trick pony … because if that's the only thing that we can talk about, well, bloody hell, we can't be doing a very good job, can we? That should be just one good component of the stuff that we're doing … and the stuff that we're talking about. And for a long time unfortunately, we were only famous for that…. Now we're famous for some other stuff, and that's important.

Ron, a senior officer at Oldham Council, put his emphasis on what Oldham was known for, at least as much as on residents' experiences. He suggested that promotion of good cohesion practice had run its course as an effective strategy for creating a positive image of Oldham; Oldham should normalise its image by talking about issues other than cohesion. Although Ron said here that Oldham was now "famous for some other stuff", it's not clear what this was. He did cite positive aspects of Oldham that he suggested could be promoted:

> RON: If you're gonna show Oldham, why not show a picture of Robert Winston....[3] That's every bit as much Oldham, you know, or our fantastic countryside.

Yet, as Ron said, images of prominent local figures or the surrounding National Park and countryside were *not* regularly used in the media when talking about Oldham. His comments suggested that while these positive images existed and were "every bit as much Oldham", they were not so in the national imagination.

Barking and Dagenham: 'the BNP council'

Approaching Barking and Dagenham

> OWEN: Well, there's obviously racism. And Barking and Dagenham shows that. In a way I think that actually ... in a place like Hackney well again there will be racism, but it's nowhere near like it is in other communities.

> SAM: Obviously you know, you just go in Barking and Dagenham and that [housing]'s gonna be THE election issue ... come next May, that people are moving in and taking ... our birthrights to housing ... in the local area. I mean it's funny that you know they're what 10 miles up the road, here in Hackney, it just doesn't feature.

> SAIDA: Far right, it's not an issue so much in Hackney ... from intelligence and what we can see... [don't] really get a lot of far right kind of issues coming in ... so, it might be an issue somewhere like in Barking and Dagenham.

All three of the extracts above came from interviews with policy practitioners based in Hackney, and there were many more examples of this use of the contrast with Barking and Dagenham to represent Hackney's success at living together with difference. The immediate association was between Barking and Dagenham and the BNP, with the association so notorious that it often did not need to be spelt out beyond a reference to 'a place like Barking and Dagenham'. Barking and Dagenham and the BNP were synonyms for an alienated, marginalised and therefore racist 'white working class'. Sometimes interviewees related this to issues such as declining manufacturing or shortages of public housing. But in most cases it was a simple shorthand for a racist place that demonstrated how people in the speaker's locality were much more comfortable with contemporary difference and complexity.

In the quotation that opened this chapter, Mark referred to 'Dagenham', where "they think that this is the final straw, Ford closes down ... and nobody cares about us, and now they're dumping all these foreigners on us". The story of Barking and Dagenham that is most often told is of a 'traditional white working-class' community that had relied rather heavily on the state and large paternalistic institutions such as the Ford car plant. Complacency among politicians on a traditionally solidly Labour council, coupled with industrial decline and new residents moving into the borough as overspill from the inner London housing market, were seen as leading to rapid change that overwhelmed long-standing residents. Much resentment for these changes was targeted at growing numbers of minority ethnic residents, with a great deal of myths, misinformation and resentment circulated about 'their' presence and the support 'they' receive from the state. The connection between this resentment and the election of 12 right-wing fascist BNP councillors to the local authority in 2006 is the 'perspective' that Mark referred to in the full quote as "atypical for London". It is clear from many of my interviews, and from national press coverage and policy literature (see, for example, Wynne-Jones, 2010; Chappell et al, 2010, p 3), that the BNP and Barking and Dagenham have become closely entwined in the popular imagination. This rhetorical move not only came from Hackney; as we saw in the discussion of Oldham above, both Anne and Steve described an incident where the Borough of Barking and Dagenham had asked for advice from Oldham on how to deal with BNP electoral success. Although Anne and Steve's attitudes to this approach were different, both presented narratives to me that emphasised the difference between the two authorities in that Oldham, while targeted by the BNP, had never elected one of its members to the local authority.[4]

A different perspective emerged in the following comment from Ed, a national think tank researcher:

> ED: But clearly ... if the BNP's winning 12 seats on Barking
> and Dagenham council, may win more ... may win a seat
> in the European Parliament ... that's not a very good ...
> sign about the health of good relations in Britain.

Here, Ed makes a similar move to that discussed above of equating the borough with the presence of the BNP. Although Barking and Dagenham had the most elected BNP representatives of any local authority in the country, it is by no means the only place where they have been elected.[5] The association between the place and the party is so strong that the place has become a national symbol of disharmony, at least for Ed. The locally based policy practitioners I spoke with who associated the place with racism and the BNP used it to illustrate the differences from their own locality. Ed, on the other hand, suggested this was potentially the future for Britain as a whole.

Inside Barking and Dagenham

> PHIL: You can see the sort of grief curve really, denial, anger. Fear and then – all those sorts of things, which people have gone through because of the change. And it's happened so quickly. And when you talk to people they hanker after this [*pause*] past which frankly didn't really exist, but all imagined with rose-tinted spectacles, everyone playing happily in their garden, sticking out there with their doors open and all the rest of it … which as I say didn't really exist, but it is very much this backward look, something that's been lost.

As in Oldham, the outsiders' narrative is not necessarily disputed head-on. Policy practitioners in Barking and Dagenham engaged especially with the explanatory elements of a broad narrative of post-industrial decline leading to exclusion and resentment. They tried to differentiate Barking and Dagenham from its national associations by arguing that support for the BNP might be a symptom of this malaise, but was not as significant for the borough as it had been made out to be.

In the quote above, Phil, a senior local authority officer in Barking and Dagenham, engaged with this pervasive narrative of loss. He suggested that the local population was mourning a golden age – even if this golden age "didn't really exist". When Phil refers to 'change' here, it is in the context of discussing the changing ethnic composition of the borough. He had talked about nearby Redbridge changing from "a very white traditional sort of place, to a predominantly Asian borough" over the course of 20 years, but suggested that the challenges in Barking and Dagenham were different, particularly because the change in population there was much faster. Phil related this population change to a sense of grief, of mourning attributed to a long-established white (and implicitly working-class) community. He described local reactions in therapeutic terms ('the grief curve'), with anger as a natural emotion to be worked through, and perhaps associated with the violence of far right politics. Phil took these emotions seriously, even as he argued that the idyllic past that was being mourned didn't exist in the terms it was remembered. This is not to say that changes in the economy, family structures and local area had not occurred, but Phil's point was that these changes, and changes in the ethnic make-up of the local population, had become associated by some with the loss of an idealised past that was entirely without strife.

June, another senior local authority officer in Barking and Dagenham, continued in a similar vein. Her account coupled structural and material changes related to housing and employment with a sense of mourning for the past that she considered "particularly marked" in Barking and Dagenham:

> JUNE: As society changed, and as Right to Buy came in which was a very very significant factor given the very significant levels of council housing, then that change was always going to be more noticeable here, because it was such a shift away from the known, and so you've got people who are kind of mourning the loss of what was there before. To an extent it's true of everywhere, but it is particularly marked here.
> HANNAH: And I mean does that come out – do people express that when they talk about the place itself, or that's....
> JUNE: People certainly express regret that things aren't ... the way they were. When we said to people how can we improve your area, there was a very significant number of people who said, make it the way it was X years ago, and X varied from anything from 8 to 80 years ago, but it was always make it the way it used to be.... So, that is a sign of a community that is mourning its past.

June did not spell out exactly what 'the past' entailed for the people who were characterised as grieving for it. She referred to the Right to Buy, the policy allowing social tenants to buy their properties from the local authority which was promoted by the Conservative government in the 1980s, reducing the amount of housing stock available for new prospective council tenants and eventually increasing the number of former council properties that were privately let, as their former residents moved to another property. This factor was suggested by a number of interviewees as helping to give rise to the myth that new migrants were 'getting council housing' when they were more likely to be privately renting but in a property otherwise indistinguishable from the state-run properties around it. Aside from the housing issue, 'the past' is not specified, is somewhat hazy, as June said that residents wanted the area to be "the way it was anything from 8 to 80 years ago."

June's analysis drew more direct attention to structural changes to life in Barking and Dagenham than Phil's. As such, it might suggest that if there were problems at the level of employment and housing, the remedy should be sought at that level. However, June also used the therapeutic language of 'mourning', suggesting policy might engage with issues in Barking and Dagenham in these terms. This differed from Ed's assessment:

> ED: We've done some focus groups in Barking and Dagenham, where obviously the BNP is quite strong on the council ... and you just listen to what people are saying you think, we're not going to solve any of this by having a statement of national values or any of this stuff, actually this is about basic social and economic issues and it needs a response at that level and ... I don't think anything that the government says about national identity or any of that will actually really cut the mustard at that level.

Ed both explicitly stated that the election of BNP representatives was a problem, and suggested that the subjects to be addressed in Barking and Dagenham were "basic social and economic ones", rejecting a response in the register of emotion or values as inadequate. This is not to say that Ed denied that feelings about place were significant in Barking and Dagenham, but his prescription was differently nuanced to those of June and Phil.

This difference in assessments may be linked to their positions as policy practitioners. Ed is a think tank commentator outside of the local place, whose professional reputation is not invested in its success; more importantly, perhaps, he is not responsible for implementing any of the policy prescriptions he makes. This enables him to suggest that social and economic issues, which are largely decided nationally, lie at the root of Barking and Dagenham's problems. June and Phil, on the other hand, are local government officers. Their positions are politically restricted, and they are required to work with councillors of whatever party is elected. More importantly, their professional positions require them not only to assess the local situation, but also to intervene. Yet the avenues available for their intervention are limited.

Their emphasis on the need to manage a local 'grief curve', rather than on addressing underlying economic and political issues they saw as contributing to this grief, was determined by what interventions seemed possible at a local level. I do not mean to suggest that the emotional grief response that these interviewees described was not real or significant, or that they did not require intervention. Rather, the emphasis on issues of emotion, presentation and narrative arose because political and bureaucratic structures made it easier for local government to intervene in those terms, than to effect large-scale structural and economic change. The perhaps counter-intuitive result is that in maintaining the guise of 'neutral bureaucrat', June and Phil were led to emphasise *emotional* techniques and outcomes of governing, in preference to more materially based ones.

Rebranding: "a positive catalyst"

> PHIL: You'll hear ... our chief exec, say this ... he didn't want Barking [and] Dagenham to only be known as 'the BNP council'.... It was only ever mentioned in that context ... and so [we] spent a lot of time trying to be known for other things. So being the most improved council last year, going to four stars and improving stronger, all that performance stuff, and getting I think quite a good reputation on the national stage around policy, developing innovation and free school meals, and pre-schooling and all this sort of stuff, it's been really important to us, obviously, for its own sake as well.... But also to say that actually Barking and Dagenham is much more than just 12 BNP councillors ... and in fact, the BNP hardly figure really in our thinking.... In many ways that's a quite positive catalyst and I think that national attention, because we have lots of people come here, ministers, senior civil servants, coming all the time now, a lot of them will come and then the first thing in their mind is BNP and how does that affect, but, very quickly, hopefully ... they see all the other stuff we're doing and actually that the BNP's a very little, very small, minor part of it and it's the other stuff that's important ... so I see it as a very positive thing, if it gets us some attention great, and then we can use that attention positively to show what we're doing.

Phil acknowledged that the BNP loomed large in outsiders' perceptions of the borough, and indeed was the reason for a lot of interest. But he insisted that not only was the BNP a 'minor' part of life in the borough, but that attention would quickly turn to the achievements of the council and partners. In some ways Phil's insistence seemed unrealistic, as it was clear that the association of the borough with the BNP had not yet been removed by this approach. Even my presence, as I discussed with him, was part of this process, and Phil cited many instances of innovative work to me, as part of the same strategy of presentation to outsiders.

This seemed to be part of a corporate strategy, providing a narrative that demonstrated a measured response to the election of the BNP. June's account is a good example:

> JUNE: The other big angle here that obviously everybody is conscious of was the election results in May 06 which brought the BNP opposition in ... now I have to say, that hasn't affected council policy, they're a tiny minority and they don't affect the policy of the council. It's brought a lot of extra attention to us. But probably what it did do was just make us particularly more conscious or refocus our efforts (a) to be concerned for how it would feel to be, say, a BME member of the public living in the borough ... but also to recognise that people voted the way that they did because they had legitimate concerns and therefore we needed to address those.

In these narratives, the importance of the election of BNP representatives was minimised (only 12 councillors on a local authority of 51 members, which remained Labour-led by a large majority) and their impact on policy dismissed. Instead, the impact of their election was described as a 'wake-up call' to local organisations to pay attention to the reasons these votes may have been cast. These were treated as protest votes about socioeconomic issues and failures of local institutions and leadership, rather than as expressing support for the policies of the BNP. Liam, a voluntary sector leader, gave one account of this:

> LIAM: A lot of our staff are volunteers, so we reflect local communities, both negatively as well as positively.... We are having to deal with those same issues within the sector ... but are not shying away from it.... If anything

the BNP are helping us to focus on the fact that we can't ignore this.

Liam argued that as a group of local organisations, the voluntary sector used the elections result to understand opinions and issues in the borough. They were also made up of local residents and so likely to replicate some of the local tensions, including representatives who may have voted for the BNP, or those who felt threatened by their presence, and residents experiencing the structural and emotional upheavals others had identified. This sense of *being*, rather than *managing*, 'the community' seemed less strong in the other accounts I gathered from Barking and Dagenham policy practitioners, who talked about the questions of mourning a lost past as something that *others* (the residents of Barking and Dagenham) were doing, and not something in which they themselves were involved. This was in marked contrast to the way many people I interviewed in Oldham, Peterborough and especially Hackney were at pains to demonstrate that they *were* part of the local community, slipping between seeing themselves as governors and part of the population being governed. Perhaps the reason for this tendency to maintain a greater distance in Barking and Dagenham was the very difficulty of finding a way to align oneself with a community that was being constituted through having elected far right representatives.

Peterborough: "All these East Europeans flooding in, picking all our tomatoes ..."

Approaching Peterborough

> PHILIPPA: The growth of the European Community and a lot of migrants coming in, they miscalculated and then suddenly there were all these ... rural communities with migrants, that had never experienced that sort of thing, and that's the background to the Community and Integration Commission.

Philippa, who worked for a local government research organisation, gave a succinct account of the relationship she saw between rurality, EU migration and the development of community cohesion policy, and how it was treated as a problem requiring attention through a national policy commission. Peterborough or 'places like it' were frequently invoked in discussions of cohesion to refer to such a rural or semi-rural place and its associations.

Philippa referred to miscalculations, by which she meant the predictions that the expansion of the EU in 2004 might lead to between 5,000 and 13,000 migrants a year to the UK from the A8 accession countries (Dustmann et al, 2003, p 57). In practice the numbers were much larger than that, with a peak of 112,000 A8 migrants arriving in the UK in 2007 (although these figures have fallen since, and there is also considerable out-migration) (Vargas-Silva, 2011, p 4). Philippa emphasised that the arrival of new migrants in rural areas "that had never experienced that sort of thing" was treated as a national problem to the extent that it was directly related to the instigation of COIC in 2006. As noted in Chapters Three and Four, other narratives of cohesion policy consider that Commission a response to the London bombings of 2005. The point here, however, is that the idea of rural communities coming to terms with substantial immigration for the first time is geographically rooted in the narratives of policy practitioners.

The association with Peterborough emerged in Mark's reference in the opening of this chapter to "the Peterboroughs of this world" where people "worry about all these East Europeans flooding in, picking all our tomatoes". It appeared again when interviewing Michelle, a leading councillor in Hackney:

> HANNAH: How this discourse on cohesion ... [has] affected your work? ... Either explicitly or implicitly changed what you do?
>
> MICHELLE: I think it's something I'm aware of in terms of newspapers and ... actually I'm from Peterborough ... I don't know if you're familiar with the issues in Peterborough and everyone is saying that all the Polish are taking their jobs and they've had lots of bad press about that so – and I guess as a councillor if you were in there or maybe Brad ... or somewhere ... you'd be asked to comment on it, I've never been asked to talk about it, explicitly.

Although Michelle drew on Peterborough partly because she was familiar with it as a former resident, she used it to illustrate a contrast with the Hackney experience in line with the narrative of newly arrived Eastern European migrants resented by existing local residents who saw them as competitors in the labour market. Note that despite her familiarity with Peterborough, Michelle emphasised *perceptions* of the place, rather than discussing immigration patterns or labour market dynamics themselves ("everyone is saying", "they've had lost of bad press"). She suggested that the narrative of new immigration, and hostility to it, was part of a landscape of cohesion, when she made (or almost made) the link with Bradford as somewhere that, like Peterborough, councillors would "be asked to comment on it". These allusions demonstrate that Peterborough and Bradford are part of the narrative of cohesion policy in a way that Hackney is not. Others (perhaps national or local press or local government organisations) who might have otherwise asked her to comment in terms of community cohesion appeared to share this understanding.

Sam, also a senior elected member in Hackney, similarly drew on Peterborough and its surrounding area as a contrast, to demonstrate a greater comfort with migration in frequently changing inner London:

> HANNAH: Just to go back to the kind of community cohesion idea itself, I mean do you see it linked to other types of policies that – say equalities, social inclusion, immigration policies even, or is it – I mean you talked about the link with the Prevent stuff....
> SAM: I can see it does nationally... hugely, particularly on Eastern Europeans in East Anglia and all that kind of thing ... on the farms and stuff, but Hackney [*4-second pause*] it's [*3-second pause*] it's never really ... come up in those terms.... Let me qualify that by saying a great deal.

Sam's reference to "Eastern Europeans in East Anglia", and to potential conflict over labour migration "on farms and stuff", situates problems with integrating new migrants in the countryside. Perceptions of migration as a cause of conflict over resources and consequent hostility to migrants had "never really come up in those terms" in Hackney, according to Sam. In this, he also made a contrast between Hackney and narratives of Barking and Dagenham, saying political arguments in Hackney about "the white working class not being able to get their kids a flat on their estate", which was "only a few steps away" from it being "because they're all going to somebody else", had never been a significant electoral issue for him; he had heard such racialised arguments about immigration and resource competition only "once or twice in ten years, I mean I've probably heard that Elvis is still alive more often".

Inside Peterborough

> HANNAH: Is that how you, how people in Peterborough think of the place, that it was kind of fairly homogeneous and suddenly had to cope with new migration?
>
> AHMED: I think to a certain extent that is true ... it was not fairly homogeneous, it was always a diverse community but that was a much more settled diverse community, there was a heavy number of Italians were here, but they were fairly well ... cohesive or at least getting on with their life ... there were a lot of Asians, relatively speaking, for a small place but they were still settled and getting on with their lives in a way, sometime, frankly, there might be a level of segregation [but] ... it was kind of not problematic, in a way, but then when with the Eastern Europeans, the wave of it, first it was the asylum seekers ... and that kind of really injected a kind of bang, what is this? ... Then this wave of migrations from the Eastern European problem, that is unprecedented for Peterborough in such a short time.

Ahmed worked on community cohesion policy in Peterborough. His narrative was at once in keeping with the narrative of a "much more settled community" confronted with "this wave of migrations that is unprecedented". However, he complicates this in two ways. The first is to suggest that the existing, settled community was not an undifferentiated white, British population but included immigrant and immigrant-heritage communities. In his account of this population (and of this time) he tried to strike a balance between presenting an overly nostalgic image or an overly problematic one. The second addition to the narrative is the first "wave" of migration from "asylum seekers" that "really injected a kind of bang, what is this?" before the politicised and publicised arrival of Eastern European labour migrants. Despite trying to take this balanced tone, and perhaps despite himself, Ahmed consistently used terms such as "Eastern European *problem*" (emphasis added) to describe migration.

A slightly different inflection was given by Colin, a Peterborough councillor who, when I interviewed him, had only days before been given responsibility for the cohesion brief with the council's cabinet. His account was extremely positive, responding to my questions about perceptions of Peterborough, by saying it was "just the opposite of the national image, it's a fantastic place" – although he did not elaborate on what he understood "the national image" of Peterborough to be, beyond my own suggestion about the narratives I had encountered of Peterborough as unused to immigration. Colin attempted to disrupt this narrative, like Ahmed describing the establishment of an Italian immigrant community following the Second World War, and the consequent presence of "third generation Italians" who are "of course British now". He also described a "huge influx" of mainly Pakistani migrants to Peterborough in the late 1980s and early 1990s, followed by a "huge influx" of economic migrants from the EU accession countries. Rather than a town unused to immigration, Colin described Peterborough as a place enveloping successive flows of migrants, and while he described the descendants of Italian migrants as "British now", his narrative was one of partial assimilation, claiming that different migrant groups were linked to particular industries (Italians largely bricklayers, Asians working in taxis, shops and clothing, and Eastern Europeans in agriculture), and that there were "areas peculiar to particular people", that is, some level of voluntary segregation. This differentiation was seen as part of a multiculturalist model of living side by side, "very multinational, almost like the UN".

Whereas Colin provided an overwhelmingly positive narrative of cohesion in Peterborough (perhaps tinged with a rather patronising tone), Amrit, who worked in race equality in Peterborough, weighed negative stories about new Eastern European migrants against positive personal encounters with them. He added that regardless of the good character or otherwise of new arrivals, the rapid change in demographics had startled existing residents:

> AMRIT: It is a fact that Peterborough was a reception centre for refugees and asylum seekers.... It is a fact that we have a large number of Polish, and East European countries, the chief constable will say to you that it is a fact that a large number of drink drunk offences are from A10 countries,[6] okay? And it is also a fact that the prison population from A10 countries is actually increasing. That doesn't mean they're a bunch of criminals.... Because some of the nicest people I've come across recently are people from Poland and the A10 countries.... Having said that, it's what I was saying to you earlier, this is the sheer scale of things that have happened ... which is beginning to frighten people. Rightly or wrongly, they are frightened about it.

Although Amrit's caveat about "some of the nicest people" coming from A10 countries may seem to echo a traditionally mocked denial of racism ("some of my best friends are black"; see also van Dijk, 1992, p 89), I think that here it was really intended to act as a 'myth-busting' technique. That is, Amrit really did want to insist that there was "a lot to learn from them". As a long-standing race equality campaigner, and a migrant himself (as a refugee from Uganda in the 1970s) Amrit was able to take a relatively sophisticated position in his narrative of cohesion and immigration in Peterborough. He acknowledged that there were difficulties with some migrants, but wanted to avoid stereotyping the whole group. He also offered an explanation of the conflict arising from migration as an emotional reaction to process and structure, rather than being rooted in individual faults ("the sheer scale of things, which is beginning to frighten people"). Amrit's account moved away from a simplified characterisation of Peterborough as a marker of new immigration, through a more detailed chronology. In his account, Amrit attempted to shift the debate from a binary idea of migration and migrants (or people fearful of migration and migrants) being either 'good' or 'bad'.

Erin, who worked for a community organisation in Peterborough, gave an example of the area's contemporary multicuture in practice. She told of a conflict that escalated in the national and local media after two nights of "what the papers called rioting but the police called disturbances" involving a group of newly arrived Kurdish migrants and some members of the established Pakistani community:

> ERIN: What they [journalists] did was they found the Kurdish café where the young lads hang out … and they interviewed the one person there who spoke the best English who happened to be a young lad that was a bit cocky … but he was actually just a young lad … interviewed by the media, stuff he said was terrible, it was things like, Pakistanis are all bad…. And for the media it was like, see, these foreign people that are involved in wars can't live like us, don't understand British values, Pakistani community have lived here so long now, they're like, they are British, you know, it was all that sort of feeling going on about new arrivals.

Here, Erin was not describing her own perception of the differences between the two groups, but the way they were characterised in the media. Part of her point was that both newly arrived groups of migrants, and established minority ethnic communities, were treated as somehow bounded entities, from which media (and government) sought spokespeople. While there was an established Pakistani Community Association whose head had been given media training and who gave a "really positive" statement about problems being with "just a few individuals", so both groups should "sit down and sort out the problems", the absence of such a structure for the more recently arrived Kurdish migrants led to a much less temperate account being sourced from "a young lad" who perhaps had thought less about how his statement might be used. Erin described this as providing an opportunity for media outlets to not only invoke an idea of a lack of "British values" among "these foreign people", but to underline their point while at the same time insulating themselves from accusations of xenophobia by contrasting the young man's response with that of the "Pakistani community" who were seen as successfully absorbing these "British values" (echoing Colin's statement about descendants of Italian migrants being "British now").

Colin's, Ahmed's and to some extent Erin's accounts all suggest that Peterborough's policy practitioners viewed the town as having been fairly comfortable with a level of relatively long-standing ethnic difference. They resisted the characterisation of the place as entirely untouched by migration in the past and so somehow unsophisticated. Instead, they suggested that what residents found hard to deal with was not the fact of migration, but the scale and character of more recent migrations. But, as previous chapters have shown, there are other aspects to community cohesion policy besides migration. In Peterborough, the local authority takes in the city and its surrounding countryside. It seemed to me that this might present particular ways of thinking about cohesion, in terms of both comfort with change, diversity and migration, and competing priorities between rural and urban residents.

At the end of my meeting with Colin, the councillor, he began to describe a 'divide' between urban and rural areas of Peterborough. He said that as the elected representative for a rural area, he had taken steps to introduce urban and rural people to one another, "and that's community cohesion too". Stuart, a senior local authority officer in Peterborough, provided more detailed comments on the subject:

> STUART: There's a massive difference between the urban and rural areas around our city. You've got one of the most deprived wards right in the centre, where you've got some really rich, affluent areas right out here on the outskirts, and their views of life will be poles apart. It's

interesting to go to [one of the village halls] for a meeting where, as a Peterborian, I'm told there – 'cos they see themselves as a separate and distinct community – we would love to put a wall around our village to prevent people from Peterborough coming into it! [*laughs*] So you really have got people that are massively different in their views and opinions, and you've gotta reflect that in the service provision that you give. And I think that's right to reflect that. But they can also become equally as scared and have really complex community cohesion issues, I mean there is a report around a potential Travellers' site[7] being built in what is probably one of the most beautiful areas that we've got on the outskirts of our city, surrounded by some of the richest houses that we've got and that will cause distinct fears and worries for that community if we don't manage it properly.

Stuart's example of controversy over the building of a Travellers' site as part of a much larger housing development brings together the entanglements between power struggles invoking class, ethnicity, belonging, nation and access to basic resources. Potentially, thinking about the rights of different groups in the countryside and the city to space and particularly to dwelling could be an opening for exploring different inflections of community cohesion policy in Peterborough, beyond the narrative of coping with new international immigration in which it is usually understood. This might open up questions of distribution of economic resources locally and nationally. However, as I discuss in the next section, the tactics for regaining control of Peterborough's community cohesion narratives that I found among local practitioners were not to reject or complicate these narratives, but to work within their logics.

Rebranding: "a city that has had massive change and found ways of dealing with it"

City MP Stewart Jackson claims Peterborough should fight back against recent negative national press by highlighting its good points. In recent weeks national newspapers have highlighted squalid migrant camps in the city and alleged Peterborough is 'overrun' with immigrants who are stretching city schools and services to breaking point.... Mr Jackson says: "Peterborough needs to hit back hard with a positive and compelling narrative about the city's strengths." (Reville, 2010)

This local press story highlights the importance that Peterborough's MP, Stewart Jackson, places on the reputation the area has nationally. Jackson is quoted as directly addressing the power of 'compelling narrative'. The article refers to a 1980s television advertising campaign which used the slogan 'The Peterborough Effect' and an actor dressed as a Roman centurion to promote positive messages about 'how the city had moved on since the Roman times'.[8] Jackson urges that this should be revived, 'to get our message across in London and beyond, to the opinion formers and decision takers who can make things happen' (Jackson, 2010). Once again, the negative stories that are to be refuted centre on immigration and link new arrivals to the city with pressure on public services and 'squalid' improvised housing. This news story and the comment piece to which it refers are not aiming to change the thinking (or practice) on 'problems with migration', but to put that narrative to one side in favour of associating Peterborough with 'strengths' instead.

Ahmed, as a local authority officer directly involved in developing local community cohesion policy, voiced a different strategy that might address the issues of housing need or stretched public services while contextualising the role of immigration in these pressures:

> AHMED: The first top priority now, is socioeconomic impact
> ... on communities, particularly vis-à-vis migration,
> economic downturn, and homelessness ... we're also
> trying to change it around [so] it's not looking at the
> migrant worker and the issues they cost ... it's as a social
> impact on the wider community.

Ahmed described how the LSP wanted to move on from simply looking at the needs of new migrants, to looking at service needs. The intention was not to remove migration from the discussion, but to think about 'social impact on the wider community', including both migrants and non-migrants, of questions such as 'economic downturn' and 'homelessness'. Despite Ahmed's suggestion that this had been agreed as the new strategy for local leaders, the examples of how the area had been 'rebranded' to change national perceptions of local community cohesion used quite different narratives.

I found that policy practitioners did describe ways they had reached 'opinion formers and decision takers' with messages that Peterborough was coping with new migration. The principal approach was not a traditional marketing campaign using advertisements to appeal to residents or investors. Rather, policy practitioners presented their local situation to national policy makers within the terms of community cohesion narratives, as a place with potential for successful government intervention promoting community cohesion. As a result, the local authority was able to promote itself as an example of good practice from which others could learn, and *this* became the narrative lens for understanding Peterborough's relationship to community cohesion policy. Erin described it thus:

> ERIN: "I think we've been seen as a city that has had massive change but has tried to find ways of dealing with it ... whereas a lot of cities have had massive change but haven't really woken up to the fact.

This reputation of having "woken up" to massive change and finding "ways of dealing with it" was one that had been negotiated through specific appeals to central government framed in the place-based community cohesion narratives with which we have become familiar:

> ERIN: So it all got a bit tense and resulted in the different agencies that were working together ... saying look we need to try and get some funding from government to deal with this before we have a Oldham and Bradford riot ... so the police, the council, and health went to the Home Office and said if you give us some money we will do lots of work to make things better in Peterborough ... projects that will help new arrivals to integrate ... and if we stop a riot, it means that we'll save Peterborough five million, because that's how much it cost the Bradford and Oldham riots per night ... I mean it's a bit – weird.

Erin described how local agencies negotiated with central government to provide funding to Peterborough for services to support the integration of new arrivals. This was initially to support the use of Peterborough as a dispersal centre for asylum seekers. Erin suggested that the most effective way to convince central government to release funds was to argue for the need to prevent disorder, with the ability to measure the projected effects of this in monetary terms. The 'Oldham and Bradford riot' was invoked not only as a spectre of the worst-case scenario of failed community cohesion, foreshadowed by previous outbreaks of racialised violence. 'Oldham and Bradford riots' were also important as a yardstick for justifying intervention in terms of good accounting, as much as good politics. Although Erin's comment that "it's a bit – weird" suggested that she saw some incongruity in deciding to prevent civil disturbances on the basis of a financial analysis, she was politically savvy enough to see this as a privileged technology of persuasion in intra-government negotiations. From being principally associated with community cohesion problems (according to another Peterborough practitioner, the city featured in the national community tension team's monitoring report every week because of the potential for a riot), Erin suggested that Peterborough was now seen as having a national reputation as a community cohesion success story.

Conclusions

Throughout this chapter I have shown how three places were used in anecdotal understandings of community cohesion policy, by policy practitioners anxious to distinguish their own locality from problem scenarios of community cohesion. I have discussed how, within each of these places, policy practitioners recognised the labels that were attached to their area, and tried to complicate these narratives by producing more nuanced accounts drawing on their local knowledge (and how resenting their area's associations with community tensions of one sort or another did not prevent policy practitioners from talking in this way about other places). In each of the three places, I have shown how policy practitioners have taken this reputational work further. Rather than devoting all of their energies to negating the associations between the place and narratives of community cohesion problems, many have tried to lever this notoriety to their locality's advantage. They have promoted Oldham as a community cohesion success story from which others can learn; they have tried to use national attention to showcase social inclusion projects in Barking and Dagenham; and they have secured national funding and support for services to new residents in Peterborough by arguing that the place's risky community cohesion status required intervention.

In each of these three examples, this rebranding has taken place within policy practitioners' professional circles. Their associations with significant events in the development of community cohesion policy exist in wider public culture, and to some extent the policy practitioners I interviewed described ways they had tried to challenge this. But their main focus was on the perceptions of their colleagues in national government, local government and associated bodies. This is, of course, the arena in which 'community cohesion policy' (in those terms) is a topic of most interest. It is where performance indicators, league tables, inspection reports, beacon status, achievement awards, sharing of good practice, conference appearances, case studies and toolkits are currencies of reputation and reward, both institutionally and individually. These are reputational tools through which local government negotiates power (on behalf of residents). They rely on persuasive (and hence affective) narratives. In order to be persuasive, and easily understood, policy practitioners often knowingly simplify such narratives, creating silences around difficult subjects which are hard to address forthrightly because of the uncomfortable positions they reveal about the limited power local government has over decisions about and reputation of its territory.

SIX

"You need to be totally objective, but you can't be"

Introduction

Previous chapters have considered how difficult subjects are narrated and negotiated in relation to different topics, times and places. In this chapter, drawing on interviews from all of my local and national research sites, I concentrate on how policy practitioners talk about community cohesion policy and the difficult subjects it invokes in relation to themselves, how they locate themselves and are located by others. I argue that for the most part, feminist thinking on the situated subject and situated knowledge – that people understand the world in specific ways depending on their experiences and social location, and that it is therefore impossible to have a completely objective or neutral view – have entered the 'common sense' of policy practice in such a way that all interviewees said, in one way or another, that their biography influenced their practice. Some interviewees appeared to feel obliged to describe their viewpoint as particular, but would then refer to this particular viewpoint as a 'neutral' one. Other interviewees emphasised values and ethics of equality and inclusivity which motivated them in their work and life; sometimes this involved resisting identity politics, at other times linking personal experiences of marginalisation to political commitments. For many, affiliation with 'difference' and ideals of equality was demonstrated through living in multicultural areas (particularly when bringing up children) or through their career choices. For others, understanding their own viewpoint as particular was not felt as a special obligation in work contexts, but experienced as a way of being in the world. This chapter explores the extent to which interviewees' own social positioning was drawn on as a resource with which to negotiate difficult subjects, and the extent to which it became a difficult subject in itself, to be negotiated around. My analysis of the positions interviewees took builds on debates about the proper role of a 'neutral' bureaucrat, demonstrating how policy practitioners often recognised the impossibility of neutrality even while it remained an ideal, and found strategies to negotiate this.

Reflexivity as reflex action

Towards the end of each interview, I asked participants whether (and if so how) they felt their own identity, background and experiences might affect their understanding of community cohesion policy. Initial reactions varied; some were taken aback and hesitated, before articulating – for what they suggested was the first time – their personal relationship to their work and these subjects. Many commented on how interesting it was to think of their work in this way, and seemed genuinely pleased to consider these subjects in what appeared to be a fresh way, albeit that most had already used personal narratives to negotiate our discussions of community cohesion policy throughout the interview. The second broad type of response was an immediate assertion: either that everyone's understandings were always influenced by their background, identity and experiences, or that this was certainly true of the interviewee personally. By far the most common reaction was agreement, more or less in one of these two forms. And even those who stated categorically that they were entirely unaffected by such influences stated elsewhere in the interview that their background *had* shaped them.

I demonstrate how the idea of situated knowledge has become a form of received wisdom using extracts from two quite different interview encounters. Alice was a long-standing colleague of mine who had been aware of and supportive of my research project for some time, and a senior officer within Hackney who therefore might well be expected to be conversant with policy and political debates about identity and inequality. Donald, a senior officer in a free market think tank, was less concerned in his day-to-day work with issues he classed as related to diversity or equality. Their (party) political persuasions were also divergent, Alice being a member of the Labour Party and Donald's work very closely associated with the Conservative Party. First, Alice:

> HANNAH: Do you think that your background or identity or whatever, affects how you think about cohesion?
> ALICE: Yeah I'm sure it does.
> HANNAH: Mmhm.
> ALICE: Erm…. [*6-second pause*] Yeah. I don't know how though, 'cos I haven't thought about that [*laughs*] erm which you obviously should do…. I don't think about my own background and identity, I think about what is fundamental to … my beliefs about what is important, which is that you treat everyone equally…. I'd rather

work and live in an environment where there's a range
of different people from different places, 'cos that's
considerably more interesting than living in a place ...
that is quite monocultural.

Here, Alice immediately agreed that she was 'sure' her background
did affect how she thought about cohesion, but was then much more
hesitant in finding the words to explore how and in what respects this
might be the case. Alice seemed to feel obliged to exhibit an awareness
of social positioning, yet not to have articulated this to herself in a
narrative that was readily drawn on in the interview situation. What I
want to note especially here is that Alice did not seem surprised by this
question, and indeed she appeared to have a strong sense of what the
answer 'should' be. Throughout the interview, she seemed to feel very
self-conscious about trying to anticipate how I might later think about
her comments, and yet this did not manifest itself as an unwillingness
to talk around the questions I raised. Rather, the stumbling over how
to express what she meant, felt or did in relation to a greater certainty
about what she *should* feel, was quite striking. The processes of self-
governing, disciplined selves clearly operate within, as well as through,
the structures of state government (see also Rose, 1999a, 1999b).

For Donald, however, the question about whether or how his own
positioning informed his ideas and practice appeared both startling and
troubling, despite his having already drawn attention to some aspects
of this earlier in the interview, in the following exchange:

> HANNAH: The government's statements on community
> cohesion often focus on race, ethnicity and faith ...
> do you think that will be something that's around in a
> Conservative version of that?
> DONALD: I think that is an interesting question, I should say
> here I'm a Catholic and I'm a governor of a Catholic
> school, I've written books on Catholic social teaching,
> so a thing such as civil society and subsidiarity I find
> very complementary to the general [name of think tank]
> philosophical beliefs.

Although Donald did not explore how he was positioned in other ways
in relation to power, he did feel the need in one sense to 'declare an
interest' related to his ethical and personal commitments that might
inform his otherwise supposedly neutral stance. But when I tried to
explore this in more depth:

> HANNAH: When I'm talking about community cohesion policy to people, they often talk about their own identity and background ... and you mentioned your Catholicism....
>
> DONALD: Yeah okay....
>
> HANNAH: So I just wondered if you feel that your own – background affects how you think about this issue?
>
> DONALD: Ooh, gosh. Er [*pause*] Marxist, isn't it? [*both laugh*] er ... [*3-second pause*] well I suppose Marx would argue that our background affects how we think about an issue even if we don't believe it does, [*laughs*] no, I mean I don't think so, no.
>
> HANNAH: ... mmhm....
>
> DONALD: No. Erm ... and I must admit it's only relatively recently that I've begun to study Catholic social teaching as an academic subject although I've always been a Catholic, and my sort of economic and political ideas were sort of formed before I started studying those things so no I, er, I, er ... I don't think so particularly.

In seeming to equate identity politics with Marxism, Donald may be thinking of 'background' as referring to class, or perhaps simply using 'Marxist' to stand in for 'left-wing' in general. Yet the question as I framed it specifically referred back to his previous references to his Catholicism and how it informed his outlook. This was partly because I already had some nervousness about asking this question to an interviewee I perceived as likely to be unsympathetic to a reading of policy making as culturally embedded. Despite my attempts to link back to earlier in our conversation and to demonstrate how the question may be relevant and perhaps relatively unthreatening, Donald chose instead to disassociate himself from his previous comments by saying that Catholic social teaching had simply become important to him as he had learned that it accorded with his pre-existing beliefs. Yet Donald's sense of needing to declare an interest in terms of his religious commitments suggests that even those who reject cultural politics as having no bearing on the possibility of 'neutrality' have been reached to some extent by critiques of objectivity (see, for example, Haraway, 1991). For Alice and Donald, the concept of situated knowledge appeared to have seeped through to become received wisdom without necessarily being engaged, theorised or put into action in the everyday. However, other interviewees reincorporated this reflexivity to reassert, paradoxically, a view from nowhere (see also Skeggs, 2004, p 131).

Reinscribing the norm

> HANNAH: I just wondered if you think your own background or experience and identity affect how you think about these kind of issues?
>
> ANDREW: In terms of my own personal background?
>
> HANNAH: Mmm.
>
> ANDREW: Right, okay. I think it probably would do, 'cos.... I think that because I'm not from any of the visibly recognised equality theme groups ... the fact that I'm able to come at it from a fresh perspective, that I don't have any particular, it sounds terrible saying, I don't have any particular axe to grind, that I can look at things in different ways.

> DAVID: I s'pose my ... life experiences, I don't know ... or lack of them....
>
> HANNAH: [*laughs*]
>
> DAVID: Means I s'pose I'm fairly open to – about it.

In the first extract above, Andrew's statement that not being part of a "visibly recognised equality group" (I presume he means protected groups under equality law) meant he had no "particular axe to grind" is particularly striking since he was speaking as an equalities officer. Later in the interview Andrew suggested that equality, diversity and community cohesion issues should be addressed as questions of customer service and efficiency, and that this would naturally reduce inequalities for those otherwise subjected to systematic discrimination and disadvantage. Thus, he was aware of the "visibly recognised equality theme groups" and that he was not part of them, but he did not describe this status as being part of an alternative (perhaps white, male, professional) "theme group". Instead, he became immediately 'normal' and invisible again; he had "no axe to grind". David, in the second extract, provided a similar account of himself. He is one of the most senior local authority officers in his borough and also agreed that "whatever your background you'll have a view", and gave some examples of backgrounds which, if he had experienced them, he thought would give him a different perspective ("if I was Orthodox Jewish ... if I was an Asian Muslim ..."). But the distinctiveness of his own life was literally invisible to him; his experiences as a white male professional were a "lack of experiences". And he went on to describe this not as a barrier to carrying out his role, but enabling him to be "fairly open", much like Andrew's lack of "axe to grind".

The treatment of white, male, middle-class identity as unmarked and unremarked has been widely noted (see, for example, Ahmed, 2004a; Hearn, 2010; Hunter, 2010; Swan, 2010), and indeed this invisibility is part of the privilege of such identities. But I want to suggest that the persisting ability to think of these identities as 'standard' requires more work in the context of my research than it may otherwise. These interviewees have to resituate themselves as the norm, rather than this position remaining entirely silent. But it does not take *much* work, and it can be a technique of reincorporating reflexivity into the service of existing hierarchies of power as a way of demonstrating knowledge and awareness, and thereby reproducing elite status (Skeggs, 2004).

This position is developed further in Thomas's account below. Thomas is a national figure, who has been involved in public discussions of community cohesion policy since 2001, and is widely seen as an expert in this area of policy. He is also a middle-aged, white, male professional.

> HANNAH: I just wondered if you felt like your own identity, experiences or background affect how you think about these issues?
>
> THOMAS: Er no, not really I mean I suppose.... I was committed to anti-racism at least by the time I was 16, and I grew up through the sixties ... and I only ever wanted to work for organisations that were progressive, that wanted change. In urban environments, where I felt comfortable, really. I suppose ... it's about what you feel comfortable with. I've never had the slightest inclination to think about my own identity, I'm not an introspective person, some people are very introspective ... if I think of myself as being white, it is only because I know that there are black and Asian people there ... and that's why of course most black and Asian people think of themselves as being black and Asian, it's because they're in a white society ... it's not how I see myself, it's how I see myself in relation to others. So I'm a bit anti all of that introspection stuff really.

Thomas's account shifted between theoretical, personal and political registers to account for his understanding of community cohesion and related subjects. Although he began by saying "not really", he then said that his values had informed his career since a young age, and that he had always felt more comfortable in 'urban' and 'progressive' environments. He also talked about identity only being defined in reaction to other categories, and went on to discuss at greater length groups identifying themselves in relation to an out-group or 'other'. Yet, while "black and Asian people" might "think of themselves as being black and Asian because they're in a white society", Thomas did not explore how his being white in a white society enabled him to follow his "inclination" not to think about his identity outside of encounters with "black and Asian people". He said dismissively that "some people are very introspective", but in positioning identity as a question of introspection, he disregarded the power relations that enabled him to do so in the first place.

The ways Andrew, David and Thomas negotiated their own status in relation to community cohesion policy and government in general reveals much about the work done by the ambiguities and silences of community cohesion policy in masking power. Andrew, David and Thomas had been exposed, through professional discourses of the public sector if not elsewhere, to discussions of how gendered, racialised and other categorisations had excluded certain groups from access to power and resources. But they had not taken these understandings further to imagine either how their own inclusion might be part of the process of exclusion, or what they might have *in common* with people who had been excluded in this way.

Marginalisation and double consciousness

> HANNAH: I just wondered if you think that identity, experience, background affect how you, personally, think about cohesion issues?
>
> ANTHONY: Absolutely.
>
> HANNAH: Yeah…. In what way? [*both laugh*]
>
> ANTHONY: Well…. I think anyone from, er, a minority ethnic group has had to think about these issues. I think someone from a mixed heritage background has probably articulated them more, whether that's shouting, [*laughs*] or having discussions over dinner tables about, and dad are you really a negro, or the experience of my sister who was pale and blue eyed and [said], in 1970, yeah I do wanna join a black society. Black civil society. But, why, how, no, you can't! You know. My family has had a long experience of challenging all the issues of ethnicity

and of race and questioning what they mean in different ways, being categorised as absolutely every ethnic group under the sun, so I just think that that's how it has shaped my thinking on it ... the other probably big experience is being in Tower Hamlets and the BNP got elected, and having to figure out ways of articulating many of these issues to friends and also publicly, and the whole thing around race and people saying yes, but there are different races ... and trying to explain to people ... you're wrong. Not true, it doesn't exist.

Whereas Thomas described a lack of inclination to think about his identity, background or experiences as formative influences, this was not a choice Anthony, a policy manager in Hackney, felt was available to him. Anthony's response was in two parts. First, he described how racialised constructions of his and his family's appearance were taken to embody difference in ways sometimes expressly at odds with their choosing. Anthony was not suggesting that *only* people of particular ethnicities had an authentic understanding of the complexities of identity and power. Rather, he was pointing out that for some people, such questions were immediate because they were constantly made visible (see also du Bois, 1994 [1903]).

Although Anthony described his long-standing 'double consciousness', his awareness of the shifting categorisations applied to him and to others throughout his life, he also described a second narrative of when he was moved to another relationship to racialising and differentialising processes – living in East London when a far right racist party first gained an elected position on the local council. This mobilised him not only to negotiate the constructions of himself by others, but to become politically and intellectually active in articulating, in various registers, other ways of deconstructing and understanding racialised imaginaries.

Saida, like Anthony, worked in Hackney. She also accounted for her understanding as related to a situated knowledge and positioning as a minoritised subject. But rather than Anthony's narrative of always having understood identity as challenging, she described a greater comfort in difference and change that came from being accustomed to them, growing up in London. She contrasted this with her experience of temporarily moving to Northampton, a large town in the East Midlands, when she was made aware of the perception of her own difference by others:

HANNAH: I just wondered how you think your own
background and identity and experiences affect how
you think about issues around cohesion? In your work.

SAIDA: I suppose for anyone I think that would be quite
natural, you know you can try and separate yourself
and put your professional hat on and say the things you
need to say ... but, yeah, evidently, my own experiences
form – if I was looking at my personal experiences, me
being born in this country, parents from Bangladesh,
have a Muslim faith, Sunni faith at that, and living in
an area which is changing.... So in that sense yeah, I
suppose your own experiences do shape how you think
of cohesion, for me because I've been brought up in my
own background and then had friends from different
communities you sort of think, oh, it's kind of normal
to be getting along with someone that is black or white
or Chinese, 'cos in my school everyone was so mixed ...
and university was mixed and ... where I work is quite
mixed so it was quite normal but trying to get work in
Northampton was a very different experience ... 'cos I
was seen different. So ... you think, why is it, I mean I'm
same person, nothing's changed, so why's it so difficult
for me to get work in Northampton? So, yeah. There is
that and, in that sense you can start viewing and thinking,
you start looking for justifications as to why things are
the way they are, and you try and put things together. I
suppose in [my work] that's quite important as well ...
so yeah, that's one of the things I think about.

Saida's account of her experience of growing up in multicultural
London places her both as *particular* ("born in this country, parents from
Bangladesh, Muslim faith, Sunni faith at that") and comfortable in a
shared sense of difference ("it's kind of normal"). But when she tried
to find work in a different city, the identities she was already aware of
living became visible in a different way; she was differently marked.
From Saida's other brief comments on this in the interview, she felt that
the problem was not necessarily that there were no Muslim/Sunni/
Bangladeshi heritage people in Northampton (making her the first to
present her visible difference in this way), but that attitudes to 'difference'
there were much more hostile than she was used to. It seemed she had
experienced so much discrimination in seeking employment that she
had returned to London to work, at some cost to her household and

family arrangements. Yet the way Saida described this having an impact on her work was not as a claim to an authentic identity politics, or explicitly as a commitment to oppositional anti-racism. Rather, she related her experience and her reactions to contexts in which others (her service users) might have had similar experiences and how she might empathise with them. She used her double consciousness – her awareness of others' perceptions of her and how they differed to her own – as a tool for governing others through her professional role.

Nadia, a London councillor, described how she perceived that her role as an elected member had been influenced by her structural positioning. She focused more directly on how she felt her marked identity had had a direct influence on her career path than Anthony and Saida, whose accounts were more focused on how their everyday lives and understandings had been formed.

> NADIA: But I think it also pushed me into a role where ...
> you know, there's not that many young Asian women that
> were coming into politics ... for me personally, I think
> it's put me into a position where I don't think my – the
> work that I've had to take on as a local councillor is very
> different to, you know, other ... you know, anyone else
> that may have come in at the same time as me, elsewhere.
> You know I don't think they would have been thrown
> in, in the same way.

Nadia had been appointed to a cabinet role relatively soon after being elected to the council, a role with a particular responsibility for community cohesion issues. The implication of her words here is that her status as one of the relatively few 'young Asian women' in politics had meant she was more visible, not only for promotion but potentially also as a voice seen to speak with 'authenticity' about community cohesion and related issues. The structures of power and visibility are such that Nadia not only recognised how she was positioned by others as specifically young, Asian and female; she also felt she was required to embody that identity as a form of authenticity, not only for herself, but for her political colleagues, to give residents and voters confidence in the local authority's representation and understanding of local residents. Her embodiment of this identity was made visible to her in connection with her professional position in a way that it was not visible to many of the white interviewees I spoke with (see also Puwar, 2001, 2004; Ahmed, 2007a; Hunter, 2010; Swan, 2010). Even though many white interviewees commented on their privileged status in terms of their ability or perceived ability to speak for diverse communities, not one suggested that their whiteness had any bearing on why or how they came to be in their current professional position.

Moving margins

> HANNAH: ... whether you think your own kind of background and identity affect how you think about those issues?
>
> EMMA: Yeah. I think being Irish and coming over here in the late eighties....Yeah, I think [*both laugh*] absolutely! And sitting on the number 36 bus outside Victoria station when a bomb went off, yes, there's a lot in your background makes you think about that.... So yes definitely, definitely. And in terms of working for local government ... that's actually very difficult, because the whole culture of the organisation is that you need to repress that view and you need to be totally objective but you can't be. You can't be, you've gotta temper the worst of your instincts and my instincts sometimes are just to completely rant at people, but you modify your behaviour. But no, your background is definitely, definitely a strong influence.

Emma, a senior local authority officer in Hackney, felt that in some ways a marked identity (as a 'potential terrorist') she might have once shared with Nadia had now been erased; yet she still retained the double consciousness of one who had been marked out as different by the gaze of others. She was aware of her privileged position as a policy practitioner expressly because of her previously (more) marked identity as an outsider, and perhaps had a feeling that her now more secure position within 'the establishment' presented the opportunity, whether she took it or not, to pass as an insider.

The moves Emma could make were determined by how she was positioned in social space. Emma explained that her history as a migrant from Ireland to London at the time of sectarian and nationalistic violence had influenced her understanding of being minoritised, demonised and vulnerable. Elsewhere in the interview she gave a specific example of this influencing her work, when she had explained "to this ex-intelligence officer from you know, MI whatever, who was working in the Home Office" that she would have been the target of their work 20 years ago, "you know, demonising Irish people whereas now it's Muslim. Who's next?" Describing how the 'demonisation' had moved on from Irish people to another group, Emma suggested she could now no longer pass as a threat, but still felt a responsibility to speak up as an 'othered' subject (see also Nickels et al, 2009).

Yet this speaking out was the 'rant' that she felt the need to 'monitor', in order to be 'objective'. Feeling completely embedded in her own histories, believing that "you need to be totally objective *but you can't be*" for Emma meant doing work on herself to "repress" her instincts to recognise resonances with her own life. In the same sentence in which she asserted the need for objectivity, Emma recognised its impossibility. Her professional commitment to strive towards an (impossible) impartiality came into conflict with her knowledge of this impossibility, and was held in tension as she tried to understand this as a question of working on herself ("temper the worst of your instincts"). This was the work of being a public servant, balancing public goods and individual need, balancing one's own personal, political and ethical commitments with organisational and democratically agreed priorities. Being able to manage these balancing acts was an essential skill for working in such environments, but was under-acknowledged and under-explored, perhaps because of some of the unsettled positions that might emerge (see Bonnett, 1993, p 79; Hunter, 2005; Keith, 2008b; Mayo et al, 2007).

Evan, another senior manager in Hackney, also described his understanding of community cohesion as tied up with his own subjectivity, which he narrated as at once giving him insights into the experience of difference and discrimination, and in other ways apparently disqualifying him from authoritative insights. Evan drew on biographical elements throughout our conversation, well before I asked him directly about his background, identity and experiences:

> Evan: I think it's also difficult because a lot of the people involved particularly for example in Muslim communities, younger people born here, the values are potentially very different from kind of general, liberal values that the society in Britain supposedly has. And I think it's because these haven't really been clearly set out, I think the assumption is that everybody has the same values, just rub along. From a Hackney point of view, I've lived in Hackney 30 years. And I think it is an amazing place, culturally speaking. I mean I'm a gay man. So I have that perspective on it. And I just think it's incredible that you go to Springfield Park on a Sunday afternoon,

and you see all these different communities using cultural space and as I say, rubbing along, it is impressive.

Here (in a much longer response to my question "What [do] you think about when you think about cohesion policy? How would you describe it?") Evan moved on to the subject of 'values', and how to manage perceived differences in values between 'communities'. In this context, he gave the example of Muslim communities as a potential threat to "general, liberal values that Britain supposedly has". Evan seemed to sense that this was a potentially contentious subject, and immediately reasserted both Hackney's exceptionalism as a place where people did "rub along" easily, and also his own minoritised status as "a gay man". By emphasising both his sexual identity and his personal commitment to and knowledge of Hackney as a multicultural space ("I've lived in Hackney 30 years"), Evan attempted to negotiate a safe space from which to talk about difficult aspects of diversity.

This position is not unproblematic, not least because it hints at what has been described as 'homonationalism' (Puar, 2007, p 39) or 'gay imperialism' where an 'artificially constructed gay v. Muslim divide, to contest sexual oppression in Muslim communities' means that 'homophobia is constructed as belonging to Islam', and that non-Muslim (implicitly white, Western Christian or secular) society is by implication exempt from confronting its own homophobia (Haritaworn et al, 2008, p 83). This resonates with a trend identified in narratives throughout this research, where understanding of local complexity (in this case, experiences of homophobia) are positioned against assumptions of simplified elsewhere or others (in this case, religious mores). Yet Evan appeared to be aware of the risk of projecting one form of prejudice onto another out-group, first noting that "Britain" only "supposedly" has "general, liberal values" of tolerance, and second, emphasising later that his wariness was more directed at the potential of *all* religion to discriminate against gay men and lesbians:

> HANNAH: My last question to everyone is whether you think that your particular background or identity affects how you think about cohesion?
>
> EVAN: Yes it does. It does. I mean the bit that, being gay, obviously, one is aware of, if you like, homophobic tendencies in other communities, particularly religious communities, and I'm not just talking about Judaism and Islam, I'm talking about Christianity as well … community leaders need to not just take the easy option,

talk about communities that are visible … the lesbian community in Hackney, and the gay community has had a really strong influence in the way Hackney's developed over the last 30 years. And has helped to contribute to that openness and tolerance if you like, and what I'd hate to see, is that aspect of diversity being shut down to pacify certain other communities or parts of other communities, now it's not a blanket thing for me, I don't make assumptions that people are gonna be homophobic, but one is aware that certain fundamentalists do have particular views in all religious communities, and that makes me a bit nervous.

Again, it was 'being gay' that Evan identified as making him most aware of discrimination, and that he identified as emanating from elements of potentially all religious groups. Evan earlier mobilised his sexual identity (alongside his personal commitment to the locality) as a resource to demonstrate a particular form of sameness in difference from which it was possible to speak about conflict and diversity. In the second extract, 'being gay' was addressed more directly as a position in which he might be the target of discrimination, and that informed his work on community cohesion by making him aware of the potential conflicts between the interests of different groups, but also of the subtleties of such conflict, which make assumptions on the basis of group membership unreliable.

This complexity is illustrated further in a final extract from the interview with Evan:

> EVAN: I'm aware of the irony of me as a white middle class, pretty well-off person saying that, it's almost like saying you shouldn't encourage everybody to live well, but I do think one of the things about Hackney is that … it's provided an environment for people to experiment and to mix and to develop different ways of relating, which I think is quite difficult to do in a society that's more solid. More fixed, in a way. So it's the fluidity. It is tiring, and it is difficult, and there are times I think as one gets older, I think that probably one wants that kind of fixedness, but certainly for younger people in Hackney I think it's a fantastic environment, because you've got all those different influences.

In this part of the interview, Evan was reflecting on his privileged position in terms of race and class that enabled him to opt in and out of being part of Hackney. His awareness of 'the irony' of celebrating the difficulties of life in Hackney as the grounds on which tolerance and mixing are built was that he did not have to confront many of these difficulties in his daily life, or could choose not to (particularly as he got older) where others could not (Bell and Binnie, 2000, p 105; Reay et al, 2007). This did not negate the fact that in other contexts and moments, other aspects of Evan's identity could lead to him being threatened and marginalised in ways that were harder to avoid.

Choosing the margins?

Some interviewees were even more explicit about how they moved in and out of 'marginality' (hooks, 1990), selecting parts of their identity or biography to represent an association with difference. Glen, a senior officer in Oldham, laughed when I asked him how he thought his own identity or background might affect how he thought about community cohesion issues, and said, "a week ago I would have answered that a bit differently". In the past week he had discovered ancestors who had been "very active on interethnic and interfaith issues" in previous centuries, "a strong tradition of serving the community and work in public service" in his family, which he now thought was "part of the reason why I've ended up in this job" because of "values that have come down through my parents and my family". I asked what he thought his answer might have been before he knew this history, and he said "the bit about values would have been the same" but now he had "the feeling that what I'm doing fit[s] so well with what some of my forebears did". Unlike Donald, who (earlier in this chapter) explained the connections between his religious inheritance and political beliefs as coincidence, Glen chose to present his ancestry as a backdated explanation of his values.

Phil, who had a very similar senior local authority role to Glen but in Barking and Dagenham, was also in the process of researching his family tree, and related this to the way he thought about community cohesion. The question I actually asked Phil was "How do you feel your own life experience affects how you think about these issues?", and he replied that, "it affects me totally" and explained that he grew up in London. But this was only mentioned very briefly before he began to discuss his current research into his family, which included migration histories on both his mother and father's sides, taking in India, Poland and Russia, and intertwined with histories of British colonialism and

European anti-semitism: "so it's those experiences of being displaced, being in a place where you're not necessarily part of the accepted community has very much shaped my identity and upbringing". Phil had already known about his diasporic family history, but was trying to find more information about the details and to trace earlier generations.

Both Glen and Phil suggested that their genealogies had formed their attitudes to cohesion and related issues through the perspectives imparted to them by their parents – in Glen's case, values of serving the community; in Phil's, a sense of being out of place and sensitive to difference and inequality. Yet they both reinforced their claims to these perspectives by reference to their ancestry. They presented their bonds of inherited identity as if these would be more authentic claims to understanding questions of marginality than their own observations or embodied experiences. Yet drawing on their genealogies was a choice; neither Glen nor Phil's historic identifications were marked as visible to others. Their family trees were drawn on as a tool to negotiate entry to the ranks of the authentically marginal.

Ellen, a local authority officer in Hackney, described a different relationship to her family history when I asked whether her background affected how she thought about cohesion:

> ELLEN: No. I don't think so…. Other than that maybe I've taken a direct path away from perhaps the values of my parents and grandparents. I think it is a generational thing and I think if you spoke to my parents they might talk about people using different words than I would certainly use … that's how it was then…. But one of the reasons I left Essex was…. I had a 360 degree feedback and the only criticism of my performance was about a lack of understanding of other communities. And that's because I lived, worked in a white middle-class area, you never saw somebody that wasn't white, you didn't see many people who were poor people, quite frankly. And that was one of the reasons I took a definite decision to come to somewhere like Hackney where I knew it would be very different, and that's one of the reasons I really like Hackney.

An important contrast here with the work being done by Phil and Glen to situate themselves as marginal in their accounts was that they suggested this positioning was secure and authentic because of its inheritance from their families; they did not express it as a choice.

Ellen, on the other hand, made a claim to an affinity with marginality precisely because she had made an active choice.

A joint interview with Karen and Angela in Hackney brought into sharper focus the questions of choosing, who gets to choose and what the consequences of choosing 'the margin' were. Both worked for the local authority; Angela was Karen's manager.

> KAREN: I think Hackney schools are a fantastic example of cohesion. When it works well, you have got a classroom of 30 pupils from real diverse backgrounds and certainly my own children, having been brought up in Hackney, had just such great experiences of primary education, they met children from a vast range of cultures, and there were tensions and differences, but things were worked through.
>
> ANGELA: But I think with that, having [been] someone who's been kind of born and brought up here, and been in school what is quite telling is that within the school environment those relationships tend to be good, I think the measure is if you were doing a longitudinal study, if you go back 10, 20 years after people have gone through the schooling system are they still in close relationships with people from other communities?
>
> HANNAH: Yeah....
>
> KAREN: Mm.
>
> ANGELA: And very often ... they're not [*all laugh*] erm.
>
> KAREN: Yeah.... I think it would be really interesting to do the sort of thing that Angela talks about, taking the temperature now, and then looking forward, because I remember reading an interview with Doreen Lawrence, and she was saying the boys who attacked and killed Stephen were brought up in this multicultural area, so what's going wrong? And I remember that really struck me, that my own experience is a really positive one, and you like to think that other people have the same openness, but we know there are both extreme groups but also extreme opinions.

This interchange is inflected not just by the class privilege involved in Karen's choice to send her children to local schools as a middle-class mother able to provide cultural capital to support their educational success while providing them with the 'multicultural capital' of familiarity with diversity (see Skeggs, 2005a, p 971; Crozier et al, 2008; Reay, 2008). Karen is white and Angela is black, and their speaking positions are also refracted through this aspect of their structural positioning. This is highlighted when Karen reacts to Angela's comments about different experiences of schooling by talking about an instance where it "really struck" her that her own positive experience might be particular, relating her thoughts about the history of the racist murder of Stephen Lawrence (see Chapter Two, this volume). Thus Karen acknowledged, after the indirect prompting from Angela, that both her whiteness and her class position[1] were particular, and perhaps did not give her the authentically and authoritatively marginal position she first claimed.

"Cohesion's for everybody"

> ANGELA: And so I think what the cohesion agenda does is allow people to park their differences for however long they want to park them with a view to the common good, 'cos this is about the value benefit for everybody whereas when you talk about social inclusion you can opt out of that, you can say well actually they're the ones who need to be included and I'm fine ... so it's not about me, it's about them. And when you talk about multiculturalism again it's another issue, it's about 'them', whereas the benefit around community cohesion is that of all of the agendas it's the most inclusive 'cos everybody has a personal stake in it.

For some practitioners, community cohesion policy offered the possibility of at once acknowledging difference and inequality, and removing the need to talk about it altogether. Angela, who I also quoted above in the joint interview with Karen, argued that the opportunity to put differences (or difficult subjects) to one side and instead focus on commonality was an advantage of the concept of community cohesion policy. She suggested that discussions of community around social inclusion or multiculturalism had become too associated with 'otherness', and that she saw an opportunity for community cohesion policy to be interpreted as being about 'the common good'. There had, of course, been attempts to promote both social inclusion and multiculturalism as universally inclusive as well as critiques of them for reverting to a focus on a reified 'other' – a critique that has equally been made elsewhere to applications of community cohesion (see Chapter

Two). Angela said that community cohesion did not let anyone off the hook, because it was about inclusive community, about everyone – including those who might otherwise be seen as unproblematic. But it was not clear from Angela's statement what she then imagined 'the cohesion agenda' to be, what it aimed to achieve. If it was to "allow people to park their differences" to come together (temporarily) for the 'common good', what becomes of the 'common good' when those differences are picked up again?

Ruth, who worked on policy issues in Hackney, presented a related analysis of the workings of community cohesion rhetoric – but she was more sceptical about its progressive potential. Considering the extent to which the language of 'community cohesion' might be a way of avoiding talking directly about questions of class or of race, she said:

> RUTH: It's more comfortable, if you're a white middle-class person, talking about cohesion … because it's about people getting on, whereas if you're that same person, talking about race equality and race justice, it's much more obvious that you're not on the receiving end of injustice and race hate and all those sorts of things, so your position, your ability to talk about those issues, is [*pause*] questionable.… I used to think that also with human rights, a little bit … human rights [representation at meetings] was often white middle-class people. And it's 'cos it's an arbitrating concept about reconciling the competing interests … there's something about it which is a little bit neutral, it's not about a struggle, or it should be, but it's not … whereas I think issues around specific equality, and injustice, is much more toothy and political … these kind of cross-cutting discourses … everybody together, all citizens, they kind of neutralise that, they kind of slightly cover up the kind of real injustice that people face. Every day.
>
> HANNAH: Yeah. And you think that's also easy for some people to talk about?
>
> RUTH: Yeah, it's easier for me to talk about.
>
> HANNAH: Yeah. [*both laugh*]
>
> RUTH: … people don't say who are you to talk about cohesion, 'cos cohesion's for everybody, you know … whereas if I was to stand up and start saying, I'm doing strategy on race equality … I don't think that would be quite such a comfortable position to be in.

Ruth described how the apparent neutrality of concepts such as community cohesion and human rights, which are about "everybody together" "cover up the kind of real injustice that people face". She, personally, found it "easier to talk about" community cohesion because this vocabulary did not require her to expose her own privilege as a "white middle-class person". Unlike Angela, Ruth didn't seem to be saying that this neutrality or comfort was a good thing; she was expressing concern that "injustice that people face every day" might be neglected. Ruth also suggested that not being "on the receiving end of injustice" might make one's ability to talk about those things "questionable". Here she reverted to an idea of the politics of authenticity that suggested that for her to challenge injustice as a privileged subject would be not only uncomfortable, but also impossible. Yet in this conversation, Ruth was putting herself back into an uncomfortable position by acknowledging not only her race and class privilege, but that even her professional work intended to address this privilege was embedded in, and reinforced, existing structures. It *is* possible to experience a disjuncture of belonging even when objectively privileged (Christie, 2006; Puwar, 2004, p 131).

Rachel, who we met in the Introduction to this book and who worked as a senior service manager in Hackney, took a position that was almost a mirror image of Ruth's. Ruth saw herself as embedded in structures of inequality and in that respect as part of the problem, and yet (and therefore) able to hide behind structures of invisibility. Rachel, on the other hand, described her home and family life as embedded in an almost 'picture perfect' narrative of urban multiculture – and yet instinctively separated this from her work within the paradigms of community cohesion and social care.

> HANNAH: Do you think your background or identity affects how you think about cohesion?
> RACHEL: God it must do. It must do! I suppose I think that it's not really about me, you know that it's something other ... we talk about communities ... I probably think about ethnic minority communities, and people who are poor.... And it's something other, to me ... something that I watch rather than partake. Although actually, that's just so not true, I mean for me personally.

Even when she surprised herself by reflecting on how her own life – in a religiously and ethnically mixed area, with her mixed race children with her female partner, where neighbours respected one another's difference and looked out for one another's welfare – could fit into narratives of community cohesion as a subject of policy, Rachel insisted that not just her class but her specific *professional* status marked her out (or rather, made her invisible) as not a subject but as a practitioner of policy:

> RACHEL: And I suppose it's different for people that are in professional worlds because so much of my work is about … very very vulnerable, very poor, high risk group of people … not that it's an attractive attribute, but it's seeing them as something other.

Rachel did, on reflection, point to ways in which her home life had become visible in relation to policy and issues of difference, belonging and inequality. She felt uncomfortable acknowledging this privilege (and with it facing up to her role in actively governing the selves of others). But she also said that in everyday practice, her home life seemed like a completely different – or invisible – realm. This is different, of course, to saying that her personal identity and experiences did not influence her practice. The point is that the technology of community cohesion policy suggests it is relevant to everybody, but does not trouble the power relations of governing that led Rachel to see herself instinctively as set apart from populations to be governed.

"Think about it on a human level"

Yet it was not only interviewees relating experiences of direct discrimination against themselves who expressed personal and emotional commitments to an understanding of context-laden complexity and power struggle. My final two examples here are Erin, a service manager in Peterborough, and Sally, a voluntary sector manager in Hackney. Both talked about experiences that informed their commitments and ethics, drawn from their observations in both their work and their personal lives, which became intertwined:

> HANNAH: … whether you think your own identity and background affect how you think about cohesion?
>
> ERIN: [*dramatic intake of breath*] That's a good one! Yeah, my father was a big trade unionist and … you know that famous poem, first they came for the Jews [*coughs*] he used to carry that everywhere on him, if you don't look out for your neighbour, how can you expect them to look out for you when you're in trouble, and ultimately when,

trouble is there's nobody there.... But he always said you question everything that you read and everything that you hear and everything that you see.... So yes, my background, I've been very fortunate. Very fortunate to have been brought up with that ... and when I was very young, well a teenager, I saw a black guy being beat up in the street by two white guys. And he was a friend of mine. You know you see that as a youngster, you don't forget it really. For no reason.

Erin here described formative political influences of growing up in a household with a commitment to an ethic of social solidarity, which she credited with forming her political attitudes and providing her with an instinct to question received wisdom. When she said she had been "very fortunate" with regard to her background, she seemed to be referring to this political outlook. Erin then described witnessing a racist attack on a friend. Her account suggested that this was a formative moment in her understanding of power relations in society, although she did not elaborate on this as we were interrupted at that point by a telephone call. The attack on Erin's friend was inexplicable – "for no reason" – yet it happened, and she could see it was motivated by racism. Although Erin was not the subject of the attack, and she did not assume the position of victim or target of racism, she clearly felt the shock of this event strongly ("you see that as a youngster, you don't forget it really").

Erin went on to describe other incidents, this time in her working life, which had brought into focus for her the discrimination and violence faced by marginalised people, and which she herself felt as emotional, if not physical, pain. When she was working with asylum seekers:

> ERIN: I just was amazed about how badly they were treated, and the services that were turning them away, without even asking them, 'cos they didn't speak English, telling them that they couldn't help them when they were entitled to things, and I'd sit and they'd lift up their shirts some of them and show me their torture.... One of them had a diary that they'd drawn the pictures of their journey here and they all had photos of their families in their wallet and it was just heartbreak – and then you'd phone up somebody and they'd say well I'm not prepared to talk to them unless they bring somebody that speaks

Eng ... you know, it was just like, do you realise, this person's been, you know....

This extract captures Erin's shock and outrage, as well as her "heartbreak" and disbelief at the lack of empathy of service providers who would not see her clients. Similarly, at another point when she had been working with unemployed young people, Erin had been struck by the racism they faced when unable to get a job interview simply as a result of their "foreign-sounding" names, and she had resorted to arranging interviews for them using false "English" names: "I'm sat with people who didn't stand a chance. Just by nature of their name." Given Erin's description of her upbringing which taught her to "look out for your neighbour", it seems that these attacks on and humiliations of people she cared for were also felt as attacks on herself. Yet she did not make an identity claim to the margin, to belong to an essentialised category herself. Nor did she claim to know what these experiences felt like for those directly under attack. Rather, having "sat with people who didn't stand a chance", Erin joined them in solidarity.

Sally, similarly, described an upbringing with politically involved parents, her "dad had a kind of burning commitment to socialism – democratic socialism of course!" and both parents were very committed to education, which she connected to the "left-ish" political commitments she and her siblings had in adult life. But again, like Erin, Sally explained this ethical and political commitment as a background that she connected with concrete experiences in her life, although they might not have been experiences that had a direct impact on her:

> SALLY: This goes for my husband as well, most of the rest of our families are working class. And so we're still in touch with working-class roots that a lot of people in our position – Labour Party people – are not in touch with, and I think gives me a totally different perspective.... The fact that three members of [our] family, when the minimum wage was introduced, received increases of 50 per cent in what they earned. And so people say oh, the minimum wage, what does that mean, that's what it means. The money that's gone into schools and health service, what has that meant? Because I think if you're middle class and London-based, you get a very different picture ... it also means that when I talk to family members who are openly racist I'm able to say, You may say, people come over here from Africa and they

> get everything but there are people living across from
> where I work, N families to a flat, women who've been
> deserted by the fathers of their children, who've brought
> them over here, who find themselves in a very difficult
> situation 'cos they don't have any legal status here any
> more and, etc, etc. Just think about that. Just think about
> what you'd be like in those circumstances....Think about
> it on a human level.

Sally described two instances in which witnessing the struggles and
triumphs of others (who were less privileged than her) gave her a
perspective from which she spoke, not necessarily on their behalf,
but with a knowledge that challenged people who were otherwise
close to her position – whether "middle class and London-based" or
"family members". Although it is a difficult and uncomfortable line
to walk, I don't think that either Erin or Sally were taking the role
of 'the institutional interlocutor who frames the self of the subaltern'
(Skeggs, 2004, p 126; see also Spivak, 1988). Rather, they used their
own experiences of coming into contact with others as a resource for
understanding social reality. In this they recognised implicitly their
(race and class) privilege but also chose to ally themselves with others
who were under direct attack from this privilege. Indeed, as Skeggs
points out, 'narrativization of one's experience is a resource; some are
unable to present themselves as the subject of narrative' (2004, p 126)
– yet this does not necessarily mean that the most progressive course
of action for those who *do* have a voice is to relinquish it. Rather, like
Erin and Sally seem to be (giving an account of) doing here, they could
also try to find ways of putting this reflexivity to use in the service of
addressing power inequalities (Skeggs, 2002, p 369).

Conclusions

Interviewees whose accounts showed the most potential for developing
an approach to difference that neither reified nor ignored constructed
identity categories and power differentials were those whose accounts
suggested a sociological imagination, that is to say, 'the capacity to shift
from one perspective to another ... to range from the most impersonal
and remote transformation to the most intimate features of the human
self – and to see the relations between the two' (Mills, 1999 [1959],
p 7). Hunter argues that 'failure to reach resolution can be read as a
strength, rather than a weakness' (2010, p 469) when contemplating
such encounters. There is a parallel here with Sara Ahmed's celebration

of the 'killjoy feminist' as the rupturer of consensus, the voice that draws attention to the oppressive or objectionable contents of a conversation or practice and is thereby seen as a negative presence herself (2010, p 582). Ahmed also argues that opening up, and keeping open, areas of vulnerability or 'sore points' is a progressive move (Ahmed, 2010, p 591).

For some, the awareness of one's own privileged status is present, but can have a paralysing effect. Srivastava, in her examination of the possibilities for anti-racist feminism, argues that a predominant strain of anti-racist feminism has become focused on the production of a virtuous anti-racist self. This results in dilemmas about how to present oneself as a white anti-racist feminist:

> If she were to say with complete ease "I am racist" … she risks criticisms that she is complacent or glib about racism. If she were to outright deny being racist, she knows she would be stuck in an unacceptable ethical position. (2005, p 53)

Srivastava argues that this dilemma, and the preoccupation with the creation and presentation of an ethical self, becomes an obstacle to institutional progress towards anti-racist goals. She suggests that a more productive approach would be to upset the apparent certainties of a dichotomous choice of 'innocence versus evil, knowledge versus ignorance' (p 58) and instead recognise the possibility of a less settled position, 'more interested in why antiracist change is not happening and less interested in her own moral acceptability' – while still acknowledging that 'individual preoccupations … may impede that work' (p 57). This potentially uncomfortable position, between acknowledging a situated, limited and compromised standpoint, and trying to move beyond this acknowledgement to intervention, is one I found many research participants to be experiencing (see also Mayo et al, 2007; Keith, 2008b). Processes of governmentality encourage policy practitioners to behave (and feel) in appropriate ways in their professional, as well as personal, lives. The continual pull to be 'neutral' or to have a fixed, correct position mitigates against attempts to retain ambiguity and 'sore points' or uncomfortable positions, which might involve stepping into the margins or challenging the power inequalities that underlie marginalisation.

SEVEN

Thinking inside the box

Introduction

In this final chapter I draw together four key arguments of the book. First, community cohesion policy, as I have demonstrated, is concerned with *enabling citizens to behave in appropriate ways* (which entails, of course, the unspoken question of who determines what is appropriate). Importantly, for the perspective of this study, governing through governmentality is a practice and a process itself. It involves individuals taking decisions within regimes of power and truth. Those regimes help to form individual selves; individuals are able to amend regimes through their actions to differing extents; and they are also (made to feel) responsible for these regimes of truth and what changes they make or do not make within them.

Second, community cohesion policy easily slips into a language of 'celebrating diversity' without necessarily considering *why* some types of difference are seen as important while others are not, and what power relations lie behind (and result from) that. This can have the effect of assuming that 'diversity' is banal, unproblematic and shared – without addressing inequalities and discrimination. This research was conducted in a period of structural, political, economic and social change and multiple, unpredictable shifts in the ways that government and individuals considered 'community', 'cohesion', 'belonging', 'identity' and 'inequality'. Discussions of these subjects at the beginning of the 21st century often cite changing technology and the consequent ease of global travel, communication and commerce as challenging long-standing (senses of) locally rooted communities (see, for example, MacKinnon et al, 2011). As we have seen, such developments, most especially international migration, were very relevant to the ways that the policy practitioners I interviewed constructed narratives about the need for and achievement of community cohesion. Yet there is a more specific question, I think, about the development of 'super-diversity' in populations. It is a question about what types of 'difference' are made visible – most often, as we have seen, connected to race, ethnicity and religion – and what types of 'difference' remain invisible or are silenced. My focus has been on the processes whereby forms of difference are created or silenced in the narratives of policy practitioners. When difference or diversity is identified (whether to be regarded with suspicion or celebration) without attention to power relations, this complicates 'community cohesion' further. Equally, recognising that differential power relations exist and that one is implicated in them can be uncomfortable for policy practitioners – particularly where, despite their professional positions, they lack the means to address underlying structural inequalities.

The third point I develop in this conclusion is how the role of local government is imagined by those narratives and voices that we have encountered throughout the book. Here I open the discussion further to consider how this is seen as both changing and staying the same through a variety of successive 'policy agendas' from shifting national government administrations. As this research reached its conclusion, it seemed the 'community cohesion' era in the UK may be coming to an end – perhaps to be replaced by David Cameron's 'Big Society' as a goal. The concepts are similarly slippery and capable of being recast in different moulds. The policy practitioners I interviewed (before the election of the Coalition government in 2010) anticipated change as a result of the global financial crisis and an expected new government (and reflected on change as a perennial process even with the same party in power). The question that concerned them was how, situated in their local area and in their professional roles, they would find ways to deliver the goals that they connected to community cohesion (or opposed to it) within whatever might come next.

Finally, I conclude by considering briefly where we might be taken by using C. Wright Mills' lens of the sociological imagination and accepting that changing the world might involve some uncomfortable positions – positions that might depart from imagining academia or academic research as separate from 'the real world'. And I build on Mills' treatment of the sociological imagination by paying greater attention to the emotional and affective elements of imagination and the links that an emotional lens can either enable or obscure between the intimate and the global (see also Back, 2007b). The role of participant observer that I took in approaching this research has drawn out narratives that rely on emotional commitments to ideas, ideals, places and processes of governing. Recognising the role of emotion in governing belonging, identity and inequality is essential because power relations are experienced through emotional, embodied registers. That I have conducted this research as at once a social researcher and a policy practitioner has helped me to analyse the similarities and discontinuities between the two roles. It has also produced a precarious line to negotiate, as does any experience of participant observation, maintaining both intimacy with the research field and enough detachment to produce informed analysis. Including an analysis of the role of emotion in governing could be subjected to parallel criticisms, that emotional responses risk obscuring material inequalities. I agree that this is a risk, and throughout this chapter I reflect on a number of moments when this elision can be seen within negotiations of community cohesion policy. But I conclude that such risks, while serious, should not prevent us from attempting to find ways of practising public sociology that intervene in society – and in doing so, it is important to recognise how affective commitments interact with structural power relations, sometimes in unexpected or contradictory ways.

'Building people'

A research participant and former colleague who works on cohesion policy tells me she has something for me that I might find interesting, something she picked up at a recent training event about community cohesion. She hands me a small tin, 6 × 6 × 2 cm. It doesn't weigh very much, and it has a hinged lid, like something that might contain mints. But the lid shows a government crest and the words 'Government Office for London'. Underneath that, in block capitals, it asks 'What is community cohesion?'. Perhaps the answer is inside the box.

I open the box and am presented, not with mints, but with a USB stick displaying the same logo and the same question. It is held within protective foam like a piece of jewellery might be. It invites me to discover the answer to its question, by plugging it into my computer to see what happens. Will I find out the answer to this question?

What I find is a film lasting six-and-a-half minutes. It begins with a statement from Hazel Blears MP, Secretary of State for CLG at the time, with responsibility for community cohesion. She stands in a computer-generated landscape with a silhouette of the London skyline in the background. Between Blears and the horizon there is a screen-within-a-screen, on which play images of (I suppose) community cohesion. Blears explains what she thinks community cohesion means and why she thinks it is important:

"Community cohesion's really important to me in the work that I do in the Department, because it's really about bringing people together, whatever their age, their 'race', their religion, and trying to really build on the shared values that people have, rather than concentrating on the differences between people. Everybody knows, if they live in a place where they feel comfortable, they feel at home, they know their neighbours, they feel that they share very much the same values as the people around them, but at the same time being able to celebrate the things that make them unique and different, and I think that community cohesion, particularly in a time of great change, is something that's really precious to us, and absolutely essential to building the kind of communities that we all want to see." (from the film 'What is Community Cohesion?', a Bold Creative production for GOL)

We then hear what seem to be extracts from interviews with local authority workers, talking about what community cohesion means to them. Unlike Blears, who appeared as herself, the visual accompaniments to these voices are two-dimensional cartoon figures (see Figures 7.1 and 7.3). There are six of these avatars in the film (although there appear to be at least 10 different voices), and they seem to represent 'diversity' in cartoon form. In order of appearance, there is an 'Asian man' in smart-casual shirt and trousers; a 'white woman' in a business suit and glasses with her hair pulled back severely; a 'young (Asian?) Muslim woman' in a hijab and jeans; another 'white woman' in jeans and t-shirt; an 'African-Caribbean woman' wearing sandals and carrying a shopping bag; and a stocky 'white man' in shorts, t-shirt, sunglasses, a hat and a high visibility jacket. They hold up cards with various words extracted from the voiceover, in the style of the Bob Dylan video to 'Subterranean Homesick Blues' (see Figure 7.1). The cards say:

Building people; Relationships; Shared understanding; Shared belonging; YOUNG OLD (and then a line is drawn between 'YOUNG' and 'OLD' saying 'understanding and dialogue'); Get to know each other; Three major stakeholders; Your ethnicity and my ethnicity living in harmony; We; Are; ALL; Stakeholders; Police; Health; Housing; Perception of services; Your community; Different understanding; Appropriate language; that's the language they talk; Services; No one understands me; Community cohesion is…; Love; Respect; Understanding.

In between the sign saying 'No one understands me' and the one saying 'Community cohesion is …', the woman in a suit holds a card with a schematic female figure who in turn holds a placard reading 'I am responsible'; then in the rest of the placard four more stick figures (two male and two female) appear, holding a sign saying 'So are we' (see Figure 7.2).

**Figure 7.1: Still from the film 'What is Community Cohesion?',
a Bold Creative project commissioned by GOL (available at
http://vimeo.com/2981426)**

**Figure 7.2: Still from the film 'What is Community Cohesion?',
a Bold Creative project commissioned by GOL (available at
http://vimeo.com/2981426)**

Over these visuals, a woman's voice explains: "It's not the responsibility of someone sitting in the centre, it's the responsibility of everybody who delivers services and also all residents as well." The last thing we hear is a man saying: "If we spend time trying to understand people and deliver the services that they want, then what we will find is that we will get the cohesion that we're looking for. Because it's about relationships." Then the music plays out to an image of the six avatars standing together holding blank pieces of paper (see Figure 7.3). Perhaps now it is over to you, the viewer to fill them in? Or is this the answer to 'What is community cohesion?'

**Figure 7.3: Still from the film 'What is Community Cohesion?',
a Bold Creative project commissioned by GOL (available at
http://vimeo.com/2981426)**

If we treat this film as a text in itself, there is ample material to analyse its construction of community cohesion as a 'thing' that can be defined (without actually providing any clear definition anywhere in the text). As I explored in Chapter Two, there are multiple narratives, meanings and resonances of community cohesion. This applies whether conceptualising 'community cohesion' as an observable state of populations, as a goal to be achieved or worked towards or as a set of policy proposals and techniques. The voices in the film seem to be discussing techniques designed to achieve community cohesion, *and* the observable state of community cohesion; these two senses of the term overlap as they do in many such discussions. However, very few of the narratives that I drew out in Chapter Two from more traditional policy documents and discourses appear explicitly in this film. There is no reference to 'tension', 'riots', 'violence'; there is no discussion of 'discrimination', 'equality' or 'extremism'; there is no mention of the specificity of local place. There is very limited reference to migration – the only specific example of what cohesion might mean at the level of interaction is a statement that "for some people community cohesion is about different ethnicities and how they get on together. A group that people often look at is refugees, and they see the need for refugees to integrate into life with other Londoners"; but what this might mean is not explored. Another speaker says that refugees are her clients, and one set of "stakeholders" in community cohesion; the other two groups of stakeholders she cites are people working in service delivery, and "the general public".

Economic inequality is only mentioned in the film very fleetingly
– there is a statement that "there are examples of very successful areas
which have high levels of deprivation but also have high levels of
cohesion". The only connection between community cohesion and
questions of inequality or discrimination in this presentation is when
a voice accompanying the woman in the suit suggests that "your
perceptions of who is getting what" from local housing services could
impact on community cohesion. The implication is that the group seen
to be getting more (or the group feeling hard done by) is defined on
ethnic or racial lines. This example also demonstrates an unspoken
class bias in who is made a concern for community cohesion policy:
principally people who live in social housing. "Services" are mentioned
but only in relation to people's *perceptions* about how services are
delivered, and whether they *feel* they are being treated fairly. This is
a narrative of community cohesion as a policy to manage residents'
feelings about how they are treated, not about whether they actually *are*
being treated differently. The overwhelming answer this video gives to
the question 'What is community cohesion?' is encapsulated by Hazel
Blears' statement at the beginning: it's about "trying to really build on
the shared values that people have, rather than concentrating on the
differences between people". This is reflected in the voiceovers and
the way they are summarised in the captions listed above; all focus on
affective relationships.

The video presents a narrative that can be understood in relation
to those in Chapter Two, but which does not directly refer to the
histories or relationships implicated in those narratives. The concept
of community cohesion is presented as free-floating, unattached to
particular events or places. Tensions, conflicts and the inequalities that
provoke them are absorbed into a discussion of diversity and acceptance
or celebration of difference. What is more, this diversity is literally
embodied in the narrators of this film. The six cartoon figures each
represent an archetype of diversity based on a set of simplified visual
clues that place them as having specific ethnic, gender, religious and
professional statuses. Most interesting, perhaps, is the figure of the 'white
man' in outdoor clothing including shorts and a high visibility jacket.
Although there is no explanation in the video of who the speakers
are, their comments suggest that they are practitioners who work in
community cohesion policy in various guises. This man in his outdoor
work-wear seems to represent an 'identity group' which is not included
in the other visual representations of the video (the white working-class
male) while it is unclear what role his outfit suggests as a community
cohesion worker. That at least 10 different voices accompany the six

avatars suggests that they are not simply representations of the speakers, but that the voices we hear have been amalgamated into this collage of professional diversity. The personal backgrounds, identity or status of the voices or their visual avatars are not mentioned at all in the script of the film. Yet the way the figures have been differentiated and physical clues to status have been distributed suggests that there is a level at which their personal identities are important.

The first sign saying 'Building people' makes an analysis of the film as a tool of governmentality via affect almost too obvious. The end of the film, where the principles of cohesion are described as 'love', 'trust' (which doesn't receive a caption), 'respect' and 'understanding', drives home this presentation of community cohesion as a policy that aims to manage populations through their emotional responses. But it also suggests that the role of the policy practitioner (the neutral bureaucrat?) is not just to find ways to manage the emotions of populations. The practitioner must engage in these emotional *relationships* with those populations; love, trust, respect and understanding all carry the implication of a two-way relationship and commitment. This resonates with Emma's comments about the impossibility of the role of the neutral policy practitioner in Chapter Six: "you need to be totally objective, but you can't be."

Thus the practitioner must embody difference, and perform love and relationships. The sign in Figure 7.2 makes it clear that not only is community cohesion a form of governmentality in which individuals must take responsibility for themselves and behave in ways which embrace 'shared values' and 'celebrate difference'; it is a framework of governmentality in which the governors themselves are expressly subject to these same requirements of self-monitoring and performance of personal attributes. This is not quite the 'evacuation of subjectivity through the policy construction of cardboard cut-out characterizations ... that runs across the struggle over citizenship between those who govern and those who are governed' that Gail Lewis describes (2005, p 538), since here the 'cardboard cut-outs' are at once those who govern *and* those being governed.

Yet it remains a contradictory relationship. It is clear that *some* individuals and groups are expected to perform community cohesion more ardently, because they are the (often unspoken) examples of potentially problematic difference that supposedly we all embody. A very clear example of this was the demand that Muslim people demonstrate antipathy to terrorism and commitment to 'the wider community' through the PVE programme, discussed in Chapter Three. The 'everybody' whose values are shared echoes Jacqui Smith's comment (quoted in Chapter Four) that to walk down the street alone in Hackney after midnight was "just not something people do". In Chapter Six, Thomas's reference to "urban environments where I feel comfortable" and Alice's preference for living in cities which are "more interesting" than elsewhere, echo this treatment of a white, middle-class self as a norm, even when this normative habitus is being described as "comfortable" with difference. 'People' and 'everybody' are imagined in these statements as "people like" the speaker, and indeed, if the values and experiences that they refer to *were* universal, there would presumably be no need for community cohesion policy to be addressed at all. The places experienced by this 'everybody' are in turn 'comfortable' or to be avoided, in relation to a normative white middle-class self.

The production of the film itself is an act of governmentality, as through its design and performance those involved present themselves as embodiments of good practice in administering and engaging in cohesion. The film is both made by and aimed at policy practitioners, and it features policy practitioners, promoting themselves as performing appropriate normative behaviours, and helping to regulate the behaviour of colleagues – who will, in turn, use these lessons in the management of populations. As I considered in Chapter One, 'good practice' can be critiqued as a technique for reincorporating reflexivity into practice in a way that shuts down critique (see, for example, Strathern, 2006, p 200). This may indeed be what is happening in the production and dissemination of this video. However, the methodological approach I have taken, and much of the practice that I have discussed, have aimed to find ways of understanding 'good practice' as an opportunity to keep open critical inquiry, to continue to negotiate uncomfortable positions and to find new ways to approach difficult subjects. Although this more open approach is not presented in the film, it is a central question for how to negotiate ethical policy practice (in the sense of unstable, ongoing negotiation and questioning; see Back, 2007b). In the next section, I consider a specific example of how the uncomfortable overlaps between professional and personal roles can be experienced, and the different ways this can be understood when thinking through a sociological imagination that recognises the links between personal actions and experiences, and structural power dynamics.

"My existence is under threat"

> HANNAH: So I just wondered if your own background and identity and experience affect how you approach these issues?
>
> JACK: Totally, one hundred and ten per cent.... Every day, when I think about community cohesion, I can honestly say I challenge myself ... people tell you all the time, that they're not racists ... now I've just got one question for those people and that's how do you know? How do you know you're not a racist 'cos how the hell do you tell that? When you talk about communities so, I live in Barking. I've always lived in Barking except for when I was at [university].... I am a Barking boy. My whole town has completely and utterly and totally changed. Doesn't look the same, smell the same, feel the same.... This afternoon, I will put my house on the market to sell it to move.... So then when you think about that in terms of your own personal experience, well, what's that all about? Why do I wanna do that, why do I wanna move? ... And I suppose it's about [*pause*] for me [*pause*] and my experiences of community cohesion [*pause*] my community no longer exists.... They're all part of the white flight, bang, they've all gone.... So all my friends have gone, I'm the last man standing, that's what they say ... and something, when I've been dealing with [my work] that I've thought about a lot is [*pause*] ... my children are now a significant minority in their schools. I think my little boy is one of four white kids in his class that he's going into.... We talk about understanding of and engagement with Muslim communities. Well, I'm a minority, aren't I, where is the understanding and engagement with my community?

Jack asked for these comments to be anonymised further than others he made. I have removed some of the identifying features, and should point out simply that he was working on cohesion-related policy but *not* in Barking and Dagenham; that was simply where he lived. I did not include this material in the discussion of Barking and Dagenham because it is about a different relationship to the place from that I was discussing in the main – Jack was speaking as a local resident, about how his experiences as a policy practitioner had affected how he thought about aspects of his home life. Although I asked Jack, as I asked others, whether he thought his own background affected how he thought about related issues, he seemed to be talking here about how his work affected his thoughts about his life outside work. He described an unsettling feeling, that the area he had lived in all his life had changed, principally describing a change in the ethnic mix of the local population as new residents moved in and previous (white) residents took flight into towns further outside London, into Essex. He described a sense of isolation, and how his children, as white English children, were in a minority in their school. Adding emphasis to this, he told me of his shock when his son came home from school one say to tell him what he had learned about Christmas:

> JACK: What he said was, he said CHRISTIANS believe.... And for me that's like – that's a real check up.... That is really hard for me to accept that. Not because I don't understand the fact that there are different faiths and different religions, but I kind of – expected, unconsciously, that my kids would be brought up in the same tradition that I was brought up in, collective acts of worship, this, that, and then when my son comes home, well Christians believe, so oh my god, don't say that when your nan's here because that will be it, that will be uproar over that....And I keep asking myself the same time, are you racist, is that what this is, are you actually a racist? And you think, well, hang on a minute, I suppose the Asian community are coming together 'cos they wanna be together, why should it be any different for me?...
>
> HANNAH: And does that make you feel [*pause*] does that kind of make – help you understand how other communities are ... or is it making you feel....
>
> JACK: No, I think it makes me feel how communities may feel under threat.... And attacked. And it's a terrible way to say it isn't it ... but actually my way of living, my existence, is under threat, is under attack, it has been threatened.

Jack described how his certainties about life and his place in the world had been shaken by changing circumstances in Barking and Dagenham. He had tried to think about this using the framework of community cohesion policy, as he understood it. In his account, the problem for him was not that his children had learned about a range of different religions and cultures, or even that their school was ethnically mixed; it was that within this mix, his 'tradition' was no longer the norm. Nowhere in our conversation did he suggest that he had a strong religious faith. What he described was identifying with Christianity as a default background faith. When he expected that his children would be brought up in "the same tradition" as him, he meant "collective acts of worship" at school – that is, a background of white (Protestant) Christian normativity within which they were unremarkable and "normal".

Jack's narrative has similarities with the narratives of a dispossessed 'white working class' disturbed by rapid demographic and social change who turn to far right voting patterns as a defence against economic and social upheaval they are not ready for, as a protest vote against their neglect by a liberal middle-class elite, or as a demonstration of their fundamentally xenophobic core. I discussed these narratives and the work they do in Chapter Two, and the work that policy practitioners do to understand, negotiate and reposition them (from within Barking and Dagenham specifically) in Chapter Five. Jack's narrative is not the same as those ideal types, however.

First, he stated several times in the interview his strong antipathy towards the BNP ("I hate those bastards as much as anyone"), and he began the comments quoted here by referring to an ongoing struggle with himself over whether his feelings stemmed from unconscious or deep-seated racism; he reiterated this struggle later in the interview. Second, Jack is not 'white working class', at least in a material sense; while we did not discuss his class identification, he certainly cited aspects of his life (his university education and home ownership, as well as his professional position) which meant that the situation of powerlessness and marginalisation usually associated with the discourse of 'white working class' disillusionment was less pronounced.

Finally, and of course connected to these other two factors, Jack was speaking in relation to a professional role in which he had become accustomed to a particular form of 'diversity talk' and practice. That is, he was expressing feelings of isolation and discomfort with (ethnic demographic) change more usually understood within the narrative of a 'white working class' turning to the far right for refuge, but using his professional habitus he attempted to make sense of his experience in a version of community cohesion discourse that emphasised affect and bounded identities in lieu of power relations – a discourse bearing a strong relationship to that in the video discussed above. Here, structural power relations and discrimination were rejected as subjects for community cohesion policy, and instead the elements of affective group belonging were emphasised as determining factors – and as shared by 'everybody'.

Jack's description of his experience emerged when I asked if his own background informed how he thought about community cohesion policy. His reply was eventually that, feeling "under attack" by changes in the "feel", "look" and "smell" of the area where he had lived all his life, he was able to empathise with "other communities" who may feel attacked. The 'threat' to Jack was not a physical attack. It was not clear what 'understanding and engagement' Jack felt was lacking for 'his' community. Nor was anyone removing his children's ability to learn about the traditions in which he grew up, in their schools. The threat was that this was no longer learned about as necessarily the dominant tradition, but one among many. 'His' community no longer felt like his, "doesn't exist any more" because he was not the one agreeing to 'tolerate' others (Lewis, 2005, p 540; Wemyss, 2006), but one of many being 'tolerated' by one another. He described a loss of his 'community' but the population of Barking had not disappeared; it had changed.

An alternative way for him to view the situation might have been to find ways to adapt his own sense of what constituted 'his' community. What he had lost was a feeling of superiority and security that he didn't even realise he had, and which many people never have had. This resonates with analyses of post-colonial melancholia (Gilroy, 2001, 2004) which suggest that feelings of alienation such as those described by Jack arise from an unmet expectation of entitlement to power and privilege which Britain as a whole has suffered with the loss of Empire and the demise of British international influence, and which those subjects who identify themselves as embodying Britishness (or more specifically Englishness), most often white men, are most likely to experience.

By imagining this within a narrative of community cohesion policy which privileges identity and belonging to bounded communities linked by 'tradition', Jack seemed to be setting himself an impossible task. As his reflections demonstrate, he had not resolved his feelings within this or any other explanatory framework to his own satisfaction. Indeed, he had decided to exit the site of his immediate discomfort by moving his family out of Barking, but this decision made him uncomfortable when he tried to understand it in the terms of his professional practice. His resolution appeared to be that "the Asian community are coming together" as were his (white English) Barking community (albeit in new locations outside of Barking), and that therefore a population living in ethnically differentiated 'communities' was acceptable. But as we have seen, the genesis of community cohesion policy is premised on such arrangements being problematic, sometimes because of a recognition that they may be linked to or exacerbate structural inequalities, more often because such separation is seen to be caused by or to increase discrimination and mistrust between communities so defined. Jack's narrative demonstrates some of the contradictions at the heart of community cohesion policy. By 'celebrating difference' without recognising that some differences are treated differently to others, one can simply reinforce division and ignore inequalities of power.

Thinking about one's role within the ethical negotiations of power as a policy practitioner can increase discomfort as one is forced to confront one's own privilege. Although some practitioners dealt with this by resilencing such questions, others tried to practice a kind of public sociology by incorporating a sociological understanding of difference and power into the way they understood their work within government. Doing so might entail recognition that there may not be a comfortable, neutral position from which to speak or act, but that words and action are necessary nonetheless. These negotiations and dilemmas go to the heart of questions about the role of government, and UK local government in particular.

What is local government for (in the Big Society)?

> HANNAH: Do you think cohesion's going to stay around as a big policy issue in the next few years?
>
> BEVERLEY: I think a great deal will depend on the change of government ... if it's the same administration [*laughing*] then I'd expect it to continue. But if we had a change of administration, I think it would qualify in some way, partly because I think that Conservatives would have their commitment to reducing funding, and this is the kind of discretionary thing that could go. And of course some of the authorities that are doing excellent work in this field are Conservative authorities, but that doesn't mean quite the same thing as national government policy.

> HANNAH: And do you think that [community cohesion policy] will have a future, can you see where that might go?
>
> ALISON: Depends who gets elected of course. It's gonna be such a mysterious [*both laugh*] I don't know whether the

Tories will hang on to the concept. They have a shadow communities minister, so that's – I think the terminology will inevitably will evolve, and change, and we'll talk about different things, but I think it will be a gradual shift if there is a shift, and I think we will continue to talk about the kinds of issues that are currently encapsulated under the umbrella term of community cohesion because I don't think local government can do its job in the current political, geopolitical, ideological environment, without having some way of talking about the diversity of their communities, and the widening class divide and the impact of the 'credit crunch'.

My fieldwork ended before the Conservative–Liberal Democrat national coalition government took power in May 2010, and my discussions here cover the way that community cohesion was understood in the years before that. But in many of the interviews and observations of policy events and discussions that I conducted, there was growing anticipation of how an expected new government might approach issues connected to community cohesion policy. Impacts of the international financial crisis and the likely effect on public spending in Britain were anticipated, both for how communities lived, and how policies for promoting cohesion would be prioritised.

The two quotes above are from separate interviews with Beverley and Alison, who worked in similar roles in two different national-level local government lobbying organisations. They gave very similar answers to my question about what might happen to community cohesion as a policy agenda in the coming years. Indeed, both laughed wryly at the idea that there was any doubt that there would be change of national government at the forthcoming general election (I interviewed Alison in June 2008 and Beverley in April 2009). They both suggested that a new (Conservative) government was likely to 'qualify', 'evolve', 'change' or 'shift' the policy programme.

Both suggested that despite their expectations of a change in terminology and focus, the issues that community cohesion connected to would continue to be political concerns – because the issues dealt with through community cohesion policy were central to the role of local government. All main UK political parties champion 'localism' in various forms, arguing that decisions about places should be made by the people who live in them (see, for example, Miliband, 2006; Cameron, 2010; Clegg, 2011). Yet, as we saw in the negotiations between local and central government in Chapter Three, this does not necessarily translate into practice; local decisions are made within the parameters set by central government. Indeed, as Beverley and Alison indicated, the predominant influence of the national political situation over what happens locally was not even up for discussion – even though they both lobbied on behalf of local government, they both suggested that local authorities were likely to alter their approaches to community cohesion policy with a change in national government, whether or not existing local approaches were seen as successful.

The close association between the purpose of local government and the practice of community cohesion policy that Beverley and Alison expressed has echoes elsewhere in my research. There are numerous examples throughout the book of how meanings and practices of community cohesion have been contradictory and contested. Perhaps less overtly, the meaning, purpose and practices of local government have also been put in question by the practitioners I interviewed and observed. This is most clearly exemplified in Chapter Three, where the extremely controversial language and design of the PVE programme provoked a clear division between many local government practitioners and their national government colleagues. That is not to say that there was a clear consensus from either group about what the role of (local) government should be – some, like the comments I quoted in Chapter Three from a television interview with the leader of Bradford Council, emphasised service delivery, while others argued there was a duty to "bring people together"; some national narratives emphasised security while others suggested structural inequality should be a greater concern. The point is that the disagreements and negotiations were not simply about what community cohesion policy is, was, or should be, or whether it was a relevant or appropriate activity for local government. Within these arguments lay a deeper question of the purpose of democratic institutions, public services and administration, and of their *local* dimension in terms of responding to the needs of specific places and populations and the levers of power available to them. Community cohesion policy is one lens through which to contemplate these issues.

As Beverley and Alison anticipated, the question of how to deliver community cohesion (whatever that might mean) has become less central to policy discussions *in those terms*. Yet questions of belonging, identity and inequality – and of the role and aims of government in these questions – have by no means disappeared since the 2010 general election:

> For a long time the way government has worked ...
> has turned many motivated public sector workers into

disillusioned, weary puppets of government targets.... It has turned lively communities into dull, soulless clones of one another.... So we need to turn government completely on its head ... these are the three big strands of the Big Society agenda. First, social action ... [g]overnment ... must foster and support a new culture of voluntarism, philanthropy, social action. Second, public service reform ... we've got [to] give professionals much more freedom, and open up public services to new providers like charities, social enterprises and private companies.... And third, community empowerment. We need to create communities with oomph – neighbourhoods who are in charge of their own destiny, who feel if they club together and get involved they can shape the world around them. (Cameron, 2010)

Although the term 'Big Society' has been much lampooned (see, for example, Guru-Murthy, 2011; Stephens, 2011; Wheeler, 2011) as without substance, the extract from Cameron's speech, given two months after he became Prime Minister, lays out its assumptions rather clearly. It begins from a premise that 'the way government has worked' had been damaging to both practitioners and citizens; that this was a result of regulation, 'targets' and centralisation. The prescription was to ask – and require – individual non-professionals to take responsibility for their own and others' well-being. That this would be promoted through a 'new culture of voluntarism' suggests some element of 'obliging people to be free' in the mode of practices and policies of governmentality within which community cohesion policy exists, as discussed in Chapter One. The second element of the Big Society project is that the idea of public services as projects of the state, that is, of government with a link to democratic institutions, would be weakened. Again this is framed in the language of 'freedom' – freedom for 'professionals' to meet needs they define (presumably with communities) rather than assessing these against national frameworks – but such 'freedom' to decide would again be obligatory, and would come with the responsibility to deliver. The responsibility (and potential culpability) associated with freedom is also evident in the third element of the Big Society, that 'communities' would be 'empowered'.

That local government is adept at adapting to the changing national policy environment is a theme that has been important throughout my discussions, around the presentation of purpose – language, narrative, myth-making or branding. The questions raised by interviewees in Chapters Four, Five and Six about the proper and actual roles of local government were not always framed directly in terms of community cohesion policy. But as we examined the subjects being debated, they were clearly about how to handle and distribute power; about the right to belong; about how to constitute communities; about how to imagine places where communities are constituted. Likewise, in Cameron's Big Society discourse, the language is not that of community cohesion policy, but the concerns are closely related. There is no mention here of many of the keywords that have become central to community cohesion (although 'communities', or more often 'neighbourhoods', are central). There is very little mention of diversity, except around 'diverse models of service provision' (that is, reducing direct government provision of public services). 'Power' is, in fact, mentioned here – but in relation to a supposed redistribution of power of decision making to more local levels, and not in relation to a distribution of social, cultural or economic resources within and across populations. Like community cohesion policy, the Big Society is a flexible policy vocabulary with its own linguistic lacunae that can leave silences to be ignored, mobilised or over-written.

The dominance of 'community cohesion policy' may be over as a central term used by government, but the term itself has stuck in places, at least for the time being – statutory duties for schools, some job titles, institutions and publications. More importantly, the issues that people tried to address through 'community cohesion policy' have not disappeared (any more than they appeared when the term did). Populations may be problematised differently, using different language and concepts, but equally, language and programmes themselves may be bent to address reimagined problems and solutions through the negotiation of policy. My research shows how, far from Cameron's vision of 'public sector workers [as] disillusioned, weary puppets of government targets', many negotiate difficult subjects with skilled manoeuvres around, within and through government targets and narratives. In doing so, they often make use of what might be called a 'sociological imagination' – an idea of how personal narratives connect to structural power relations.

This research also provides findings that contradict Cameron's sense that 'lively communities' have been turned into 'dull, soulless clones of one another'. I have shown at length in Chapters Four and Five how narratives of place are manoeuvred, negotiated and reincorporated by policy practitioners. In Chapter Four, we saw how multiple narratives of Hackney were intertwined in negotiations over the meaning of the place. Notably, each of these narratives was dependent on a sense that Hackney was *special*, that its internal diversity and changeability was connected to a kind of 'sameness in difference', if not solidarity in diversity. In Chapter Five, I discussed the negotiations of policy practitioners first projecting and using images of Oldham, Barking and Dagenham and Peterborough as metaphors in narratives of community cohesion policy, and second reincorporating these images into new narratives with more positive connotations. Neither of these chapters suggests that the places considered or their populations are 'dull, soulless clones'.

Cameron does not describe what he means by 'the way government has worked', but implies that this has been about the central control of local activities. I have shown how national policy narratives and techniques shape local understanding of priorities, needs and populations. But importantly, I have also shown that this is far from a direct relationship of command-and-control. Rather, narratives within policy and government incorporate existing meanings and resonances while individuals and groups of policy practitioners reflexively interpret, and sometimes deliberately subvert, the meanings of national policy narratives in the context of their own professional, personal, political and ethical experiences, knowledge and priorities.

This is not to say that nationally mandated government priorities have not had an effect on how local government operates – they are deeply entangled. But local authorities, or more accurately, the practitioners who make up local governance, do not have their practices or interpretations fixed in place by national governing techniques. Rather, they operate within regimes of governmentality. Governmentality has most usually been used as a way of understanding the management of populations by 'obliging them to be free', that is, requiring self-government where individuals *choose* how to behave, but where behaviour within normative frameworks and parameters is the only thinkable 'choice' (Rose, 1999b). Such techniques do not usually require forcible coercion, because populations, in the main, choose to behave in normative ways of their own accord in order to avoid expected penalties for moving outside of the norm, but because the rules are often unspoken, there remains room for incremental change and manoeuvre. This book builds on the considerable work on governmentality as a technique for managing *populations*, to demonstrate how such dynamics also operate *within* practices of government – my research develops the study of *the conduct of conduct* to engage with *the conduct of the conduct of conduct*. The policy practitioners in this study were engaged in finding ways to get populations to behave as cohesive communities, but they were doing so because this was part of the normative expectations of them within the regime of governmentality of their professional statuses.

Imagining sociologically, thinking emotionally and staying uncomfortable

I began the book by setting my research in the context of early 21st-century policies of governmentality, suggesting that to develop such techniques of governing, policy practitioners must have a sense of the relationships between individual choice and structural constraint; that is, they must have a sociological imagination (Mills, 1999 [1959]). Using a sociological imagination within practices of government does not necessarily mean always coming to the same conclusion. It seems to create a variety of uncomfortable positions for those involved in practices of governing, if only because looking at society and one's place in it this way can reveal contradictions that may be impossible to resolve. Jack's narrative of dislocation in this chapter is just one example.

We might also think of Emma's reflection in Chapter Six that, as a theoretically neutral arbiter of government she felt the need "to be totally objective, but you can't be". Or perhaps the way that many research participants in Chapter Five discussed their local areas as obviously linked to community cohesion narratives at the same time that they tried to establish new narratives. The negotiations of policy practitioners and others in Hackney in Chapter Four, as they tried to find ways to address power inequalities (while recognising their ability to do so relied on their own relative power and privilege) are another example. The ways that research participants (including myself) reflected on the compromises required and made around the implementation of the PVE programme in Chapter Three (and the moments when limits of compromise were reached) showed practitioners working within the limits of governance regimes while simultaneously able to reflect on these limits, and using their understanding of the limits to attempt some changes within the rules of the game. And Chapter Two, which describes the sets of narratives and resonances that slip past and through one another in practitioners and others' understandings of community cohesion policy, demonstrates how the sociological imagination (the ability to make links between historic resonances and current problematisations, specific crises and longer-term trends) is both relied on and confounded by the languages and techniques of policy which use silences and implication to create links that can still be denied. The ongoing tension about a definition of community cohesion, the repetition that this 'goes beyond "race" and faith', at that very moment indicating the expectation that race and faith are at the heart of its concerns, is an excellent example of this reliance on implicit meanings to communicate the unspoken.

My work extends the theorisation of brand into the sphere of government, into the importance of narrative building and presentation, and government through *emotion*. Finally, the apparent intangibility of many techniques of branding, and the importance of the slipperiness and unruliness of brands, their unpredictability, potential for reincorporation and subversion of meaning – their retention of the 'margins of indeterminacy' (Lury, 2004, p 162) – is a characteristic of branding and also of policy practice. As discussed in Chapter One, the concept of 'community' in itself is attractive precisely because of its 'ambiguous potential' (Schofield, 2002, p 680). It can connote both nostalgia for a lost past and excitement for building an alternative future. It can suggest absolute difference or commonality across difference. It can be a tool of self-organisation or of oppressive control. This book demonstrates how such ambiguities constitute both the meanings and practices of community cohesion policy.

We need to take seriously the narratives – and feelings – of policy practitioners because these are the tools they use to conduct government, with consequences for the populations they govern. This should not be confused with the growing trend to 'measure happiness', largely associated with behavioural economics, which tends to treat emotional responses (of populations) as more important than material measures of well-being or inequalities of power. Rather, my research builds on what is sometimes known as 'the affective turn' in the sociological literature which pays attention to the importance of embodied emotions in social processes to extend existing insights on the role of affect in management of self; to understand the centrality of emotional techniques to the processes of government; and to pay attention both to how individuals operating within governance structures are subject to difficult negotiations of affect and power, and that they often recognise the complications and incommensurabilities of their work, but find ways to do it anyway.

Recognising these ambiguities and indeterminacies means recognising the difficult, unstable balances that many policy practitioners (and sociologists) attempt to make when interpreting and intervening in social worlds. Through the application and honing of skills and techniques they might aim to deliver ever more definite and precise definitions and solutions to social problems and questions of government. Yet context and interpretation is shifting, and therefore it can be important to remain open (and vulnerable to) the unknown (Gunaratnam, 2009). This vulnerability can be lived as an emotional reaction, but this does not necessarily mean it is against reason, or reactionary. As discussed in Chapter One, if we treat emotion and affect as embodied commitments or reactions to ideas and situations, we may see how their power can also be harnessed to resist dominant norms (Sayer, 2005). Recognising emotion within practices of both (public) sociology and policy practice is important not for the sake of sentimentalism or even sympathy, but because structural and political power dynamics are experienced through emotional filters within the everyday. Taking seriously emotional or affective commitments within government does, of course, produce yet another precarious line to walk. It can slip into a masking of power relations, as in the video discussed earlier in this chapter, or more significantly in some of the manoeuvres associated with Third Way communitarianism, discussed in Chapter One.

Negotiating such precarious lines is part of the role of a reflective policy practitioner. It is also a negotiation central to critical sociology. While they overlap, the roles of critical researcher and applied policy practitioner are, of course, distinguished from one another by their different aims: as a social researcher, to delineate and investigate theoretical and empirical questions and seek their answers; as a policy practitioner, to effect changes which address empirical social problems, within the parameters available. I am certainly not the only person who moves between these roles, and indeed my research uncovered many practitioners speaking in the language of, or using models of, sociological theory and research. Yet the conclusions to which this led them might not necessarily be possible or thinkable in the context of governing. For some, this was approached by silencing the difficulties of the space between ethical commitments as felt and as practised, or developing other languages to talk about and bypass such uncomfortable positions. For others, it meant creating new narratives that attempted to bring conflicting imaginaries together. And yet others attempted to live on a precarious line they felt might not be achievable, but which was worth striving towards, by keeping in mind both the contradictions of their position and attempts to intervene in the world and distributions of power and meaning despite these contradictions. Perhaps this attention to working within contradiction, of staying uncomfortable, is essential to living according to a sociological imagination, and to practising public sociology.

Notes

Introduction

[1] Rachel was a senior manager in a local authority interviewed during this research. Her name, like the names of other interviewees mentioned in this book, has been changed to preserve anonymity.

Chapter One

[1] See, for example, DCLG (2006) and Lyons (2007).

[2] Although under the subsequent Coalition government from 2010 the major focus has been on 'efficiency' rather than the detailed performance measures of the previous administration (see, for example, Pickles, 2010).

Chapter Two

[1] At that time, the Department of Environment.

[2] From 2006, the Department for Communities and Local Government.

[3] With some of the same members as the Community Cohesion Review Team that authored the Cantle Report, and again chaired by Ted Cantle.

[4] Most notoriously, 'If you want a nigger neighbour vote Labour', a slogan the candidate refused to condemn (Solomos and Back, 1995, p 54).

[5] Although two of the killers were finally sentenced for Stephen Lawrence's murder in January 2012, 19 years after the crime took place.

[6] Question Time, BBC1, 22 October 2009.

[7] In the May 2010 local elections, all of the BNP councillors in Barking and Dagenham lost their seats.

[8] And one he seemed to remain keen to repeat through the magazine he edited; see, for example, Mirza et al (2010).

[9] Although see, for example, Blue (2008); Pickard (2010); Woods (2010); Webb (2011); and for a commentary on this as a New Labour agenda, see Skeggs (2004, p 54).

Chapter Three

[1] Internal document. I gained access to many documents discussed in this chapter as a result of my participant observer status, and therefore do not give full referencing details for them in the References.

[2] Twenty-six of the 33 local authorities in London were eligible to bid for PVE on the basis of the size of their Muslim populations. A total of 52 local authorities were eligible nationally (see Kelcher, 2007).

[3] Internal document.

[4] LAAs were introduced in 2004/05 and phased out by the new Coalition government in 2010. An LAA was an agreement between a local area and central government, including a set of improvement targets which local partners committed to achieving, and the funding allocations from central government that underpin them. While the local LAA signatory was the Local Strategic Partnership (LSP) that consisted of major statutory sector and other organisations in a local area, the local authority was the accountable body.

[5] Internal document.

[6] Internal document.

[7] This version of the indicators was not made public, and I no longer have a copy of the document. Measurement of the scheme's success was subsequently dramatically altered; see later in this chapter.

[8] Internal document.

[9] Internal document.

[10] Although government thinking in this area had already begun by 2004 (see FCO, 2004; Thomas, 2010, p 443).

[11] A reference to the human rights abuse of prisoners of war, by US soldiers, in a Baghdad prison, which were publicly exposed.

[12] Jean Charles de Menezes was an innocent Brazilian man who was shot in the head by police at Stockwell tube station on 22 July 2005. They had mistaken him for a terrorist suspect during a flawed surveillance operation. This occurred two weeks after four terrorist bombs on the London transport system killed 56 people and injured around 700.

[13] The Charedi community is estimated to be 7 per cent of Hackney's population (LBH, 2012b, p 1), and the largest such community in the world outside New York and Israel (Mayhew and Harper, 2008, p 5).

[14] The Charedi community was cited frequently in interviews as the most obvious example of a bounded (or 'cohesive') community in Hackney. The

Charedi community has strict rules about diet, schooling, gender roles and use of communal services, and in Hackney the community has a number of strong advocates who articulate its specific needs and lobby the council in this regard. For reasons of space I cannot provide a detailed discussion of these relationships here, but for more information see Holman and Holman (2002).

Chapter Four

[1] Because Rosen and Sinclair were both interviewed as public figures, it would have been absurd to attempt to anonymise their comments in the way I have for the other interview data. They both agreed that their comments be attributed.

[2] The policy practitioners I interviewed were, by definition, middle class themselves, and many resided in inner London; I explore in more detail how they negotiated their own personal implication in local processes of change in Chapter Six.

[3] www.hackney.gov.uk/xp-factsandfigures-geography.htm

[4] www.hackney.gov.uk/cp-community-parks.htm

[5] See Mayhew and Harper (2008), which includes a discussion of the difficulties of data collection and updated, but still not definitive, population estimates.

[6] See www.hackneygazette.co.uk/home/e-edition

[7] The 3rd March story about a cleaner chasing away would-be jewel thieves managed to combine the elements of crime and humour (and a picture of an attractive young woman) in one story.

[8] Hackney Council was judged to be a well-performing local authority by the national inspection body, the Audit Commission, in 2008.

[9] Which was itself an incredibly successful rebranding of associations of danger and desire (Kidd and Glaser, 2003), and has been copied widely.

[10] A more bizarre inflection of this, to which I referred in Chapter Two, was the unauthorised use not of the 'I Love Hackney' logo, but of the logo representing the London Borough of Hackney as a local authority, on a range of basketball shirts sold worldwide by the global sportswear company Nike – for which the local authority won damages (see LBH, 2006c; Tran, 2006).

[11] There is no room to go into the complicated history of this development here, but see Hart (2003) for one insider's account.

[12] For more on the treatment of the outer London suburb of Croydon as an abject elsewhere to the vibrant inner city, see Back (2001). The use of Manhattan and Croydon as adjacent symbols of soulless capitalism (and as

contrasting symbols to 'the way Hackney is') deserves further exploration than is possible here.

[13] See, for example, www.houseofhackney.com, 'the luxe wallpaper, bed linen and home furnishings brand which reworks traditional British homewares for a new generation'. Their 'Hackney Empire' design features sloths smoking shishas and raccoons downing bottles of tequila, and adorns teacups sold for £68 each and wallpaper at £148 per roll.

[14] Although my study, of course, differs markedly from that of these earlier researchers, who focused on middle-class residents in general, rather than policy practitioners and public figures.

Chapter Five

[1] Of course, Birmingham is still remembered for riots in the Handsworth area of the city in 1981, but Jim was here referring to an incident since 2001. Newspapers also reported rioting in Birmingham following clashes between the far right English Defence League and the anti-racist Unite Against Fascism in August 2009, but my interview with Jim took place the previous June. Similarly, the riots across England in the summer of 2011 took place after all of my research interviews were completed, and produced their own mythologies, parallels and analysis.

[2] Details of the branding exercise were also reported at: http://news.bbc. co.uk/1/hi/england/manchester/7351420.stm

[3] Robert Winston is a prominent scientist, but has no connection with Oldham that I know or can find. Ron may have meant to refer to Winston Churchill, the wartime Prime Minister. who was MP for Oldham between 1900 and 1906.

[4] Although between my interviews with Anne and Steve, the BNP did gain the North West of England seat for the European Parliament, which includes Oldham in its boundaries.

[5] In addition to two seats in the European Parliament and one in the Greater London Authority, the BNP also managed, at different times between 2006 and 2010, to elect councillors including in Blackburn, Bradford, Burnley, Calderdale, Epping Forest, Kirklees, Sandwell and Stoke.

[6] The 10 countries that gained new status as members of the EU in 2004 (Czech Republic, Estonia, Hungary, Latvia, Lithuania, Poland, Slovakia and Slovenia) and 2007 (Bulgaria and Romania), allowing their citizens to travel freely throughout the EU.

[7] An officially sanctioned space where nomadic Traveller or Gypsy people are able to live.

[8] www.youtube.com/watch?v=DnJ7K_YOu6Y

Chapter Six

[1] "What went so wrong" for the (white) boys who killed Stephen might be something to do with their class position, meaning that they experienced growing up in inner London less as a cultural resource and more as a process of marginalisation and demonisation (see Haylett, 2001, p 365; Hewitt, 2005, pp 121-30).

References

Abbott, D. (2008) 'Multicultural marvel', *Hackney Gazette*, 4 December, p 22.

Abraham, D. (2010) 'Doing justice on two fronts: the liberal dilemma in immigration', *Ethnic and Racial Studies*, vol 33, no 6, pp 968-85.

Ahmed, S. (2000) *Strange encounters: Embodied others in post-coloniality*, New York: Routledge.

Ahmed, S. (2004a) 'Declarations of whiteness: The non-performativity of anti-racism', *borderlands e-journal*, vol 3, no 2.

Ahmed, S. (2004b) *The cultural politics of emotion*, Edinburgh: Edinburgh University Press.

Ahmed, S. (2005) 'The non-performativity of anti-racism', *Borderlands e-journal*, vol 5, no 3.

Ahmed, S. (2007a) '"You end up doing the document rather than doing the doing": Diversity, race equality and the politics of documentation', *Ethnic and Racial Studies*, vol 30, no 4, pp 590-609.

Ahmed, S. (2007b) 'The language of diversity', *Ethnic and Racial Studies*, vol 30, no 2, pp 235-56.

Ahmed, S. (2010) 'Killing joy: Feminism and the history of happiness', *Signs: Journal of Women in Culture and Society*, vol 35, no 3, pp 571-92.

Ahmed, S. (2012) *On being included: Racism and diversity in institutional life*, Durham, NC: Duke University Press.

Aldred, R. and Jungnickel, K. (2010/11) 'Hackney blog: Cycling cultures' (http://cyclingcultures.org.uk/hackney-fieldwork).

Alexander, C. (2000) *The Asian gang*, Cambridge: Berg.

Alexander, C. (2004) 'Imagining the Asian gang: Ethnicity, masculinity and youth after "the riots"', *Critical Social Policy*, vol 24, no 4, pp 526-49.

Alexander, C. (2007) 'Cohesive identities: The distance between meaning and understanding', in M. Wetherell, M. Laflèche and R. Berkeley (eds) *Identity, ethnic diversity and community cohesion*, London: Sage Publications, pp 115-25.

Alleyne, B. (2002) 'An idea of community and its discontents: Towards a more reflexive sense of belonging in multicultural Britain', *Ethnic and Racial Studies*, vol 25, no 4, pp 607-27.

Anderson, B. (1991) *Imagined communities: Reflections on the origin and spread of nationalism*, London and New York: Verso.

Andersson, J. (2009) 'East End localism and urban decay: Shoreditch's re-emerging gay scene', *The London Journal*, vol 34, no 1, pp 55-71.

Aronczyk, M. (2007) 'New and improved nations: branding national identity', in C. Calhoun and R. Sennet (eds) *Practicing culture*, Abingdon: Routledge, pp 105-28.

Atkinson, P. and Silverman, D. (1997) 'Kundera's immortality: The interview society and the invention of the self', *Qualitative Inquiry*, vol 3, pp 304-25.

Back, L. (2001) 'So ... fucking Croydon' (http://web.archive.org/web/20060417083446/http://www.skylineprojections.co.uk/lesText.htm).

Back, L. (2002) 'Guess who's coming to dinner? The political morality of investigating whiteness in the gray zone', in V. Ware and L. Back (eds) *Out of whiteness: Color, politics and culture*, Chicago, IL: University of Chicago Press, pp 33-59.

Back, L. (2007a) 'Phobocity: London and the War on Terror', *Eurozine*, 15 March (www.eurozine.com/articles/2006-11-15-back-en.html).

Back, L. (2007b) *The art of listening*, Oxford: Berg.

Back, L. (2008) 'Sociologists talking', *Sociological Research Online*, vol 13, no 6 (www.socresonline.org.uk/13/6/3.html).

Back, L., Keith, M., Khan, A., Shukra, K. and Solomos, J. (2002) 'New Labour's white heart: politics, multiculturalism and the return of assimilationism', *Political Quarterly*, vol 73, pp 445-54.

Bagguley, P. and Hussain, Y. (2003a) '"The Bradford riot" of 2001: a preliminary analysis', in C. Barker and M. Tyldesley (eds) *Ninth international conference on alternative futures and popular protest*, Manchester: Manchester Metropolitan University, pp 1-17.

Bagguley, P. and Hussain, Y. (2003b) 'Conflict and cohesion: constructions of "community" around the 2001 "riots"', Communities Conference, Leeds (www.leeds.ac.uk/sociology/people/pbdocs/Conflict%20and%20Cohesion%204%20conference.doc).

Ball, W. and Solomos, J. (eds) (1990) *Race and local politics*, Basingstoke: Macmillan.

Ball, W., Gulam, W. and Troyna, B. (1990) 'Pragmatism or retreat? Funding policy, local government and the marginalisation of anti-racist education', in W. Ball and J. Solomos (eds) *Race and local politics*, Basingstoke: Macmillan, pp 78-94.

Barnes, M. (2008) 'Passionate participation: Emotional experiences and expressions in deliberative forums', *Critical Social Policy*, vol 28, no 4, pp 461-81.

BBC News (1998) '£800m lifeline for "no-go" estates', *BBC Online Network*, 15 September (newsrss.bbc.co.uk/1/hi/uk/171530.stm).

BBC News (2001) 'Police official in plastic bullets call', *BBC News Online*, 25 June (news.bbc.co.uk/1/hi/uk/1407133.stm).

Bell, D. and Binnie, J. (2000) *The sexual citizen: Queer politics and beyond*, Cambridge: Polity Press.

Ben (2006) 'Dalston revisited: Report on the protest at Gillett "square" today', *Mute: Culture and Politics after the net*, 11 November (www.metamute.org/editorial/articles/dalston-revisited-report-protest-gillett-apossquareapos-today).

Ben-Tovim, G., Gabriel, J., Law, I. and Stredder, K. (1986) *The local politics of race*, Basingstoke: Macmillan.

Benyon, J. and Solomos, J. (eds) (1987) *The roots of urban unrest*, Oxford: Pergamon.

Berlant, L. (2004) 'Introduction: Compassion (and withholding)', in L. Berlant (ed) *Compassion: The culture and politics of an emotion*, New York and London: Routledge, pp 1-14.

Bhatt, C. (2007) 'Frontlines and interstices in the global War on Terror', *Development and Change*, vol 38, no 6, pp 1073-93.

Bhatt, C. (2010) 'The "British jihad" and the curves of religious violence', *Ethnic and Racial Studies*, vol 33, no 1, pp 39-59.

Blair, T. (2007) Callaghan Memorial Speech, 11 April (http://image.guardian.co.uk/sys-files/Politics/documents/2007/04/11/blairlecture.pdf).

Blond, P. and Pabst, A. (2007) 'Neither Brown nor Cameron fully understand our crisis', *Open Democracy* (www.opendemocracy.net/ourkingdom/2007/07/16/neither-brown-nor-cameron-fully-understand-our-crisis).

Blue, A. (2008) 'Which class is John Prescott?', *BBC News Magazine*, 27 October (news.bbc.co.uk/1/hi/magazine/7680063.stm).

Bonnett, A. (1993) *Radicalism, anti-racism and representation*, London and New York: Routledge.

Bonnett, A. (1998) 'How the British working class became white: The symbolic (re)formation of racialized capitalism', *Journal of Historical Sociology*, vol 11, no 3, pp 16-340.

Bonnett, A. (2009) 'The dilemmas of radical nostalgia in British psychogeography', *Theory, Culture & Society*, vol 26, no 1, pp 45-70.

Bonnett, A. (2010) *Left in the past: Radicalism and the politics of nostalgia*, New York: Continuum.

Bottero, W. (2009) 'Class in the 21st century', in K.P. Sveinnson (ed) *Who cares about the white working class?*, London: Runnymede Trust, pp 7-14.

Bourdieu, P. (1977 [1972]) *Outline of a theory of practice*, Cambridge: Cambridge University Press.

Bourdieu, P. (1986) 'The forms of capital', in J. Richardson (ed) *Handbook of theory and research for the sociology of education*, New York: Greenwood Press, pp 241-58.

Bourdieu, P. (1990 [1980]) *The logic of practice*, Cambridge: Polity Press.

Bright, M. (2006) *When progressives treat with reactionaries: The British state's flirtation with radical Islamism*, London: Policy Exchange.

Brighton, S. (2007) 'British Muslims, multiculturalism and UK foreign policy: "integration" and "cohesion" in and beyond the state', *International Affairs*, vol 83, no 1, pp 1-17.

Burawoy, M. (2004) 'Public sociologies: Contradictions, dilemmas, and possibilities', *Social Forces*, vol 82, no 4, pp 1603-18.

Burnett, J. (2004) 'Community, cohesion and the state', *Race & Class*, vol 45, no 3, pp 1-18.

Burnett, J. (2007) 'Britain's "civilising project": community cohesion and core values', *Policy & Politics*, vol 35, no 2, pp 353-7.

Burnett, J. and Duncan, S. (2008) 'Reflections and observations: An interview with the UK's first Chief Government Social Researcher', *Critical Social Policy*, vol 28, no 3, pp 283-98.

Butler, T. (1997) *Gentrification and the middle classes*, Aldershot: Ashgate.

Butler, T. and Hamnett, C. (2011) *Ethnicity, class and aspiration: Understanding London's new East End*, Bristol: The Policy Press.

Butler, T. and Robson, G. (2003a) *London calling: The middle classes and the re-making of Inner London*, Oxford: Berg.

Butler, T. and Robson, G. (2003b) 'Negotiating their way in: The middle classes, gentrification and the deployment of capital in a globalising metropolis', *Sociology*, vol 40, no 9, pp 1791-809.

Calhoun, C. (2002) 'Imagining solidarity: Cosmopolitanism, constitutional patriotism, and the public sphere', *Public Culture*, vol 14, no 1, pp 147-71.

Calhoun, C. (2005) 'The promise of public sociology', *The British Journal of Sociology*, vol 56, no 3, pp 355-63.

Calhoun, C. (2007) *Nations matter: Culture, history and the cosmopolitan dream*, London and New York: Routledge.

Cameron, D. (2010) Big Society speech, 19 July (www.number10.gov.uk/news/speeches-and-transcripts/2010/07/big-society-speech-53572).

Cantle, T. (2001) *Community cohesion: A report of the Independent Review Team chaired by Ted Cantle*, London: Home Office.

Cantle, T. (2005) *Community cohesion: A new framework for race and diversity*, Basingstoke: Palgrave Macmillan.

Chakraborti, N. (2010) 'Beyond "passive apartheid"? Developing policy and research agendas on rural racism in Britain', *Journal of Ethnic and Migration Studies*, vol 36, no 3, pp 501-17.

Chappell, L., Clifton, J., Gottfried, G. and Lawton, K. (2010) *Exploring the roots of BNP support*, London: Institute for Public Policy Research.

Cheong, P.H., Edwards, R., Goulbourne, H. and Solomos, J. (2007) 'Immigration, social cohesion and social capital: A critical review', *Critical Social Policy*, vol 27, no 24, pp 24-49.

Christie, A. (2006) 'Negotiating the uncomfortable intersections between gender and professional identities in social work', *Critical Social Policy*, vol 26, no 2, pp 390-411.

Clarke, A. (2001) *Burnley Task Force report*, Burnley: Burnley Task Force.

Clarke, N. and Cochrane, A. (2013) 'Geographies and politics of localism: The localism of the United Kingdom's Coalition government', Paper given at 'Local action in an era of localism?', The Open University, Milton Keynes, 7 March.

Clegg, N. (2011) Nick Clegg: Speech to the LG Group Annual Conference, 29 June (www.libdems.org.uk/speeches_detail. aspx?title=Nick_Clegg%3A_Speech_to_the_LG_group_Annual_ Conference_&pPK=4012290d-35f4-433d-bc16-7abe7ba9bea2).

Clifford, J. (1986) 'Introduction: Partial truths', in J. Clifford and G.E. Marcus (eds) *Writing culture: The poetics and politics of ethnography*, Berkeley, CA: University of California Press, pp 1-26.

CLG (Communities and Local Government) (2007a) *Negotiating new Local Area Agreements*, London: CLG Publications.

CLG (2007b) *Preventing Violent Extremism Pathfinder Fund: Guidance note for government offices and local authorities in England*, London: CLG.

CLG (2007c) *The new Performance Framework for Local Authorities and Local Authority Partnerships*, London: CLG.

Coffey, A. (1999) *The ethnographic self*, London: Sage Publications.

COIC (Commission on Integration and Cohesion) (2007) *Our shared future*, Wetherby: Department for Communities and Local Government.

Community Cohesion Review Panel (2004) *The End of Parallel Lives? The Report of the Community Cohesion Panel*, London: Home Office.

Cook, R. (2001) 'Robin Cook's chicken tikka masala speech', *The Guardian*, 19 April (www.guardian.co.uk/world/2001/apr/19/race. britishidentity).

Cooper, D. (1995) *Power in struggle: Feminism, sexuality and the state*, Buckingham: Open University Press.

Cooper, D. (2006) 'Active citizenship and the governmentality of local lesbian and gay politics', *Political Geography*, vol 25, no 8, pp 921-43.

Copsey, N. (2008) *Contemporary British fascism: The British National Party and the quest for legitimacy*, Basingstoke: Palgrave Macmillan.

CRE (Commission for Racial Equality) (1984) *Hackney Housing investigated: Summary of a formal investigation report,* London: CRE.

Crozier, G., Reay, D., James, D., Jamieson, F., Beedell, P., Hollingworth, S. and Williams, K. (2008) 'White middle-class parents, identities, educational choice and the urban comprehensive school: dilemmas, ambivalence and moral ambiguity', *British Journal of Sociology of Education*, vol 29, no 3, pp 261-72.

Darbyshire, N. (2001) 'These riots are not the same as Brixton 20 years ago', *The Telegraph*, 10 July (www.telegraph.co.uk/comment/4263753/these-riots-are-not-the-same-as-Brixton-20-years-ago.html).

Davies, A. (2009) 'Artists launch "Keep Hackney Crap" campaign', *Hackney Citizen*, 6 June (http://hackneycitizen.co.uk/2009/06/06/artists-launch-%E2%80%98keep-hackney-crap%E2%80%99-campaign/).

DCLG (Department for Communities and Local Government) (2006) *Strong and prosperous communities: Local Government White Paper 2006*, London: DCLG.

DCLG (2007a) *Preventing violent extremism: Winning hearts and minds*, Wetherby: CLG Publications.

DCLG (2007b) *'What works' in community cohesion*, London: CLG Publications.

DCLG (2008) *The government's response to the Commission on Integration and Cohesion*, London: DCLG.

Dench, G., Gavron, K. and Young, M. (2006) *The new East End: Kinship, race and conflict*, London: Profile Books.

Denham, J. (2001) *Building cohesive communities: A report of the Ministerial Group on Public Order and Community Cohesion*, London: Home Office.

Denham, J. (2009) 'Connecting communities', Speech given at the Institute of Community Cohesion, 14 October (http://webarchive. nationalarchives.gov.uk/+/http://www.communities.gov.uk/speeches/corporate/connectingcommunities).

Dodd, V. (2009a) 'MPs investigate anti-extremism programme after spying claims', *The Guardian*, 18 October (www.guardian.co.uk/uk/2009/oct/18/prevent-extremism-muslims-information-allegations).

Dodd, V. (2009b) 'Neo-Nazi convicted of planning terrorist bombing campaign', *The Guardian*, 15 July (www.guardian.co.uk/uk/2009/jul/15/neo-nazi-bomb-plan).

Dodd, V. (2009c) 'Police fear far-right terror attack', *The Guardian*, 6 July (www.guardian.co.uk/uk/2009/jul/06/far-right-terrorism-threat-police).

du Bois, W.E.B. (1994 [1903]) *The souls of black folk*, New York: Dover Publications, Inc.

du Gay, P. (2000) *In praise of bureaucracy*, London: Sage Publications.

du Gay, P. (2007) *Organizing identity: Persons and organizations 'after theory'*, London: Sage Publications.

Dunant, S. (ed) (1994) *The war of the words: The political correctness debate*, London: Virago.

Dunleavy, P. (1991) *Democracy, bureaucracy and public choice*, Hemel Hempstead: Harvester Wheatsheaf.

Dustmann, C., Casanova, M., Fertig, M., Preston, I. and Schmidt, C.M. (2003) *The impact of EU enlargement on migration flows*, Home Office Online Report 25/03, London: Home Office.

Dyckhoff, T. (2008) 'Let's move to … Hackney Wick, east London', *The Guardian*, 27 September (www.guardian.co.uk/money/2008/sep/27/homes).

Edelman, M. (1977) *Political language: Words that succeed and policies that fail*, New York and London: Academic Press.

Evans, G. (2006) 'Branding the city of culture: The death of city planning?', in J. Monclus and M. Guardia (eds) *Culture, urbanism and planning*, Aldershot: Ashgate, pp 197-213.

Evening Standard (2008) 'Livingstone: My 2012 bid was to snare billions of pounds for London', 24 April (www.thisislondon.co.uk/standard-mayor/article-23480071-livingstone-my-2012-bid-was-to-snare-billions-of-pounds-for-london.do).

Faist, T. (2009) 'Diversity – a new mode of incorporation?', *Ethnic and Racial Studies*, vol 32, no 1, pp 171-90.

Farrar, M. (2008) 'Analysing London's 'new East End' – How can social science make a difference?', *Sociological Research Online*, vol 13, no 5 (www.socresonline.org.uk/13/5/7.html).

FCO (Foreign and Commonwealth Office) (2004) *Draft report on young Muslims and extremism*, London: FCO.

Fekete, L. (2001) 'The Terrorism Act 2001: An interview with Gareth Pierce', *Race & Class*, vol 43, no 2, pp 95-103.

Fielding, N.G. (2002) 'Automating the ineffable: Qualitative software and the meaning of qualitative research', in T. May (ed) *Qualitative research in action*, London: Sage Publications, pp 161-178.

Fineman, S. (2000) *Emotion in organizations*, London: Sage Publications.

Finney, N. and Simpson, L. (2009) *Sleepwalking into segregation? Challenging the myths about race and migration*, Bristol: The Policy Press.

Flint, J. and Robinson, D. (eds) (2008) *Community cohesion in crisis? New dimensions of diversity and difference*, Bristol: The Policy Press.

Flood, S. (2010) *The government funding relationship: Its impact on the sector and the future challenges and opportunities*, London: National Council for Voluntary Organisations.

Fortier, A.-M. (2005) 'Pride politics and multiculturalist citizenship', *Ethnic and Racial Studies*, vol 28, no 3, pp 559-78.

Fortier, A.-M. (2007) 'Too close for comfort: loving thy neighbour and the management of multicultural intimacies', *Environment and Planning D: Society and Space*, vol 25, no 1, pp 104-19.

Fortier, A.-M. (2010) 'Proximity by design? Affective citizenship and the management of unease', *Citizenship Studies*, vol 14, no 1, pp 17-30.

Foucault, M. (1982) 'The subject and power', in H.L. Dreyfus and P. Rabinow (eds) *Michel Foucault: Beyond structuralism and hermeneutics*, Chicago, IL: University of Chicago Press, pp 208-26.

Foucault, M. (1991 [1978]) 'Governmentality', in G. Burchell, C. Gordon and P. Miller (eds) *The Foucault effect: Studies in governmentality*, Chicago, IL: University of Chicago Press, pp 87-104.

Foucault, M. (2002 [1969]) *The archaeology of knowledge*, London and New York: Routledge.

Frankenberg, R. (1993) *White women, race matters: The social construction of whiteness*, London: Routledge.

Fraser, N. (2000) 'Rethinking recognition', *New Left Review*, vol 3, May-June, pp 107-20.

Garland, J. and Chakraborti, N. (2006) '"Race", space and place: Examining identity and cultures of exclusion in rural England', *Ethnicities*, vol 6, no 2, pp 159-77.

Garner, S. (2009) 'Home truths: the white working class and the racialisation of social housing', in K.P. Sveinnson (ed) *Who cares about the white working class?*, London: Runnymede Trust, pp 45-51.

Gane, N. and Back, L. (2012) 'C. Wright Mills 50 years on: The promise and craft of sociology revisited', *Theory, Culture & Society*, vol 29, nos 7-8, pp 399-421.

Gavrielides, T. (2011) 'The new politics of community cohesion: making use of human rights policy and legislation', *Policy & Politics*, vol 38, no 3, pp 427-44.

Giddens, A. (1998) *The third way: The renewal of social democracy*, Cambridge: Polity Press.

Gillborn, D. (2009) 'Education: The numbers game and construction of white racial victimhood', in K.P. Sveinnson (ed) *Who cares about the white working class?*, London: Runnymede Trust, pp 15-22.

Gilroy, P. (1987) *There ain't no black in the Union Jack: The cultural politics of race and nation*, London: Hutchinson.

Gilroy, P. (1990) 'The end of anti-racism', in W. Ball and J. Solomos (eds) *Race and local politics*, Basingstoke: Macmillan, pp 191-209.

Gilroy, P. (2001) 'Joined-up politics and postcolonial melancholia', *Theory, Culture & Society*, vol 18, nos 2-3, pp 151-67.

Gilroy, P. (2004) *After empire: Melancholia or convivial culture?*, London: Routledge.

Goodhart, D. (2004) 'Discomfort of strangers', *The Guardian*, 24 February (www.guardian.co.uk/race/story/0,11374,1154684,00.html and www.guardian.co.uk/comment/story/0,3604,1154693,00.html).

Gordon, P. (1990) 'A dirty war: the New Right and local authority anti-racism', in W. Ball and J. Solomos (eds) *Race and local politics*, Basingstoke: Macmillan, pp 175-90.

Greater Peterborough Partnership (2008) *Sustainable community strategy 2008-2021*, Peterborough: Greater Peterborough Partnership.

Greco, M. and Stenner, P. (eds) (2008) *Emotions: A social science reader*, London: Routledge.

Grillo, R. (2007) 'An excess of alterity? Debating difference in a multicultural society', *Ethnic and Racial Studies*, vol 30, no 6, pp 979-98.

Gunaratnam, Y. (2009) 'Narrative interviews and research', in Y. Gunaratnam and D. Oliviere (eds) *Narrative and stories in health care: Illness, dying and bereavement*, Oxford: Oxford University Press, pp 47-62.

Guru-Murthy, K. (2011) 'So what does the Big Society mean to you?', *Channel 4 News*, 13 February (www.channel4.com/news/so-what-does-the-big-society-mean-to-you).

Hall, S. (1998) 'The Great Moving Nowhere Show', *Marxism Today*, November/December, pp 9-14.

Hall, S. (2000) 'Conclusion: The multi-cultural question', in B. Hesse (ed) *Un/settled multiculturalisms: Diasporas, entanglements, transruptions*, London and New York: Zed Books, pp 209-41.

Hall, S., Critcher, C., Jefferson, T., Clarke, J.N. and Roberts, B. (1978) *Policing the crisis: Mugging, the state, and law and order*, London: Palgrave Macmillan.

Haraway, D.J. (1991) 'Situated knowledges: The science question in feminism and the privilege of partial perspective', in D.J. Haraway (ed) *Simians, cyborgs and women: The reinvention of nature*, London: Free Association Books, pp 183-201.

Haritaworn, J., Tauqir, T. and Erdem, E. (2008) 'Gay imperialism: Gender and sexuality discourse in the "War on Terror"', in A. Kuntsman and E. Miyake (eds) *Out of place: Interrogating silences in queerness/raciality*, York: Raw Nerve Books, pp 71-95.

Harris, A. (2012) 'Art and gentrification: pursuing the urban pastoral in Hoxton, London', *Transactions of the Institute of British Geographers*, vol 37, no 2, pp 226-41.

Harrison, P. (1983) *Inside the inner city: Life under the cutting edge*, London: Penguin.

Hart, A. (2003) 'A neighbourhood renewal project in Dalston, Hackney: Towards a new form of partnership for inner city regeneration', *Journal of Retail and Leisure Property*, vol 3, no 3, pp 237-45.

Harvey, D. (1989) 'From managerialism to entrepreneurialism: The transformation in urban governance in late capitalism', *Geografiska Annaler, Series B, Human Geography*, vol 71, no 1, pp 3-17.

Haylett, C. (2001) 'Illegitimate subjects? Abject whites, neoliberal modernisation, and middle-class multiculturalism', *Environment and Planning D: Society and Space*, vol 19, no 3, pp 351-70.

Hearn, J. (2010) 'Reflecting on men and social policy: Contemporary critical debates and implications for social policy', *Critical Social Policy*, vol 30, no 2, pp 165-88.

Hesse, B. (1993) 'Black to front and black again: Racialization through contested times and spaces', in M. Keith and S. Pile (eds) *Place and the politics of identity*, London: Routledge, pp 160-79.

Hewitt, R. (2005) *White backlash and the politics of multiculturalism*, Cambridge: Cambridge University Press.

Hickman, M. (1998) 'Reconstructing deconstructing "race": British political discourses about the Irish in Britain', *Ethnic and Racial Studies*, vol 21, no 2, pp 288-307.

Hickman, M. (2007) 'Multiculturalism in one country?', *Economy and Society*, vol 36, no 2, pp 318-24.

Hill, D. (2008) 'Jules Pipe defends the Dalston Project', *Clapton Pond Blog* (http://davehill.typepad.com/claptonian/2008/05/hackney-mayor-j.html).

HM Government (2006) *Countering international terrorism: The United Kingdom's strategy*, Norwich: The Stationery Office.

HM Government (2008) *The Prevent strategy: A guide for local partners in England: Stopping people becoming or supporting terrorists or violent extremists*, London: HM Government.

HM Government (2009a) *Pursue, prevent, protect, prepare: The United Kingdom's strategy for countering international terrorism*, Norwich: The Stationery Office.

HM Government (2009b) *Self-assessing local performance against NI 35: Building resilience to violent extremism. Guidance for local partners*, London: Home Office.

HM Government (2011) *Prevent strategy*, London: The Stationery Office.

Hochschild, A.R. (1983) *The managed heart: Commercialization of human feeling*, Berkeley, CA: University of California Press.

Hoggett, P. (2000) 'Social policy and the emotions', in G. Lewis, S. Gewirtz and J. Clarke (eds) *Rethinking social policy*, London: Sage Publications, pp 141–55.

Hoggett, P. (2001) 'Agency, rationality and social policy', *Journal of Social Policy*, vol 30, no 1, pp 37–56.

Hoggett, P., Mayo, M. and Miller, C. (2006a) 'Private passions, the public good and public service reform', *Social Policy & Administration*, vol 40, no 7, pp 758–73.

Hoggett, P., Beedell, P., Jimenez, L., Mayo, M. and Miller, C. (2006b) 'Identity, life history and commitment to welfare', *Journal of Social Policy*, vol 35, no 4, pp 689–704.

Hollway, W. and Jefferson, T. (2000) *Doing qualitative research differently*, London: Sage Publications.

Holman, C. and Holman, N. (2002) *Torah, worship and acts of loving kindness*, Leicester: De Montfort University.

Holt, D. and Cameron, D. (2010) *Cultural strategy: Using innovative ideologies to build breakthrough brands*, Oxford: Oxford University Press.

Home Office (2005a) *Community cohesion: Seven steps, A practitioner's toolkit*, London: Home Office.

Home Office (2005b) *Improving opportunity, strengthening society: The government's strategy to increase race equality and community cohesion*, London: Home Office.

Home Office (2005c) *Integration matters: A national strategy for refugee integration*, London: Immigration and Nationality Directorate.

Hood, C. (1991) 'A public management for all seasons?', *Public Administration*, vol 69, no 1, pp 3–19.

Hood, C. (1998) *The art of the state*, Oxford: Oxford University Press.

hooks, b. (1990) 'Choosing the margin as a space of radical openness', in b. hooks (ed) *Yearning: Race, gender and cultural politics*, Boston, MA: South End Press, pp 145–54.

House of Commons Communities and Local Government Committee (2010) *Preventing violent extremism: Sixth report of the Session 2009-10. Report, together with formal minutes, oral and written evidence*, London: The Stationery Office.

Hunter, S. (2003) 'A critical analysis of approaches to the concept of social identity in social policy', *Critical Social Policy*, vol 23, no 3, pp 322–44.

Hunter, S. (2005) 'Negotiating professional and social voices in research principles and practice', *Journal of Social Work Practice*, vol 19, no 2, pp 149–62.

Hunter, S. (2010) 'What a white shame: Race, gender and white shame in the relational economy of primary health care organizations in England', *Social Politics*, vol 17, vol 4, pp 450-76.

Hunter, S. (2013) *Power, politics and the emotions: Impossible governance?*, London: Routledge.

Husband, C. and Alam, Y. (2011) *Social cohesion and counter-terrorism: A policy contradiction?*, Bristol: The Policy Press.

IDeA (Improvement and Development Agency) (2009) 'Branding and place shaping' (www.idea.gov.uk/idk/core/page.do?pageId=7816272#contents-2).

Independent, The (2006) '1,000 foreign prisoners escape deportation after release', 25 April (www.independent.co.uk/news/uk/crime/1000-foreign-prisoners-escape-deportation-after-release-475559.html).

Ipsos MORI (2009) *Assessing Hackney's performance: Results of the Place Survey for London Borough of Hackney and partners*, London: London Borough of Hackney.

Jackson, S. (2010) 'Stewart Jackson: on Peterborough's past, present and future', *peterboroughtoday.co.uk*, 20 August (www.peterboroughtoday.co.uk/news/columnists_2_17117/stewart_jackson_on_peterborough_s_past_present_and_future_20_08_10_1_814218).

Jacobs, J.M. (1996) *Edge of empire: Postcolonialism and the city*, London and New York: Routledge.

Jeffers, S. and Hoggett, P. (1995) 'Like counting deckchairs on the Titanic: A study of institutional racism and housing', *Housing Studies*, vol 10, no 3, pp 325-44.

Jessop, B. (2003) 'Governance and metagovernance: On reflexivity, requisite variety, and requisite irony', in H.P. Bang (ed) *Governance as social and political communication*, Manchester: Manchester University Press, pp 101-16.

Kalra, V. (2002) 'Riots, race and reports: Denham, Cantle, Oldham and Burnley inquiries', *Sage Race Relations Abstracts*, vol 27, no 4, pp 20-30.

Keith, M. (1993) *Race, riots and policing: Lore and disorder in a multi-racist society*, London: UCL Press.

Keith, M. (2005) *After the cosmopolitan? Multicultural cities and the future of racism*, Abingdon: Routledge.

Keith, M. (2007a) 'Don't sleepwalk into simplification: what the Commission on Integration and Cohesion really said', *Open Democracy* (www.opendemocracy.net/ourkingdom/articles/commission_on_integration_and_cohesion).

Keith, M. (2007b) 'Nostalgia isn't what it used to be', *Open Democracy* (www.opendemocracy.net/ourkingdom/2007/07/21/nostalgia-isnt-what-it-used-to-be).

Keith, M. (2008a) 'Between being and becoming? Rights, responsibilities and the politics of multiculture in the new East End', *Sociological Research Online*, vol 13, no 5, p 11.

Keith, M. (2008b) 'Public sociology? Between heroic immersion and critical distance: Personal reflections on academic engagement with political life', *Critical Social Policy*, vol 28, no 3, pp 320-34.

Keith, M. and Murji, K. (1990) 'Reifying crime, legitimising racism: Policing, local authorities and left realism', in W. Ball and J. Solomos (eds) *Race and local politics*, Basingstoke: Macmillan, pp 115-131.

Keith, M. and Pile, S. (eds) (1993) *Place and the politics of identity*, London and New York: Routledge.

Keith, M. and Rogers, A. (1991) 'Hollow promises? Policy, theory and practice in the inner city', in M. Keith and A. Rogers (eds) *Hollow promises: Rhetoric and reality in the inner city*, London and New York: Mansell Publishing, pp 1-30.

Kelcher, S. (2007) *Preventing Violent Extremism Pathfinder Fund*, London Councils Executive, 23 April (www.londoncouncils.gov.uk/London%20Councils/PVEDFrepor.doc).

Kettle, M. and Hodges, L. (1982) *Uprising! The police, the people and the riots in Britain's cities*, London: Pan Books Limited.

Khan, O. (2007) 'Policy, identity and community cohesion: How race equality fits', in M. Wetherell, M. Laflèche and R. Berkeley (eds) *Identity, ethnic diversity and community cohesion*, London: Sage Publications, pp 40-58.

Kidd, C. and Glaser, M. (2003) 'Chip Kidd talks with Milton Glaser', *The Believer*, September (www.believermag.com/issues/200309/?read=interview_glaser).

Knight, S. (2005) 'Shot Brazilian's lawyers demand inquiry over police "lies"', *The Times*, 17 August (http://www.thetimes.co.uk/tto/news/uk/article1936967.ece).

Knowles, C. (2008) 'The landscape of post-imperial whiteness in rural Britain', *Ethnic and Racial Studies*, vol 31, no 1, pp 167-84.

Koutrolikou, P.-P. (2012) 'Spatialities of ethnocultural relations in multicultural East London: Discourses of interaction and social mix', *Urban Studies*, vol 49, no 10, pp 2049-66.

Kundnani, A. (2002) 'The death of multiculturalism', *Race & Class*, vol 43, no 4, pp 67-72.

Kundnani, A. (2009) *Spooked! How not to prevent violent extremism*, London: Institute of Race Relations.

Lansley, S., Goss, S. and Wolmar, C. (1989) *Councils in conflict: The rise and fall of the municipal left*, Basingstoke: Macmillan Education.

Law, J. (2003) *Making a mess with method*, Lancaster: Lancaster University (www.lancs.ac.uk/fass/sociology/papers/law-making-a-mess-with-method.pdf).

Layard, P.R.G. (2005) *Happiness: Lessons from a new science*, London: Allen Lane.

LBH (London Borough of Hackney) (2006a) *Hackney Borough profile 2006*, London: LBH.

LBH (2006b) *Mind the gap: Hackney's strategy to reduce inequalities and poverty. Community strategy 2005-2015. Review and update: July 2006*, London: LBH.

LBH (2006c) 'On your bike, Nike!', *Hackney News* (www.hackney.gov.uk/xc-news-may06-nike.htm).

LBH (2012a) *Hackney census data: Population and households November 2012*, London: LBH (http://tiny.cc/lbhcensus).

LBH (2012b) *Facts and figures leaflet December 2012*, London: LBH (www.hackney.gov.uk/Assets/Documents/facts-and-figures.pdf).

Le Grand, J. (2003) *Motivation, agency and public policy: Of knights and knaves, pawns and queens*, Oxford and New York: Oxford University Press.

Levitas, R. (2005) *The inclusive society? Social exclusion and New Labour* (2nd edn), Basingstoke: Palgrave Macmillan.

Lewis, G. (2000) *Race, gender, social welfare: Encounters in postcolonial society*, Cambridge: Polity Press.

Lewis, G. (2005) 'Welcome to the margins: Diversity, tolerance, and policies of exclusion', *Ethnic and Racial Studies*, vol 28, no 3, pp 536-58.

LGA (Local Government Association) (2002) *Guidance on community cohesion*, London: LGA.

Lipsky, M. (1980) *Street-level bureaucracy: Dilemmas of the individual in public services*, New York: Russell Sage Foundation.

Lister, R. (2001) 'New Labour: a study in ambiguity from a position of ambivalence', *Critical Social Policy*, vol 21, no 4, pp 425-47.

Lury, C. (2004) *Brands: The logos of the global economy*, London: Routledge.

Lyons, M. (2007) *The Lyons Inquiry into local government: Place-shaping: A shared ambition for the future of local government*, London: The Stationery Office.

Mac an Ghaill, M. (2001) 'British critical theorists: The production of the conceptual invisibility of the Irish diaspora', *Social Identities*, vol 7, no 2, pp 179-201.

MacKinnon, D., Cumbers, A., Featherstone, D., Ince, A. and Strauss, K. (2011) *Globalisation, labour markets and communities in contemporary Britain*, York: Joseph Rowntree Foundation.

Macpherson, W. (1999) *The Stephen Lawrence Inquiry*, London: The Stationery Office.

McGee, S. (2008) 'Binmen in Muslim areas ordered by terror police to snoop in residents' rubbish bins', *Mail Online*, 19 April (www.dailymail.co.uk/news/article-560727/Binmen-Muslim-areas-ordered-terror-police-snoop-residents-rubbish-bins.html).

McGhee, D. (2003) 'Moving to "our" common ground – a critical examination of community cohesion discourse in twenty-first century Britain', *The Sociological Review*, vol 51, no 3, pp 376-404.

McGhee, D. (2005) 'Patriots of the future? A critical examination of community cohesion strategies in contemporary Britain', *Sociological Research Online*, vol 10, no 3 (www.socresonline.org.uk/10/3/mcghee.html).

McGhee, D. (2008) *The end of multiculturalism? Terrorism, integration and human rights*, Maidenhead: Open University Press.

McKee, K. (2009) 'Post-Foucauldian governmentality: What does it offer critical social policy analysis?', *Critical Social Policy*, vol 29, no 3, pp 465-86.

McLaughlin, E. and Neal, S. (2004) 'Misrepresenting the multicultural nation: the Parekh Report, the media and the policy making process', *Policy Studies*, vol 25, no 3, pp 155-73.

McLean, M. (2008) LGA office holders meeting, 16 April, Strategic issues: Preventing violent extremism, London: Local Government Association.

Malik, S. (2009) Speech given at Capita's 4th National Preventing Violent Extremism Conference, 22 October, London (http://webarchive.nationalarchives.gov.uk/20100104223119/http://www.communities.gov.uk/speeches/corporate/capitaprevent09).

Manzi, T. and Jacobs, K. (2009) 'From a "society of fear" to a "society of respect": the transformation of Hackney's Holly Street Estate', in R. Imrie, L. Lees and M. Raco (eds) *Regenerating London: Governance, sustainability and community in a global city*, London: Routledge, pp 273-88.

Markova, E. and Black, R. (2007) *East European immigration and community cohesion*, York: Joseph Rowntree Foundation.

May, J. (1996) 'Globalization and the politics of place: place and identity in an inner London neighbourhood', *Transactions of the Institute of British Geographers*, vol 21, no 1, pp 194-215.

May, T. (2012) *Outcome of the Equalities red tape challenge and reform of the Equality and Human Rights Commission*, Written Ministerial Statement, London: Home Office (www.homeoffice.gov.uk/publications/about-us/parliamentary-business/written-ministerial-statement/red-tape-reform-ehrc).

Mayhew, L. and Harper, G. (2008) *Estimating and profiling the population of Hackney*, London: Mayhew Harper Associates Ltd.

Mayo, M., Hoggett, P. and Miller, C. (2007) 'Capacities of the capacity-builders: should training frameworks include ethical and emotional dimensions?', in J. Diamond, J. Liddle, A. Southern and A. Townsend (eds) *Managing the city*, London and New York: Routledge, pp 133-45.

Mercer, K. (1994) *Welcome to the jungle: New positions in Black cultural studies*, London and New York: Routledge.

Miles, R. (1993) *Racism after race relations*, London: Routledge.

Miliband, D. (2006) 'Building community in a diverse society: Scarman lecture', Scarman Trust (www.thescarmantrust.org/Scarman%20final.doc).

Mills, C.W. (1999 [1959]) *The sociological imagination*, Oxford: Oxford University Press.

Mirza, M., Sewell, T., Singh, S. and Dyer, S. (2010) 'Rethinking race', *Prospect*, October, pp 31-7.

Modood, T. (2007) 'Multiculturalism, citizenship and national identity', *Open Democracy* (www.opendemocracy.net/faith-terrorism/multiculturalism_4627.jsp).

Mouffe, C. (2000) *The democratic paradox*, London: Verso.

Mouffe, C. (2005) *On the political*, London and New York: Routledge.

MPA (Metropolitan Police Authority) (2007) *Counter-terrorism: The London debate*, London: MPA.

Muir, H. and Butt, R. (2005) 'A rumour, outrage and then a riot. How tension in a Birmingham suburb erupted', *The Guardian*, 24 October (www.guardian.co.uk/uk/2005/oct/24/race.ukcrime).

Muir, R. (2008) *One London? Change and cohesion in three London boroughs*, London: Institute for Public Policy Research.

Mulgan, G. and Davies, W. (2011) 'Why happiness? An interview with the co-founder of Action for Happiness', *Open Democracy*, 7 June (www.opendemocracy.net/ourkingdom/geoff-mulgan-william-davies/interview-with-co-founder-of-action-for-happine).

Mumford, K. and Power, A. (2003) *East Enders: Family and community in East London*, Bristol: The Policy Press.

Neal, S. (2002) 'Rural landscapes, representations and racism: multicultural citizenship and policy making in the English countryside', *Ethnic and Racial Studies*, vol 25, no 3, pp 442-61.

Newman, J. and Clarke, J. (2009) *Publics, politics and power: Remaking the public in public services*, London: Sage Publications.

Newsnight (2008) 10 September, BBC2.

Nickels, H.C., Thomas, L., Hickman, M.J. and Silvestri, S. (2009) *A comparative study of the representations of 'suspect' communities in multi-ethnic Britain and of their impact on Irish communities and Muslim communities – Mapping newspaper content*, Working Paper 13, London: Institute for the Study of European Transformation, London Metropolitan University (www.londonmet.ac.uk/fms/MRSite/Research/iset/WP13%20H%20Nickels%203.pdf).

Noble, M., McLennan, D. and Whitworth, A. (2009) *Tracking neighbourhoods: The Economic Deprivation Index 2008*, London: Communities and Local Government.

Oakeshott, I. (2008) 'Jacqui Smith admits "I won't walk down a street alone at night"', *The Times*, 20 January (www.thesundaytimes.co.uk/sto/Test/politics/article78856.ece).

Orwell, G. (1949) *Nineteen Eighty-Four*, London: Penguin.

Ouseley, H. (1990) 'Resisting institutional change', in W. Ball and J. Solomos (eds) *Race and local politics*, Hampshire: Macmillan, pp 132-52.

Ouseley, H. (2001) *Community pride, not prejudice: Making diversity work in Bradford*, Bradford: Bradford Vision.

Paley, J. (2009) 'Narrative machinery', in Y. Gunaratnam, and D. Oliviere (eds) *Narrative and stories in health care: Illness, dying and bereavement*, Oxford: Oxford University Press, pp 17-32.

Parekh, B. (2002) *The future of multi-ethnic Britain: Report of the Commission* (2nd edn), London: Profile Books.

Phillips, T. (2004) 'Genteel xenophobia is as bad as any other kind', *The Guardian*, 16 February (www.guardian.co.uk/world/2004/feb/16/race.equality).

Phillips, T. (2005) 'After 7/7: Sleepwalking to segregation', Speech to the Manchester Council for Community Relations, Manchester: Commission for Racial Equality (www.humanities.manchester.ac.uk/socialchange/research/social-change/summer-workshops/documents/sleepwalking.pdf).

Philo, C. and Kearns, G. (1993) 'Culture, history, capital: A critical introduction to the selling of places', in G. Kearns and C. Philo (eds) *Selling places: The city as cultural capital, past and present*, Oxford: Pergamon Press, pp 1-32.

Pickard, J. (2010) 'Official: Everyone is middle class now', *Financial Times Westminster Blog*, 10 August (blogs.ft.com/westminster/2010/08/official-everyone-is-middle-class-now).

Pickles, E. (2010) *Local government accountability*, London: Communities and Local Government (www.communities.gov.uk/statements/newsroom/localgovaccountability).

Pratt, A.C. (2009) 'Urban regeneration: From the arts "feel good" factor to the cultural economy: A case study of Hoxton, London', *Urban Studies*, vol 46, no 5-6, pp 1041-61.

Preventing Extremism Together Working Groups (2005) *Preventing Extremism Together Working Groups*, London: Home Office (www.communities.gov.uk/documents/communities/pdf/152164.pdf).

Puar, J.K. (2007) *Terrorist assemblages: Homonationalism in queer times*, Durham, NC: Duke University Press.

Puwar, N. (2001) 'The racialised somatic norm and the senior civil service', *Sociology*, vol 35, no 3, pp 651-70.

Puwar, N. (2004) *Space invaders: Race, gender and bodies out of place*, Oxford: Berg.

Ratcliffe, P. and Newman, I. (eds) (2011) *Promoting social cohesion: Implications for policy and evaluation*, Bristol: The Policy Press.

Reading Muslim PVE Crisis Group (2008) Letter to Reading Council (http://pvecrisisgroup.com/letter-to-reading-local-authority).

Reay, D. (2008) 'Psychosocial aspects of white middle-class identities: Desiring and defending against the class and ethnic "Other" in urban multi-ethnic schooling', *Sociology*, vol 42, no 6, pp 1072-88.

Reay, D., Hollingworth, S., Williams, K., Crozier, G., Jamieson, F., James, D. and Beedell, P. (2007) '"A darker shade of pale?" Whiteness, the middle classes and multi-ethnic inner city schooling', *Sociology*, vol 41, no 6, pp 1041-60.

Reid, S. (2008) 'Merchants of hatred: On the anniversary of 9/11 this terrifying investigation reveals the hatred of Britain's enemies within', *Mail Online*, 13 September (www.dailymail.co.uk/news/article-1055422/Merchants-Hatred-On-anniversary-9-11-terrifying-investigation-reveals-hatred-Britains-enemies-within.html).

Reville, M. (2010) 'The Peterborough effect: MP calls for city to defend itself', *peterboroughtoday.co.uk*, 20 August (www.peterboroughtoday.co.uk/community/ex_pats_2_17170/the_peterborough_effect_mp_calls_for_city_to_defend_itself_1_814212).

Rhys-Taylor, A. (2010) 'Coming to our senses: A multisensory ethnography of class and multiculture in East London', Unpublished PhD thesis, London: University of London.

Rhodes, R.A.W. (1988) *Beyond Westminster and Whitehall*, London: Unwin Hyman.

Riles, A. (2006) '(Deadlines): Removing the brackets on politics in bureaucratic and anthropological analysis', in A. Riles (ed) *Documents: Artifacts of modern knowledge*, Ann Arbor, MI: University of Michigan, pp 71-94.

Rimmer, S. (2008) 'Preventing violent extremism: March 2008 update', Letter to Government Office Regional Directors and Deputy Directors, Chief Officers of Police and Chairs of Police Authorities, 13 March, Director of Home Office Prevent and Research, Information and Communications Unit.

Ritchie, D. (2001) *Oldham Independent Review Panel report: One Oldham, one future*, Manchester: Government Office for the North West.

Robinson, D. (2005) 'The search for community cohesion: key themes and dominant concepts of the public policy agenda', *Urban Studies*, vol 42, no 8, pp 1411-27.

Robinson, D. (2008) 'Community cohesion and the politics of communitarianism', in J. Flint and D. Robinson (eds) *Community cohesion in crisis? New dimensions of diversity and difference*, Bristol: The Policy Press, pp 15-33.

Robinson, D. and Reeve, K. (2006) *Neighbourhood experiences of new immigration: Reflections from the evidence base*, York: Joseph Rowntree Foundation.

Rose, N. (1998) *Inventing our selves: Psychology, power and personhood*, Cambridge: Cambridge University Press.

Rose, N. (1999a) *Governing the soul: The shaping of the private self*, London and New York: Free Association Books.

Rose, N. (1999b) *Powers of freedom: Reframing political thought*, Cambridge: Cambridge University Press.

Rosen, M. (2007) 'Michael Rosen: Interview', *Time Out London*, 9 July.

Rosen, M. (2008a) 'Michael Rosen: New Labour's private degeneration', *Socialist Worker Online* (www.socialistworker.co.uk/art.php?id=14820).

Rosen, M. (2008b) *Regeneration blues* (opendalston.blogspot.com/2008/07/new-poem-by-dalston-resident-michael.html).

Samuel, R. and Thompson, P. (1990) 'Introduction', in R. Samuel, and P. Thompson (eds) *The myths we live by*, London and New York: Routledge, pp 1-22.

Savage, M., Bagnall, G. and Longhurst, B. (2005) *Globalization and belonging*, London: Sage Publications.

Sayer, A. (2005) *The moral significance of class*, Cambridge: Cambridge University Press.

Scanlon, C. and Adlam, J. (2008) 'Refusal, social exclusion and the cycle of rejection: A cynical analysis?', *Critical Social Policy*, vol 28, no 4, pp 529-49.

Schofield, B. (2002) 'Partners in power', *Sociology*, vol 36, no 3, pp 663-83.

Shaw, S., Bagwell, S. and Karmowska, J. (2004) 'Ethnoscapes as spectacle: Reimaging multicultural districts as new destinations for leisure and tourism consumption', *Urban Studies*, vol 41, no 10, pp 1983-2000.

Silverman, D. (1998) *Harvey Sacks: Social science and conversation analysis*, Cambridge: Polity Press.

Sinclair, I. (2008a) 'Banned in Hackney – for going off-message about the Olympics', *The Guardian*, 22 October (www.guardian.co.uk/books/2008/oct/22/hackney-library-book-ban).

Sinclair, I. (2008b) 'The Olympics scam', *London Review of Books*, vol 30, no 12, pp 17-23.

Sinclair, I. (2009) *Hackney, that Rose Red Empire: A confidential report*, London: Hamish Hamilton.

Skeggs, B. (1997) *Formations of class and gender: Becoming respectable*, London: Sage Publications.

Skeggs, B. (2002) 'Techniques for telling the reflexive self', in T. May (ed) *Qualitative research in action*, London: Sage Publications, pp 349-75.

Skeggs, B. (2004) *Class, self, culture*, London: Routledge.

Skeggs, B. (2005a) 'The making of class and gender through visualizing moral subject formation', *Sociology*, vol 39, no 5, pp 965-82.

Skeggs, B. (2005b) 'The re-branding of class', in F. Devine, M. Savage, J. Scott and R. Crompton (eds) *Rethinking class: Culture, identities, lifestyle*, Basingstoke: Palgrave Macmillan, pp 46-67.

Smith, D.P. and Holt, L. (2005) '"Lesbian migrants in the gentrified valley" and "other" geographies of rural gentrification', *Journal of Rural Studies*, vol 21, pp 313-22.

Solomos, J. (1986) *Riots, urban protest and social policy: The interplay of reform and social control*, Coventry: Centre for Research in Ethnic Relations.

Solomos, J. (1988) *Black youth, racism and the state: The politics of ideology and policy*, Cambridge: Cambridge University Press.

Solomos, J. (2003) *Race and racism in Britain*, Basingstoke: Palgrave Macmillan.

Solomos, J. and Back, L. (1995) *Race, politics and social change*, London and New York: Routledge.

Solomos, J. and Ball, W. (1990) 'New initiatives and the possibilities of reform', in W. Ball and J. Solomos (eds) *Race and local politics*, Basingstoke: Macmillan, pp 210-24.

Solomos, J. and Singh, G. (1990) 'Racial equality, housing and the local state', in W. Ball and J. Solomos (eds) *Race and local politics*, Basingstoke: Macmillan, pp 95-114.

Spencer, S. (2011) 'Integration in the UK: why the silence?', *Open Democracy*, 6 April (www.opendemocracy.net/5050/sarah-spencer/integration-in-uk-why-silence).

Spivak, G.C. (1988) 'Can the subaltern speak?', in C. Nelson and L. Grossberg (eds) *Marxism and the interpretation of culture*, Urbana, IL: University of Illinois Press, pp 271-313.

Srivastava, S. (2005) '"You're calling me a racist?" The moral and emotional regulation of antiracism and feminism', *Signs: Journal of Women in Culture and Society*, vol 31, no 1, pp 29-62.

Stenner, P., Barnes, M. and Taylor, D. (2008) 'Editorial introduction: Psychosocial welfare: Contributions to an emerging field', *Critical Social Policy*, vol 28, no 4, pp 411-14.

Stephens, P. (2011) 'Memo to Cameron: tactics are not enough', *Financial Times* (www.ft.com/cms/s/0/95a838e4-a671-11e0-ae9c-00144feabdc0.html#axzz1RN8sxBeE).

Stiglitz, J., Sen, A. and Fitoussi, J.-P. (2009) *The measurement of economic performance and social progress revisited*, Paris: Commission on the Measurement of Economic Performance and Social Progress.

Stoker, G. (2004) *Transforming local governance: From Thatcherism to New Labour*, Basingstoke: Palgrave Macmillan.

Stone, C.N. (1995) 'Political leadership in urban politics', in D. Judge, G. Stoker and H. Wolman (eds) *Theories of urban politics*, London: Sage Publications, pp 96-116.

Strathern, M. (ed) (2000) *Audit cultures: Anthropological studies in accountability, ethics and the academy*, London and New York: Routledge.

Strathern, M. (2006) 'Bullet-proofing: A tale from the United Kingdom', in A. Riles (ed) *Documents: Artifacts of modern knowledge*, Ann Arbor, MI: University of Michigan, pp 181-205.

Swan, E. (2010) 'States of white ignorance, and audit masculinity in English higher education', *Social Politics*, vol 17, no 4, pp 477-506.

Swyngedouw, E. (2010) 'Apocalypse forever? Post-political populism and the spectre of climate change', *Theory, Culture & Society*, vol 27, no 2-3, pp 213-32.

Temple, M. (2000) 'New Labour's Third Way: pragmatism and governance', *British Journal of Politics and International Relations*, vol 2, no 3, pp 302-25.

Theodoropoulou, S. and Zuleeg, F. (2009) *What do citizens want? Well-being measurement and its importance for European policy-making*, Brussels: European Policy Centre.

Thomas, P. (2010) 'Failed and friendless: The UK's "Preventing Violent Extremism" programme', *British Journal of Politics and International Relations*, vol 12, no 3, pp 442-58.

Thompson, C.J., Rindfleisch, A. and Arsel, Z. (2006) 'Emotional branding and the strategic value of the Doppelgänger brand image', *Journal of Marketing*, vol 70, no 6, pp 50-64.

Tran, M. (2006) 'Hackney wins logo case against Nike', *The Guardian*, 11 September (www.guardian.co.uk/business/2006/sep/11/politics. money).

Travis, A. (2010) 'Ministers dismantle £60m programme to prevent violent extremism', *The Guardian*, 13 July (www.guardian.co.uk/ politics/2010/jul/13/ministers-dismantle-programme-prevent-violent-extremism).

Trouillot, M.-R. (1995) *Silencing the past: Power and the production of history*, Boston, MA: Beacon Press.

Turley, A. (2009) *Stronger together: A new approach to preventing violent extremism*, London: New Local Government Network.

Urry, J. (1995) *Consuming places*, London and New York: Routledge.

van Dijk, T.A. (1992) 'Discourse and the denial of racism', *Discourse & Society*, vol 3, no 1, pp 87-118.

Vargas-Silva, C. (2011) *Briefing: Migration flows of A8 and other EU migrants to and from the UK*, Oxford: The Migration Observatory.

Vertovec, S. (2007) 'Super-diversity and its implications', *Ethnic and Racial Studies*, vol 30, no 6, pp 1024-54.

Ward, S.V. (1998) *Selling places: The marketing and promotion of towns and cities 1850-2000*, Abingdon: Spon Press.

Ware, V. (2002) 'Seeing through skin/seeing through epidermalization', in V. Ware and L. Back (eds) *Out of whiteness: Color, politics and culture*, Chicago, IL and London: University of Chicago Press, pp 60-93.

Ware, V. (2008) 'Towards a sociology of resentment: A debate on class and whiteness', *Sociological Research Online*, vol 13, no 5 (www.socresonline. org.uk/13/5/9.html).

Watson, S. (2009) 'The magic of the marketplace: Sociality in a neglected public space', *Urban Studies*, vol 46, no 8, pp 1577-91.

Watson, S. and Wells, K. (2005) 'Spaces of nostalgia: the hollowing out of a London market', *Social and Cultural Geography*, vol 6, no 1, pp 17-30.

Webb, B. (2011) 'We are all working-class now', *The Guardian*, 10 February (www.guardian.co.uk/commentisfree/2011/feb/10/ working-class-lord-lang-cuts).

Wemyss, G. (2006) 'The power to tolerate: contests over Britishness and belonging in East London', *Patterns of Prejudice*, vol 40, no 3, pp 215-36.

Wemyss, G. (2008) 'White memories, white belonging: Competing colonial anniversaries in "postcolonial" East London', *Sociological Research Online*, vol 13, no 5 (www.socresonline.org.uk/13/5/8.html).

Wemyss, G. (2009) *The invisible empire: White discourse, tolerance and belonging*, Farnham: Ashgate.

Wessendorf, S. (2010) *Commonplace diversity: Social interactions in a super-diverse context*, Working Papers 10-11, Göttingen: Max Planck Institute for the Study of Religious and Ethnic Diversity.

Wetherell, M. (2008) 'Speaking to power: Tony Blair, complex multicultures and fragile white English identities', *Critical Social Policy*, vol 28, no 3, pp 299-319.

Wetherell, M., Laflèche, M. and Berkeley, R. (eds) (2007) *Identity, ethnic diversity and community cohesion*, London: Sage Publications.

Wheeler, B. (2011) 'Big society: More than a soundbite?', *BBC News*, 14 February (www.bbc.co.uk/news/uk-politics-12163624).

Wilkinson, R. and Pickett, K. (2009) *The spirit level: Why equality is better for everyone*, London: Penguin.

Williams, R. (1973) *The country and the city*, London: Chatto and Windus.

Williams, T. and Keith, M. (2006) *'British people live on the 14th floor' (BNP): Building a new community in Barking and Dagenham following the May elections – The implications for English Partnerships of development at Barking Riverside*, London: English Partnerships.

Wolman, H. (1995) 'Local government institutions and democratic governance', in D. Judge, G. Stoker and H. Wolman (eds) *Theories of urban politics*, London: Sage Publications, pp 135-59.

Woods, J. (2010) 'We're all middle class now, darling', *The Telegraph*, 22 January (www.telegraph.co.uk/news/politics/7053761/Were-all-middle-class-now-darling.html).

Worley, C. (2005) '"It's not about race. It's about the community": New Labour and "community cohesion"', *Critical Social Policy*, vol 25, no 4, pp 483-96.

Wright, P. (2009) *A journey through ruins: Last days of London* (2nd edn), Oxford: Oxford University Press.

Wynne-Jones, R. (2010) 'What would life be like under a BNP council? The ugly truth revealed', *The Mirror*, 23 March (www.mirror.co.uk/news/top-stories/2010/03/23/what-would-life-be-like-under-a-bnp-council-the-ugly-truth-revealed-115875-22132109).

Young, K. (1990) 'Approaches to policy development in the field of equal opportunities', in W. Ball and J. Solomos (eds) *Race and local politics*, Basingstoke: Macmillan, pp 22-42.

Young, M., Young, H., Shuttleworth, E. and Tucker, W. (1980) *Report from Hackney: A study of an inner city area*, London: Policy Studies Institute.

Yuval-Davis, N., Anthias, F. and Kofman, E. (2005) 'Secure borders and safe haven and the gendered politics of belonging: Beyond social cohesion', *Ethnic and Racial Studies*, vol 28, no 3, pp 513-35.

Appendix: A note on methods

The research for this book was never intended as a prescriptive study, an analysis of how to 'do' policy or government better, or a vision of 'what should be'. The project was formed from my own experience of uncomfortable positions in local government, and curiosity about what it might mean to make these discomforts explicit. I wanted to get at the work policy practitioners do to create, maintain, obstruct, manipulate or change policies and institutions – including, often, work on themselves.

Project origins

Before the research began, I was employed as a policy manager in a local authority (London Borough of Hackney, LBH). My work involved working with the chief executive and senior management, the elected Mayor and his cabinet, people in similar roles in partner organisations such as health and the police, and other interest groups within and outside the local authority. Much of the time my work was about working out compromises of policy, intervention or simply language, in which all of these interest groups could feel that their own interests, and the demands on each of them from outside agencies (such as central government) had been met. This is where my interest in the knowingness of uncomfortable positions in local government began.

An illustrative example was an incident when I was involved in developing new governance arrangements for children's services. This emerged after sitting with a group of the most senior managers from health, education and social services and trying to agree on a shared definition of 'commissioning', a term each of the three professions used to describe slightly different relationships to designing and delivering services. There were many meetings on this subject, covering similar ground and objections, after which I or other colleagues would draft another version of a policy paper attempting to reconcile different definitions and practices, only for it to be discussed and revised again. Finally, in one meeting it seemed all three heads of service had reached agreement about the word 'commissioning' and how it could be used in joint planning. But as we left the room, I realised that what had actually been agreed was that colleagues would not dispute the others' use of the word 'commissioning', yet would continue to operate within each service with the existing practices. This wasn't necessarily a problem in itself (although it had taken a long time to reach this situation).

The point is that all those involved were aware of the different uses of language and meaning which they were negotiating individually and together, and reconciled that while they may not have reached agreement, they had reached something that they could treat *as* agreement (Young, 1990, p 33).

It is clear that when operating in this environment, the ability to hold several contradictory opinions at once is necessary. But this is different to Orwell's 'doublethink' (Orwell, 1949) in the dystopian *Nineteen Eighty-Four.* There is a sort of self-policing involved, but there is also recognition among (many) policy practitioners that sometimes these manoeuvres can be contradictory. I certainly felt (but was also able to operate within) the cognitive dissonance of this necessary discomfort. So did many of my colleagues who could reflect on the sometime absurdity of the policy process, but also see it as a form of negotiation necessary to develop shared meanings or to cope with competing prerogatives. This was not a realisation that came on me suddenly, but a habitus formed by and forming the policy process. Thinking about the importance of this way of being, how it functions and what work it enables seemed like an important area for exploration in a research project.

Project formation

There are two concrete ways in which my relationship to this research project and its subjects require particular consideration. First, having worked as a policy practitioner in Hackney I had existing relationships with many research participants, and perceptions about how policy negotiations work. This experience informed and enriched my data and provided opportunities for ethnographic description based on participant observation. These histories also provided credentials that undoubtedly helped me to achieve access to interviewees, both within and outside Hackney that would otherwise have been much more difficult. But there was a risk that these connections could blur my analytic lens through over-familiarity or lack of questioning of norms and practices.

A more unusual aspect of my relationship to the research was that my research became funded, after its initial stages, through a collaborative (Centre for Analysis of Social Exclusion, CASE) doctoral studentship, by the Economic and Social Research Council (ESRC), with an annual contribution from LBH. CASE studentships were an initiative of the ESRC meant to encourage doctoral research to be connected to arenas beyond academia. To set one up, a university department and a non-academic partner organisation (in this case, LBH), agree a research proposal for a PhD thesis that will also provide work that is of use to the non-academic organisation, and alongside this a programme of support from, and involvement in the work of, the organisation for the research student. In this case, I worked up the research and support proposals with both partners and received approval and funding from the ESRC, that provided the majority of the funds for my tuition fees and living costs, with a smaller contribution from LBH. Prior to the CASE studentship, I had begun the research on a part-time basis, while working for LBH part time and with an agreement that they would pay my part-time tuition fees. That prior agreement, however, did not include any formal discussions of the subject of my studies, or of arrangements for cooperation with fieldwork.

At the outset of the CASE arrangement, all partners signed an agreement about ethics and intellectual property that stated that my research for the PhD would be guided ultimately by my academic supervisors. While I would share findings with the non-academic supervisors from LBH throughout the research, and discuss any matters of contention, they would not have a right of veto over writing or publications. A studentship panel was held quarterly involving LBH, my Sociology Department and me, at which we reviewed progress on fieldwork and writing, and work I was doing for the local authority. This work, which also formed part of the studentship arrangement, involved sharing my expertise as an academic researcher with the local authority in practical ways. For example, I produced a position paper that was used as a basis for discussion of how Hackney might approach the concept of community cohesion in a locally relevant way. I also gave advice and comments on research design and research reports that were commissioned by the council from outside organisations as part of their consultation on a community cohesion strategy. This model of research collaboration suggests some expectations about research that will be practical, applied or technocratic, producing measurable, quantifiable or obviously 'useful' outputs (Burawoy's idea of 'policy sociology'; see Chapter One). As a CASE student, I was constantly thinking about the 'usefulness' of my research, even as I tried to ensure this did not limit my methodology or analysis. The example of our specific project shows that such collaborations do not have to close down opportunities for freedom of intellectual inquiry. To a large extent, this freedom was dependent on a partnership between individuals within organisations who saw value in finding time and space for reflection without predetermined utilitarian applications. Its success also depended on my ability to participate in more instrumental activities linked to the research while developing critical theoretical underpinnings for my own research.

Sources and resources

My study began with documents because policy documents are tangible tools around which policy processes are organised. Policy practitioners treat and create policy documents as tools to shape debate, as starting points to be worked with and as sources of meaning. There have been a number of attempts to define community cohesion in landmark policy documents, which have become embedded in wider narratives, and these are discussed in Chapter Two. These definitions are used by policy practitioners, not as demonstrations of the 'truth' of what community cohesion is, but as artefacts around which to base their constructions of what community cohesion means.

Similarly, I analysed policy documents not as records of what happened, what is, or what should be, but rather as tools whose production, consumption and use is part of the negotiation of cohesion, inequality and change. I do not assume that they present a definition of what the institutional authors believed community cohesion to be. I suggest instead that they represent an outcome (at a particular point in time) of negotiations around what can and cannot be said about the project of community cohesion, presented in a particular form which is intended to push debate in one direction or another – and which may or may not manage to do so. This treatment of documents follows Foucault's reconceptualisation of documentary sources as a resource for history that allow scholars to treat the text as *part* of history, rather than simply a (perhaps unreliable, perhaps partial) representation of it (Foucault, 2002 [1969], pp 6-7).

Securing the documentary data (policy documents and media sources) to work with was relatively straightforward. General web searches using important key words, the use of online alert services for key words ('Hackney' and 'community cohesion') to identify new web postings and manual searches of relevant government departments and policy organisations supplemented my existing archive of key documents built up through working in the field. In addition, I secured local policy documents through my collaboration with Hackney Council, while a large amount of other documentation is publicly available for all local authorities and policy organisations via their websites. I consulted and analysed over 57 separate government reports, speeches or letters, 52 separate media or news items and 12 additional policy documents (such as those produced by think tanks).

I began with looking at the document to consider its potential uses, but by stepping outside of the study of documents I could start to consider the other elements of negotiating difficult subjects in practice. This is why I linked the study of policy documents to ethnography and interviews. However, these other methods themselves produce documents – field notes and interview transcripts – which not only make an account of 'what happened' but also do work on 'what happened', turning it into text, noting some elements and leaving out others (Clifford, 1986; Trouillot, 1995, p 26).

Coffey (1999, p 127) argues that 'ethnography is an act of memory', that even detailed field notes, or physical mementoes, are tools that enable memory, rather than 'pure' sources themselves. Although my work in Hackney prior to embarking on 'official' research was not framed as an ethnography, it serves as a source of data both for understanding the esoteric knowledge of how local government policy works, and the specific research setting and occupational priorities, behaviours and languages. This experience is supplemented by observations made in and around the process of conducting interviews, including participation in the policy process, attendance at conferences, events and meetings, and informal conversations. These data and experiences helped to produce relationships I would later rely on in fieldwork.

This experience provided me with a 'feel for the game' (Bourdieu, 1990 [1980], p 103) of policy practice and institutional life within the organisations of local government and their interactions with other organisational forms. Taking a step outside of this common-sense framework by choosing to study these processes with an element of ethnographic distance was an ongoing process. Access primarily as a practitioner allowed me to account for my own direct experiences (including affective ones) in Chapter Three. This involvement enabled both privileged access to the research site and an embodied understanding of policy processes, which became data for research as I reflected on the notes, records and memories I had of those experiences, and considered what they could tell us about policy practice.

Participation as a practitioner also allowed me access to privileged materials that might otherwise have been held as confidential, some of which I refer to in Chapter Three as 'internal documents'. I have tried to strike a balance between using these materials as integral to demonstrating the practices I was researching, and maintaining some level of confidentiality with respect to the trust placed in me by research participants, by referring to these documents and events with some level of discretion. As the research was produced in cooperation with colleagues at LBH through my studentship, some of these documents were passed to me specifically because they might be of use to me in my research, and as such I have respected this relationship by using the documents in this way. I have contextualised these documents where I use them as far as is necessary to make sense within the analysis, without adding extraneous details that would only serve to identify individuals. Since the ethnographic work I conducted was, in part, done before I knew it would become research, and because of its nature, I was unable to obtain 'consent' from others who formed part of my experience. For that reason, I have tried to ensure that the discussions that were based on participant observation do not identify any specific people who had not agreed to be included in the study at some point.

Uncomfortable positions emerge when reflexive subjects are faced by contradictions between their taken-for-granted understandings of the world and their empirical experiences. The interview encounters I engineered often enabled policy practitioners to occupy such uncomfortable positions, whereas in day-to-day life (as studied through the ethnographic component of this research), they might have less time to dwell on these positions, because of the demands of fulfilling professional duties. This is not to say that such discomforts were not present in daily interactions, just that a space to examine and elaborate on them was created in the interview encounter.

Interviews gave participants an opportunity to reflect on, as well as to engage in, these negotiations. I treated the interview encounters as constructed space in which I took seriously what the interviewees said. I did not dismiss their arguments as simple self-justifications ("they would say that, wouldn't they"). But nor did I take the interview transcript as a straightforward explanation of "how it really is". Rather, taking seriously the interview encounter meant understanding it as a negotiation, in which both interviewer and interviewee reflected on *and reproduced* elements of the policy- and self-making process. Interviews thus provided concentrated access to such negotiations in process, rather than an unquestioned explanation of the situation "from the horse's mouth". The interview encounter produced a particular kind of frame in which personal narratives of self were produced by participants, and perhaps more emphasised than in their daily work. It was a separate space from daily ethnography, set aside to consider the construction of policy practice from a different angle. Participants found a mode of talking about policy issues when one-to-one, and used personal narratives both to remake themselves and to claim a form of authenticity often associated with the confessional account.

The main body of data in the thesis is formed of 85 interviews with 'policy practitioners'. Although the choice of interview participants was my own, I sought guidance and cooperation from 'gatekeepers' whose endorsement helped me to identify myself as a legitimate researcher, as well as triangulating my own views on who the relevant people within an organisation or locality might be. Table A1 shows the roles of the people I interviewed. The typical interview lasted around an hour, although they ranged from between half an hour to almost two hours. I recorded all of these events with a digital voice recorder, except for one interview where the participant preferred not to be recorded and where I took detailed notes as we talked. Immediately after every interview I made detailed notes on the context, body language and any elements of the interaction that had struck me as particularly important at the time. I later transcribed all of the interviews myself, taking account of all pauses, stutters and exclamations.

The interviews were semi-structured and based around four broad questions:

- How would you describe community cohesion policy/What is your understanding of community cohesion policy?
- (How) has community cohesion policy and its development affected the work that you do?
- How do you think community cohesion policy will develop in the future?
- People often describe community cohesion policy as being about identity, background and experiences; do you think your own identity, background or experience affect how you think about cohesion policy?

For each of these areas of questioning I had a number of related prompts in case the thrust of the questions was unclear to interviewees or they were hesitant to expand. In most cases, however, these broad questions prompted initial responses that I could follow up with more reactive questions. I tried, as far as possible, to follow the directions of discussion that seemed most relevant to the interviewee, while keeping in mind the structure and focus of the interview. For instance, if an interviewee began talking about what might seem a relatively unrelated issue of policy, or their own experiences in a previous job, I would follow their line of thought but if necessary provide prompts or questions relating this back to the main line of questioning. Because of this reactive style of interviewing, in different interviews the amount of time spent on each area of interest differed.

The final question listed (how one's own identity, background or experiences informed thinking about community cohesion) was added after six pilot interviews, where participants had talked unprompted about their own experiences in relation to their understanding of cohesion policy. Reviewing the pilot interviews, I saw that this was an important area of investigation, and decided to incorporate a specific question to tease out more reflections on it. I spent some time considering the wording of this question, and while I did not always stick exactly with the script for all of the questions (for example, perhaps adapting some of the vocabulary to that which had already been used by an interviewee, or elaborating on aspects of the question if they were unclear), the language of 'identity, background or experience' was an important combination. The broad interpretations this made possible are common to the language of much community cohesion policy documentation, which tends to avoid the language of 'equality categories' (such as gender, race or sexuality), instead using terms with which 'everyone' can identify (see, for example, COIC, 2007, p 4). I did not want to subscribe to the idea that those identified with 'unmarked' categories such as male or white are unaffected by questions of gender or race, and wanted interviewees to feel as comfortable as possible to relate their own viewpoints whatever these might be, while allowing them to choose whether this was expressed by drawing on identity politics, ethical commitments, material events, some other formation or a combination of these. While some interviewees initially expressed surprise or embarrassment at this question (one reason why I couched it with the preface that this was especially relevant to cohesion policy), most had already begun to answer it with comments throughout the interview, to which I would sometimes refer back as prompts if they struggled. However, I also gave interviewees the opportunity to say that they did not see how any of these issues affected their understandings of cohesion policy, and some did say this.

Analysis

As discussed, the transcripts became documents, and I paid attention to the process that went into creating them. I understood the conversations I recorded as encounters in a specific, created research encounter. When analysing the language used by both me and the people I was interviewing, I tried to view it in this context, and to consider hesitations, intonation and laughter, for example, as part of the process of performance and conveying of meaning. In this sense my analysis was influenced by traditions of conversation analysis (Silverman, 1998). This was an influence or epistemological starting point, rather than a strict prescriptive method. I used inductive understandings and communicative strategies to develop my analysis, and demonstrate the reasons for my analysis and conclusions with close reference to the transcript texts, as you will see throughout.

I have contextualised the data to the extent that it makes sense within my analysis (for instance, describing the professional role or other characteristics of an interviewee), while not providing additional unnecessary information that would only serve to identify individual research participants. All of the names of interviewees have been changed (except for two who were expressly interviewed as public figures and who gave consent to be named – see Chapter Four). Where an interviewee asked me not to attribute specific comments to them, I either took further measures to obscure their identity, or avoided using the material altogether. I obtained consent (written or verbal) from every participant I interviewed; I anonymised the interviews; I explained the purpose of the research both in writing before the interview and verbally when we met.

The process of transcribing enabled me to think back over the interviews and to become intimate with the large amount of data I had collected. This way, I avoided the fragmentation of data that can be a risk of relying on qualitative data analysis programmes, retaining my overview of themes and my ability to recognise subtle resonances and use intuitive and inductive strategies for analysis (Hollway and Jefferson, 2000, p 68).

As a way of organising my data, I created 'codes' for the themes that emerged from the data, both from interview transcripts and other documentary sources. These codes were created and administered within the qualitative data analysis programme NVivo, which made it possible to systematically apply these codes to the transcripts as I re-read each one in turn. In the process of coding, further themes emerged inductively and I created new codes for them to help to organise the data. In all, I had 93 different codes by the end of this process. For an idea of how I handled these codes, the first five in my NVivo file when organised alphabetically were '2001 riots, Oldham, Bradford, Burnley', 'age as diversity', 'barking [and dagenham]', 'beneath the surface' and 'bnp, far right'.

Reviewing these five codes gives a reasonable idea of the complexities of this coding strategy. First, the codes were created inductively and were shorthand for my own use, thus they did not necessarily form fully fleshed-out analytic categories that I would use in my final write-up. Second, they are a mixture of types of ideas, based on the formations that emerged from the data. For example, the first code listed here ('2001 riots, Oldham, Bradford, Burnley') is a cluster around narratives of the emergence of community cohesion policy that comes out consistently in the data and is located in time and space. The second ('age as diversity') is a way of talking about diversity by reference to age, which emerged as a tactic in some data for demonstrating that community cohesion policy was not simply based in race and faith – yet in the end this was not a strong enough theme to be discussed at length here. The third ('barking') is a place which came up frequently in narratives of community cohesion policy and which I subsequently pursued as a theme of the research by developing the methodology to investigate perspectives from within that place; the fact that in my own shorthand I left off 'Dagenham' may be revealing of my own lack of attention to the specificities of place, but also to the ways that interviewees in particular might talk more about one than the other part of the local authority in Barking and Dagenham. The fourth code ('beneath the surface') is a category I created to group together narratives that seemed to form around themes of unspoken tensions, when practitioners or documents alluded to cohesion as potentially just 'on the surface', with more sinister or difficult subjects concealed or silenced. This code included a variety of different subjects, constructed within resonant narrative forms. The final code listed here ('bnp, far right') refers to narratives and allusions to the British National Party and other far right groups which were identified in some sources as specific, or primary, threats to cohesion.

Finally, it is worth pointing out that as I went through this coding process, much of my data was given several different codes. A different methodology might have investigated systematic correlations between codes (Fielding, 2002, p 165), but my coding system was not a tool to scientise or quantify this data on narratives and meaning. I coded the data as a way of sorting and thinking about it, of organising my thoughts and interpretations, and so where codes overlap, I have discussed these associations in my analysis, but I do not pretend this shows some independent variable at work, because, of course, all of the codes themselves and their application emerged from my own inductive decisions.

Table A1: Interviews conducted for the research

Research site	Hackney	National	Barking and Dagenham	Peterborough	Oldham
Total number or interviews	43 (with 45 people, plus 1 large meeting)	20 (with 22 people)	5	6	7
Positions of those interviewed (For Barking and Dagenham, Oldham and Peterborough this was combined to preserve anonymity; for national interviews, I have referred to the interviewee's organisation only)	Mayor; chief executive; 4 directors; 6 cabinet members; 17 assistant directors; 3 heads of service; 6 policy officers (various directorates); 2 service managers (various directorates); 1 police officer; 1 voluntary sector rep; 2 cultural commentators (see Chapter Five); plus one large meeting of voluntary and community sector reps	2 × DCLG; 2 × Improvement and Development Agency; LGA; COIC; UK Borders Agency; Department of Industry, Universities and Skills; Institute for Public Policy Research; Young Foundation; New Local Government Network; 2 × Equalities and Human Rights Commission; 2 × Institute for Community Cohesion; Institute for Economic Affairs; Centre Forum; Department for Children, Schools and Families; 2 × Local Government Information Unit; Social Market Foundation	2 × community cohesion lead officer; 2 × directors; 2 × cabinet member; former cabinet member; assistant director; 2 × Race Equality Council head; head of equalities; head of strategy; 2 × interfaith workers; 2 × community and voluntary sector leaders; Neighbourhood and Community Engagement manager; chair of Cohesion Board		

Index